T0306005

Lecture Notes in Experimental Economics

World Scientific Lecture Notes in Economics and Policy

ISSN: 2630-4872

The World Scientific Lecture Notes in Economics and Policy series is aimed to produce lecture note texts for a wide range of economics disciplines, both theoretical and applied at the undergraduate and graduate levels. Contributors to the series are highly ranked and experienced professors of economics who see in publication of their lectures a mission to disseminate the teaching of economics in an affordable manner to students and other readers interested in enriching their knowledge of economic topics. The series was formerly titled World Scientific Lecture Notes in Economics.

Published:

Vol. 21: *Lecture Notes in Experimental Economics*
by John Duff

Vol. 20: *Public Policy and Climate Change: Politics, Philosophy and Economics*
by John Quiggin

Vol. 19: *Lectures in Applied Environmental Economics and Policy*
by Xepapadeas Anastasios

Vol. 18: *International Economics and Policy: An Introduction to Globalization and Inequality*
by Keith E. Maskus

For the complete list of volumes in this series, please visit
www.worldscientific.com/series/wslnep

World Scientific Lecture Notes in Economics and Policy – Vol. 21

Lecture Notes in Experimental Economics

John Duffy
University of California, Irvine, USA

W World Scientific

EW JERSEY • LONDON • SINGAPORE • BEIJING • SHANGHAI • HONG KONG • TAIPEI • CHENNAI • TOKYO

Published by

World Scientific Publishing Co. Pte. Ltd.

5 Toh Tuck Link, Singapore 596224

USA office: 27 Warren Street, Suite 401-402, Hackensack, NJ 07601

UK office: 57 Shelton Street, Covent Garden, London WC2H 9HE

Library of Congress Cataloging-in-Publication Data
Names: Duffy, John, 1964– editor.
Title: Lecture notes in experimental economics / John Duffy, University of California, Irvine, USA.
Description: New Jersey : World Scientific, [2024] | Series: World Scientific lecture notes in
  economics and policy, 2630-4872 ; vol. 21 | Includes bibliographical references and index.
Identifiers: LCCN 2024000273 | ISBN 9789811288463 (hardcover) |
  ISBN 9789811288470 (ebook) | ISBN 9789811288487 (ebook other)
Subjects: LCSH: Experimental economics. | Economics--Methodology.
Classification: LCC HB131 .L43 2024 | DDC 330--dc23/eng/20240111
LC record available at https://lccn.loc.gov/2024000273

British Library Cataloguing-in-Publication Data
A catalogue record for this book is available from the British Library.

For any available supplementary material, please visit
https://www.worldscientific.com/worldscibooks/10.1142/13736#t=suppl

Desk Editors: Nimal Koliyat/Catherine Domingo Ong

Typeset by Stallion Press
Email: enquiries@stallionpress.com

Printed in Singapore

To Markéta, with love and appreciation

Preface

Experimental economics is a branch of economics that uses laboratory and field experiments to study economic behavior. Experimental economists use *controlled* environments to more clearly evaluate how people make economic choices and to better identify causal relationships. The work in this field has led to insights that would be difficult to obtain using traditional archival data approaches where the information available to individuals or their payoff incentives are not clearly understood. In order to produce such findings, economic experiments have been conducted across a wide variety of different settings from traditional laboratories to online platforms and studies in the field, and cover a broad range of economic topics such as market behavior, game theory, and individual consumption and savings decisions. In recent years, the experimental method has become increasingly popular among social scientists as a means of informing public policy decisions and providing a clearer understanding of complex economic phenomena.

This book is intended to provide the reader with an introduction to the methods of experimental economics along with a broad overview of some of the major topics that experimental economists have studied. The content is based on lectures that I have given at both the graduate and undergraduate levels in semester- or quarter-length courses I have taught at the University of Pittsburgh and at the University of California, Irvine. While the material covered in this book reflects my own idiosyncratic tastes, the coverage is sufficiently broad to provide a good introduction to both the methodology and key topic areas within the field. The material presumes only a basic knowledge of economics and game theory, and mathematical details have been kept to a minimum. The primary aim of the book is to convey to the reader in a clear and concise manner the power and excitement of the experimental method for evaluating models and addressing questions of interest to economists and other social science researchers.

There are, of course, many other good books on experimental economics. These either emphasize experimental results (e.g., Kagel and Roth (1995, 2016), Plott and Smith (2008), Camerer (2011) and Holt (2019)) or methodology (e.g., Guala (2005), Bardsley *et al.* (2010), Fréchette and Schotter (2015), and Schram and Ule (2019)). For a self-contained *course* on experimental economics, I have found it useful to present both the methodology of experimental economics and some of the many applications of the experimental method. The methodological chapters reflect current best practices in the profession and will enable the reader to start conducting their own experimental research immediately. In deciding which application topics to include I have been somewhat selective, with a focus on game theory and market experiments—the research areas with which I am most familiar.

I have had many great teachers, collaborators, and colleagues over the years who have contributed in so many ways to the knowledge that is presented in this book. I would like to thank, without implicating, Jasmina Arifovic, Te Bao, Andreas Blume, Colin Camerer, Enrica Carbone, Tim Cason, David Cooper, Nick Feltovich, Eric Fisher, Guillaume Fréchette, Dan Friedman, Nobi Hanaki, Frank Heinemann, Charlie Holt, Cars Hommes, Ed Hopkins, John Kagel, Tatiana Kornienko, Michael McBride, Rosemarie Nagel, Charles Noussair, Jack Ochs, Tom Palfrey, Charles Plott, Daniela Puzzello, Alvin Roth, Arthur Schram, Vernon Smith, Shyam Sunder, and Lise Vesterlund.

Organization and Intended Audience

The aim of these lecture notes is to provide teachers of courses on experimental economics/social science with an effective means by which to organize a course on experimental social science. The book is organized as a series of twelve lectures or chapters. Each chapter can be covered in a week. The first five chapters cover the basics of experimental design and analysis while the remaining seven chapters cover various applications. These application chapters are all independent of one another and can be covered in any order. Further, supplementary readings can be readily incorporated.

The intended audience is students and researchers in the social sciences who are interested in conducting controlled experiments in the laboratory or in the field. The material is written at a level that is suitable for advanced undergraduate, masters, or PhD level courses in experimental economics, or, more broadly, experimental social science.

About the Author

John Duffy is Professor of Economics at the University of California Irvine and is also affiliated with the Institute of Social and Economic Research at Osaka University. He was previously Professor of Economics at the University of Pittsburgh. John earned a BA in Economics from the University of California, Berkeley and a PhD in Economics from the University of California, Los Angeles. His research interests lie in behavioral and experimental economics, game theory, finance and macroeconomics.

Contents

Preface   vii

About the Author   ix

1 Why Experiment?   **1**
   1.1 Causal Inference   1
   1.2 Other Reasons to Experiment   4
   1.3 The Duhem–Quine Thesis   7
   1.4 So, Why Experiment?   8
   1.5 Let's Do an Experiment!   9

2 Where to Experiment?   **15**
   2.1 Reasons to Conduct Experiments in a Laboratory 17
   2.2 Reasons to Conduct Experiments in the Field 20
   2.3 Are Student Subjects Different from Non-student Subjects? 23
   2.4 Online Workforces 25

3 How to Experiment: Methods   **27**
   3.1 Randomization 27
   3.2 Within versus Between-Subject Designs 28
   3.3 Induced Value Theory 30
   3.4 Extrinsic versus Intrinsic Rewards 32
   3.5 Payment Protocols 34
   3.6 Control of Risk Preferences 36
   3.7 Elicitation Mechanisms 39
   3.8 Robot Players 51
   3.9 Time Horizons and Discounting 52
   3.10 Matching 53

4 How to Experiment: Implementation   **57**

    4.1   Institutional Review Board Approval   57

    4.2   Planned Experimental Design   59

    4.3   Pre-analysis Plans and Pre-registration of Hypotheses . . .   61

    4.4   Power Analysis to Determine Sample Size   63

    4.5   Writing Instructions and Control Questions   66

    4.6   Deception   68

    4.7   Data Collection Methods   69

    4.8   Recruitment of Subjects   71

    4.9   How Much to Pay?   71

5 Data Analysis   **75**

    5.1   What is an Independent Observation?   75

    5.2   Preliminary Data Analysis   77

    5.3   Non-parametric Methods   78

         5.3.1   Wilcoxon–Mann–Whitney test   79

         5.3.2   Robust rank-order test   81

         5.3.3   Kruskal–Wallis test   81

         5.3.4   Fisher's exact test   82

         5.3.5   Chi-squared test   83

         5.3.6   Kolmogorov–Smirnov test   83

         5.3.7   Sign test   85

         5.3.8   Wilcoxon signed-rank test   86

    5.4   Parametric Approaches   88

         5.4.1 t-Tests   88

         5.4.2   Linear regression analysis   90

         5.4.3   Interaction effects   91

         5.4.4   Limited dependent variables and data censoring . . .   92

         5.4.5   Clustering of standard errors   93

         5.4.6   Correcting for multiple hypothesis testing   94

6 Game Theory Experiments   **97**

    6.1   Dominant Strategy, Prisoner's Dilemma Games   99

    6.2   Mixed Strategies: Matching Pennies   101

    6.3   Coordination Games: Stag Hunt, Battle of the Sexes   104

    6.4   Backward Induction: Centipede and Trust Games   107

    6.5   Contests and Over-dissipation   111

    6.6   Level-k Reasoning: The Beauty Contest Game   113

    6.7   Summary   116

7 Public Economics Experiments   **119**
7.1 Public Good Experiments 119
7.2 Variations on a Theme 123
7.3 Mechanisms to Increase Public Good Contributions 129
7.4 Tax Compliance 133
7.5 Voting 136
7.6 Summary 141

8 Social Preferences   **143**
8.1 Ultimatum Game Bargaining 144
8.2 Dictator Games 146
8.3 Market Games 148
8.4 Inequity Aversion 150
8.5 Reciprocity/Intentions-Based Models 156
8.6 Image Concerns/Social Norms 157
8.7 Social Identity 159
8.8 Social Preferences in the Field 162
8.9 Summary 163

9 Auction Experiments   **167**
9.1 Private-Value Auctions 168
9.2 Common-Value Auctions and the Winner's Curse 174
9.3 All-pay Auctions 178
9.4 Summary 181

10 Market Experiments   **183**
10.1 Double Auctions and Competitive Equilibrium 184
10.2 Call Markets 190
10.3 Sunspots and Market Prices 192
10.4 Shapley–Shubik Market Game Mechanism 196
10.5 Decentralized Markets 198
10.6 Summary 201

11 Asset Market Experiments   **203**
11.1 Informational Efficiency of Asset Prices 204
11.2 Asset Price Bubbles 206
11.3 Learning-to-Forecast Experiments 211
11.4 Consumption-Based Asset Pricing Models 213
11.5 Asset Market Experiments with Multiple Assets 218
11.6 Summary 219

12 Macroeconomic Experiments **221**
12.1 Intertemporal Optimization 222
12.2 Rational Expectations 225
12.3 Inflation in an Overlapping Generations Economy 228
12.4 Poverty Traps 231
12.5 Bank Runs 233
12.6 Monetary Policies 235
12.7 Summary 239

References 241

Index 273

Chapter 1

Why Experiment?

1.1 Causal Inference

In the social sciences, we are often interested in going beyond descriptions of data or associations among data and set out instead to make **causal inferences**. For instance, do opinion polls affect voter turnout? Do individuals with higher cognitive abilities behave more strategically and less pro-socially? Does a change in tax policy affect tax revenues? We say that there is a causal relationship between two variables, X and Y, if a change in one variable, X, reliably causes a change in the other variable, Y. But how do we assess such causality?

In the physical sciences, causal relationships are typically studied in the laboratory, often under ideal, vacuum tube-like conditions to avoid potential confounding factors. In the laboratory, one can carefully create exogenous variation in the hypothesized independent variable, X, and observe its relationship with the hypothesized dependent variable, Y. For example, if water is heated to a sufficiently high temperature, the molecules start to move more quickly, causing the water to boil. From this we would conclude that heat is causal for the state of water. By contrast, in the social sciences, the objects of interest are less easily controlled—that is to say, they are human beings, who, unlike molecules, often have minds of their own.

In medical research, which also involves human subjects, the most widely used approach to causal inference is the **randomized control trial (RCT)**. In an RCT for a new drug, for example, a sample of subjects is randomly drawn from the population of individuals who may benefit from that drug. This sample, or **subject pool**, is then randomly and unknowingly assigned to one of two groups: the **treatment group** which is given the new drug and the **control group** which does not receive the new drug. To prevent human subjects from being able to determine which group they are assigned to, participants assigned to the control group are typically given a **placebo** (i.e., a fake drug that appears in all respects similar to the real drug). Since the sample pool of subjects is randomly assigned to treatment and control groups and a placebo device is used as well, the RCT is considered the "gold standard" for evidence-based medicine. If a pre-defined **outcome variable** (e.g., some health measure) indicates that outcomes are better for patients treated with the drug than those who are not, and the differences in the outcome variable are statistically significant given the sample size, then one can be reasonably confident in the efficacy of the drug treatment since the only difference between treatment and control is which group was given the drug. Indeed, such RCT testing is typically required before government approval of the use of any new drug.

Over the last 50 years, RCT-type methods have also been used to make causal inferences in the social sciences.[1] Human subjects are randomly sampled from some population and from this sample there is random assignment either to a baseline, "control treatment," or to one or more different treatment conditions, $T_1, T_2, \ldots, T_k$, as illustrated in Figure 1.1. The control treatment may consist of "no treatment," a placebo, or some benchmark treatment. The non-control treatments vary in a *single dimension* from the control treatment or from one another. Random assignment ensures that there are no selection biases. The aim of such experimentation is to determine whether and how the various treatment conditions affect subjects' behavior relative to the baseline control case. For instance, the control setting might be a first-price sealed-bid auction, where all n bidders simultaneously submit sealed bids; when the bids are opened, the highest bidder wins. This control setting could be contrasted with a treatment condition where the auction bidding is sequential, with the bid being increased by a clock until only one bidder remains, the one willing to pay the highest amount as in an English ascending price auction. A further treatment might maintain the sealed bid auction design but increase the number of bidders, n, to explore the effects of greater competition on bidding.

The key elements of control in experimentation are: (1) random assignment of subject participants to control or treatment groups and (2) ensuring

---

[1]For a history of this development, see Svorenčík (2015).

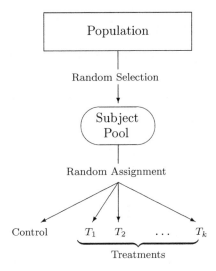

Figure 1.1: Random sampling and assignment to control and treatment conditions.

that treatments differ from the control in a single dimension, representing the hypothesized causal factor(s).

Laboratory methods are certainly not the only means of assessing causality. Indeed, the most common approach to causal inference in the social sciences involves **regression analysis**. This is where, on the basis of a theory, one posits a causal relationship (e.g., that a change in X causes a change in Y). In the case where that relationship may be endogenous, instrumental variables approaches can be used. A further common practice is to control for other possible confounding factors (that the researcher is aware of) by including a set of control variables on the right-hand side of the regression specification. Still, this approach is far from perfect. What is often missing is *truly exogenous* variation in the independent variable X, which is important because it is this variation where controlled experiments with different treatment conditions can often claim an advantage.[2]

---

[2] As labor economists (Angrist and Pischke, 2008, pp. 4–5) observe, an important question for empirical researchers working with *non-experimental* field data to ask is as follows: "What experiment ... could ideally be used to capture the causal effect of interest?" The suggestion here is that researchers using non-experimental field data to make causal inferences should still be thinking in terms of an experiment that, if it were possible to carry it out, would enable an answer to the research question. Angrist and Pischke refer to research questions that cannot not be answered by an experiment as "fundamentally unidentified questions."

1.2   Other Reasons to Experiment

While the advantages of the experimental method for making causal inferences are perhaps the main reason for conducting experiments, there are several other reasons to conduct experiments in the social sciences. **Vernon Smith**, a Nobel laureate in Economics and one of the founders of experimental economics, argues that laboratory-type economic experiments are real-life economic systems that are behaviorally richer than any theory. Smith (1982) sees the principal value of laboratory experiments as: (1) providing accurate measures, e.g., of efficiency or welfare; (2) testing theoretical or behavioral hypotheses; and (3) assessing the comparative performance of different *institutions*, e.g., do the rules of some market mechanism matter? Do different mechanisms perform differently, e.g., first- versus second-price auctions?

Alvin Roth, another Nobel laureate in Economics and pioneer in the use of experimental economic methods, proposes a slightly broader typology of experiments with respect to the researchers' aims. Roth (1995) suggests that experiments can be conducted with the aim of (1) speaking to theorists, (2) searching for facts, and/or (3) whispering in the ears of princes.

Researchers conducting experiments that "speak to theorists" try to utilize an experimental environment that closely matches that used in a theory, dispensing with the need to consider any real-world features, just as theorists do. This theory testing approach, common in the natural and life sciences, involves evaluation of the model in all its abstraction, using controlled experimental methods. For instance, the researcher might evaluate the comparative statics predictions of the model while maintaining its assumptions (e.g., rational choice, risk-neutral expected utility maximization). If the theory and/or assumptions do not jointly hold, the researcher may consider how relaxation of the assumptions might make a difference, such as by supposing that agents are boundedly rational or risk-averse with respect to uncertain monetary payoffs. **Charles Plott**, another pioneer in experimental methods, argues that economics and other social sciences only transitioned from being a non-experimental science to an experimental science with the development of models and theories that could be tested using controlled methods. (Plott, 1991, p.906) argues that, like the theory being tested, "an experiment should be judged by the lessons it teaches about the theory and not by its similarity with what nature might have happened to have created."

An advantage of having a theory to test in one's experiment is that the theory helps to motivate and frame the experimental design. Given that theories generally abstract from many real-world features, it becomes acceptable for the experimenter to do so as well. Furthermore, if the comparative statics predictions of the theory *fail* to obtain in the experiment, then, in the words of Bardsley *et al.* (2010), one can always "blame the theory" for this failure; that is, the experimenter can duck some blame for having run the experiment in the first place by arguing that the theory predicted that there would be differences across treatments.

By contrast, if one does not have a theory (say) as to why a treatment intervention should change behavior relative to the control setting, then one cannot easily blame the theory if the treatment intervention fails to deliver any difference between treatment and control. More precisely, let us define an experiment where existing theory predicts *no difference* between the treatment and control settings—as a **behavioral bet**. Many social science experiments are, essentially, behavioral bets. For example, a test of whether women are more generous than men in charitable giving is a behavioral bet as theory is generally silent on gender differences in giving. For another example, one may wonder whether non-binding "cheap talk" prior to the play of a non-cooperative game matters for behavior relative to its absence. As standard theory states that non-binding cheap talk is rationally ignored—it is cheap talk after all—testing whether such pre-play communication matters amounts to a behavioral bet.

Such behavioral bets fall into Roth's second category for performing experiments, namely, searching for facts. Researchers conducting experiments to uncover facts typically do not have a fully worked-out theory in mind. Alternatively, experiments that involve searching for facts can be viewed as lying somewhere between what can be written down in theory and real economic phenomena. For instance, in many drug trials, there is no theory or model to suggest that the drug being tested will be useful in treating humans who suffer from some affliction. Nevertheless, there may be some historical knowledge or correlations or judgments by researchers that a drug, or combination of drugs, might be useful in treating the affliction. Similarly, while there may be no a priori reason to think that women are more generous than men, a researcher might observe that women are socialized to take care of their families and communities and that such socialization could lead women to be more generous than men (e.g., in terms of their willingness to give to charity).

One aim of conducting such behavioral bet experiments may be to assemble a body of empirical evidence on a particular phenomenon (e.g., gender differences). Alternatively, one might use experimental evidence to develop *new theories*, such as exploring the conditions under which cheap talk might be useful and when it might not be.

Finally, researchers whispering in the ears of princes use experiments to address policy questions or to design market institutions, which are of interest to policymakers. One of the most famous examples of the use of experiments to address policy questions was the design and testing of various auction formats, some of which were adopted by the U.S. Federal Communications Commission (FCC) to auction off licenses to use the certain bands of the electromagnetic spectrum beginning in the 1990s (see, for example, Plott (1997),Goeree *et al.* (2007)). Another important example is the use of experiments to design and improve upon centralized mechanisms for the matching of new doctors with hospitals (Kagel and Roth (2000)) or for the matching of students with universities (Hakimov and Kübler (2021)).

In this book, we adopt a pluralistic view. All three reasons to experiment are quite reasonable. Roth's classification is useful for thinking of the different *types* of economic experiments. However, there are other reasons to experiment that are not conditional on the type of experiment one conducts or whether the audience includes princes.

One of the most fruitful reasons to experiment is to provide evidence in settings where theory cannot make any precise predictions. For instance, the folk theorem of infinitely repeated games asserts that if players are sufficiently patient, then every feasible and individually rational payoff for the game corresponds to some sub-game perfect equilibrium of the repeated game. The empirical question that experimentalists have explored pertains to *which* equilibrium strategies players may be using. Similarly, in macroeconomics, Nobel laureate **Robert Lucas** observed (Lucas (1986)) that many macroeconomic models have multiple equilibria, limiting further theoretical claims. As Lucas puts it:

> "Economic theory does not resolve the question. One can imagine principles that would, but this cannot rule out the possibility that still other principles might resolve it quite differently. It is hard to see what can advance the discussion short of assembling a collection of people, putting them in the situation of interest and observing what they do."

Ken Binmore, a mathematician and economist (Binmore (1999)), makes a strong case for experimentation by *practitioners in the field*, e.g., psychologists doing psychology experiments, and economists doing economic experiments, as these researchers are more knowledgeable about the theories and assumptions to be tested. Binmore argues also for clean and transparent experimental designs. He observes that "just as we need to use clean test tubes in chemistry experiments, so we need to get the laboratory conditions right when testing economic theory." To that end, he suggests that experiments should be designed so that the problem subjects face is simple and clear, that adequate incentives are provided, and that there is sufficient time allowed for trial-and-error adjustment. As Binmore observes, it is easy to "bamboozle" subjects with complicated designs that serve only to confuse subjects, ultimately leading to easy refutation of theories. For this reason, there may be some value to experimentation by researchers with some stake in the outcome, or at least having some deep knowledge of the theory or hypothesis being evaluated. Thus, economists should not outsource experiments to psychologists, just as psychologists should not outsource experiments to economists. On the other hand, researchers with too vested an interest in the theory may unintentionally (or even intentionally) design the experiment or interpret the data in the manner that is most favorable to the theory being tested.

1.3   The Duhem–Quine Thesis

In discussing reasons to experiment, we have so far assumed that experimentation can yield data that would enable us to falsify theoretical claims. However, the **Duhem–Quine thesis** (named after Pierre Duhem, a French physicist who first proposed the thesis in 1906, and Willard V.O. Quine, an American philosopher who expanded upon it in 1951) asserts that no scientific hypothesis can be unambiguously tested independent from a range of additional and required auxiliary assumptions. This "non-separability" argument means that we have to be careful when making claims as to what a single experimental test actually reveals. For instance, if one evaluated the hypothesis that water boils at 100 degrees Celsius by conducting experiments in Denver, Colorado (the Mile High City), one might be led to reject that hypothesis in favor of the alternative that water boils at a lower temperature of 94 degrees Celsius. Of course, the missing, auxiliary assumption is atmospheric pressure. The 100 degree Celsius boiling point applies only at sea level. As one ascends in altitude, atmospheric pressure drops, meaning that less energy is required for water to boil, resulting in a lower boiling point.

Similarly, in social science experiments, we may have a model with clear testable predictions, but treatment differences may rely on many auxiliary assumptions (e.g., that individuals are not short-sighted, do not make calculation mistakes, and can apply Bayes's Rule). In essence, the thesis asserts that theories cannot be proven or disproved beyond all doubt.

One response, suggested by the Austrian and British philosopher Karl Popper, is to acknowledge the Duhem–Quine thesis but to seek to minimize the futility of the thesis for hypothesis testing via carefully controlled experimental testing. As (Popper, 1957, p.132) writes: "Admittedly Duhem is right when he says that we can test only huge and complex theoretical systems rather than isolated hypotheses; but if we test two such systems which differ in one hypothesis only, and if we can design experiments which refute the first system while leaving the second very well corroborated, then we may be on reasonably safe grounds if we attribute the failure of the first system to that hypothesis in which it differs from the other."

A second response to the Duhem–Quine thesis is for experimentalists to conduct further experiments to test whether violations of auxiliary assumptions are the cause of changes or the *lack* of changes in behavior across treatments or whether observed changes in behavior instead follow from theoretical predictions. For example, suppose it is unclear whether one's opponent in the Prisoner's Dilemma game is a rational, self-interested player who always plays his or her dominant strategy of Confess. This uncertainty might lead a player to choose Don't Confess (even though it is not his dominant strategy). To address this issue, we can conduct further experiments where we remove such uncertainty by replacing the "other player" (prisoner) with a robot player.

My own view is that experimentalists must recognize Duhem and Quine's non-separability argument when assessing and reporting on their findings. One should avoid claims that a theory is disproved by experimental evidence. Indeed, if all of the auxiliary assumptions of the theory were to hold, and if the proofs are correct, then the *theory* is true. However, that says little about whether the theory is empirically relevant to the subject matter.

1.4   So, Why Experiment?

Experiments are useful for understanding the *empirical relevance* of a theory and/or its auxiliary assumptions as a collection of hypotheses. After all, that is how theorists also view the world. Alternatively, one can use experiments to establish empirical regularities upon which to build new theories. Finally, many experimenters employ "experimental models" that are simplified versions of theoretical models or that make use of behavioral models informed by prior experimental results. They use these experimental models to tell stories in the same manner that theorists do.

In designing experiments to test theories or model empirical phenomena, Sitzia and Sugden (2011) offer some thoughtful, practical advice. They suggest that you first ask whether what happens in your experiment could possibly be different from what happens in your model. Understanding the range of possible outcomes is important for the questions that you can ask. For instance, if the model makes a unique prediction, then what would it mean if that unique prediction was not vindicated in the experiment? Are you prepared to offer an alternative explanation? If there are multiple equilibria, there is more latitude for experimental discovery, but you should be thinking about how you might rationalize the equilibrium that subjects choose to coordinate upon. Second, are you using the *simplest model* to evaluate the theory? If not, you may be losing control due to unnecessary added complexity. For instance, if one type of player's decision is rote or uninteresting, could they be replaced by a robot player? Finally, since many experiments can be conducted, and it is costly to do so, you should have a good motive for conducting your experiment. A good motive would be to try to understand some phenomenon observed in the "real world" through the evaluation of a model of that phenomenon or through data collection (e.g., on social preferences), as these would help to better understand that phenomenon. Alternatively, your experiment might provide some evidence on equilibrium selection in settings with multiple equilibria. As for bad motives, (Sitzia and Sugden, 2011, p. 341) write: "What you should not do is implement a model just because it is interesting or insightful or famous, and because you will be the first experimental economist to do so."

1.5 Let's Do an Experiment!

To better understand causal inference and other reasons to experiment, there is no substitute for conducting an experiment and observing the outcomes. The experiment I suggest below also illustrates the ideas of treatment and control, and is sufficiently simple to conduct with paper and pencil. Moreover, it can be conducted with any number of subjects.

To begin with, let us design the experiment while considering the number of subjects in the class/group/session. Let this size be denoted by N.

Second, the experiment will utilize a baseline control parameterization followed by a different treatment parameterization, and all N subjects will participate in both treatments. This approach is known as a "within-subjects design," which will be discussed in greater detail in Section 3.2.[3]

In the setup of the experiment that follows, the experimenter must choose a single, payoff relevant parameter, c, as explained below. I suggest that for the control treatment, one choose $c_0 = 0.2 \times N$, rounded to the nearest integer, and for the treatment variation, one choose $c_1 = 0.8 \times N$, again, rounded to the nearest integer.

To conduct the experiment, the N participants need both paper and pencil or some other means of recording their choices. Once everyone is ready, the experiment can begin. Subjects should be instructed not to communicate with one another and to not reveal their choices to one another (i.e., they must keep their choices private). The experimenter then announces:

Consider the following binary choice game. You make a choice of either A or B.

If you choose "A," then you earn 40 points (or experimental currency units (ECU)).

If you choose "B," then your payoff in points is:

$$40 + 2 \times (c - m),$$

where m is the number of people out of the N participants who have chosen "B" and c is a "treatment" variable. For the control treatment: c=c_0 so the payoff to "B" is:

$$40 + 2 \times (c_0 - m).$$

All N subjects should be informed of the value of c_0 and the payoff function for a B choice. They should then write down their choice of A or B on a piece of paper, e.g., My Choice 1 is: (A or B). After everyone has written down their answers, the experiment can proceed to the next treatment.

For the next treatment, the experimenter announces that $c = c_1$, so the payoff to choosing "B" is now:

$$40 + 2 \times (c_1 - m).$$

Again, all N subjects should be informed of the new value, c_1, and the new payoff function for a B choice. They should then write down their

---

[3] An alternative approach would be a "between-subjects" design, where one sample of N subjects participates in the control and a different sample of N subjects participates in the treatment.

choice of A or B on a piece of paper, e.g., My Choice 2 is: (A or B). After everyone has written down their two choices for the control, Choice 1, and the treatment, Choice 2, the experiment is over and the pieces of paper can be collected and the data analyzed.

Spoiler alert: Please conduct the experiment before reading further!

What does this simple experiment illustrate? This experiment illustrates both experimental design and causal inference. The design involves a baseline or control setting where the payoff relevant parameter c is set to c_0. In the treatment condition, everything is held constant except that c is changed to c_1. The outcome variable of each trial (treatment or control) is the number of A and B choices among the N participants (#A, #B).

What should we predict for the outcome of this experiment? Assuming that individuals are rational, self-interested payoff-maximizers (the auxiliary assumptions), we should have a situation where the payoff from choosing action A is equal to the payoff from choosing action B (i.e., $40 = 40 + 2(c - m)$ or $c = m$). This prediction follows from standard game-theoretic reasoning that, in equilibrium, there are no profitable deviations that players can make.

As it turns out, there are many different Nash equilibria that are consistent with this prediction. Assuming c is an integer, any profile of the N players where c choose B and the remaining $N - c$ choose A is a Nash equilibrium.[4]

For our purposes it will suffice to test whether the change in the treatment variable, c, has an effect on the number of B choices. Since the only parameter that changed from the control setting to the treatment setting was the parameter c, we can be quite confident that if we observe a difference in the number of B choices between the two treatments, that the change in the c parameter was **causal** for that change in behavior. Why? We have not changed anything else, including, in this experiment, the subject participants.

If the c parameter was set to $0.2 \times N$ in the control and to $0.8 \times N$ in the treatment, then we would expect 20% of participants to choose B (the main outcome variable) in the control and 80% of participants to choose B in the treatment. These are the precise "point predictions" of the theory, and we can assess the extent to which they hold or not. While it is possible

---

[4]Another symmetric pure strategy Nash equilibrium has $m = c - 1$ subjects choosing B and the remainder choosing A. There is also a symmetric mixed strategy Nash equilibrium where each player i chooses B with probability $p_i = \frac{c-1}{N-1}$ and A otherwise.

that both point predictions hold precisely, it is more likely that $c = m$ plus or minus some small number of players due to noisy best response behavior by subjects in response to the change in incentives, or some other confounding factors (e.g., subject confusion or inattention). Further sessions with additional samples of N subjects might yield average numbers of B choices across all sessions that are closer to the point predictions, and, treating each sample of N subjects as a single observation, this is the correct way to proceed to make a convincing causal inference. Still, in the context of a single, in-class session, we might judge the predictions of the theory not in terms of whether the point predictions are precisely met or not, but whether the *comparative statics predictions* of the theory hold or not. In particular, we might simply ask whether there were more B choices in the treatment condition where $m = c_1$ relative to the control setting where $m = c_0$, since $c_1 > c_0$. This simple comparative statics prediction nearly always holds up in a single session trial provided that the sample size of subjects, N, is sufficiently large.

The game just described and played is an N-player coordination game known as the "market entry game," which was first studied experimentally by **Daniel Kahneman** (another Economics Nobel laureate) (see Kahneman (1988)). In this game, the players, or firms, simultaneously decide whether to enter (choice B) or stay out of (choice A) a market. A general finding from this literature is that the capacity of the market, c, determines the amount of entry.

To Kahneman, a psychologist, the results of this experiment, which have subsequently been reproduced by many others, was surprising. "To a psychologist," he wrote, "it looked almost like magic ... The equilibrium outcome (which would be generated by the optimal policies of rational players) was produced in this case by a group of excited and confused people, who simply did not seem to know what they were doing."

Of course, to economists, it is the incentives that ultimately explain the results. As confused or irrational as people may seem, in pursuing their own self-interest, they are able to coordinate on the equilibrium prediction of the model that $m = c$ plus or minus some small amount of noise.

The possibility of observing this equilibration result and understanding how it changes in response to changes in incentives (changes in the market capacity, c) provides a useful illustration of the power of the experimental method. Without conducting this experiment in the laboratory, we would not be able to so clearly appreciate that the aggregate outcomes we observe in terms of firms who have entered markets reflects some best responses to underlying incentives. Indeed, we might even believe it was magic.

This type of understanding reveals the power of applying the experimental method.

Chapter 2

Where to Experiment?

When conducting experiments, an important consideration is the subject population that the experimenter samples from and whether the experiment is conducted in a natural field setting or in a more artificial setting such as a laboratory.

The considerations that go into the questions of **where** and on **whom** one conducts an experiment are clearly interrelated, as the location of the experiment largely determines the subject pool. Perhaps the most important consideration that researchers must confront when choosing where (or on whom) to experiment concerns internal versus external validity.

An experiment is said to have good **internal validity** if the design enables clear, robust causal inferences and possible confounding factors have been eliminated or minimized. Typically, good internal validity requires the control afforded by a laboratory, or, at minimum, laboratory-like conditions, where the information, incentives, communication abilities, and focus of the subject population can be tightly monitored and where treatments involve a single change to the environment, holding all other factors constant (the *ceteris paribus* assumption in economics). However, good internal validity can also be accomplished in the field, such as when the major instrument of control is simple randomization of subjects across treatments and there are no other differences in the environment that subjects face across treatments.

By contrast, **external validity** is concerned with whether causal relationships can be generalized to different subject populations or to different settings, e.g., to settings with higher stakes or with longer decision times, or those that occur in more natural settings. Thus, external validity is also known as "generalizability." The extent to which experimental evidence is generalizable will most often be a matter of some speculation. We cannot conclude that the results of an experiment generalize unless and until the experiment has been conducted on a wide cross-section of different populations and ideally by different experimenters using the same protocols.

It is important to stress that external validity or **generalizability** are not properties that are inherent to naturally occurring, non-experimental data; we might have such data, for example, for one country, but it would still remain unclear whether such data and the findings for that one country can be generalized to or are externally valid for other countries. That is, external validity or generalizability are concerns for all types of datasets, not just those generated by experiments.

Figure 2.1 places several different types of experiments on the internal-external validity spectrum.

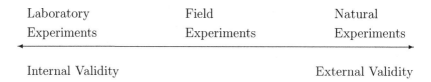

Figure 2.1: Validity of experimental designs.

As noted, laboratory experiments have good internal validity because potentially confounding factors (context, subject distractions, the interdependence of subject choices) can be minimized. However, the same conditions that enhance internal validity, such as a controlled laboratory environment with limited communication and close supervision, can hinder external validity. For instance, subjects may struggle to make decisions in a context-free setting or feel uneasy in the unnatural laboratory environment where they are aware of being observed. Additionally, if the incentives provided are not sufficiently large, it can also affect external validity.

At the other extreme, as shown in Figure 2.1, lies natural experiments. A natural experiment is one in which some external event (e.g., a war, plague, technological change, or a change in government policy) outside the control of any experimenter is exploited to make causal inferences. Such experiments have excellent external validity because the event and the reaction to it unfold naturally. However, it is not possible for researchers to conduct such experiments and, indeed, they are not experiments that **can be designed**. For this reason, we exclude discussion of natural experiments from these notes.

Finally, in the intermediate range on the internal-external validity spectrum of Figure 2.1 lie field experiments, which randomize subjects across treatments in a real-world economic environment. This stands in contrast to laboratory experiments, which do this in the more controlled environment of the laboratory. This randomization can be done overtly or covertly. In the language of Harrison and List (2004), discussed in further detail below, field experiments can be classified as artefactual, framed field experiments, or natural field experiments. In artefactual and framed field experiments, human subjects are aware of their participation—that is, their participation requires informed consent or clear instructions are read aloud to them.

In a natural field experiment, by contrast, assignment to the control or one of the treatment groups is covert, meaning that subjects do not know they are participating in an experiment.

The choice of *where* to conduct an experiment is also related to the subject pool that is used. In the next two sections, we will provide some of the rationales for choosing to experiment in the laboratory versus in the field—and we will also consider approaches that hybridize the two approaches.

2.1 Reasons to Conduct Experiments in a Laboratory

The primary reason to conduct experiments in laboratories is the tremendous control that a laboratory environment affords, enabling causal inferences to be effectively made. The elements of control are many. A partial and incomplete list would include the following:

1. **Control of extraneous factors and manipulation of independent variables. Extraneous factors**, also known as "confounders," are variables that may be positively or negatively correlated with both the independent variables of the experiment and the dependent outcome variables of interest that are not accounted for or are unobservable and thus unwittingly confound the making of causal inferences. For example, the gender or the speaking voice of the person conducting an experimental intervention might have an influence on the outcome variable in an experiment. Another potential confounding

factor is **selection bias**, which is where subjects who choose to participate in an experiment have certain characteristics (e.g., confidence or financial needs) that are not present among non-participants, thus generating potential confounding factors. Finally, a third type of confounding factor is the information and communication opportunities available to subjects before, during, and after an experimental intervention. While laboratory experiments are by no means immune to such confounding factors, they may be better equipped to deal with such factors than are studies conducted in the field. For instance, in laboratory studies, the experimental interventions can always be carried out by the same experimenter (or the same team), while the information that subjects have available to them and their ability to communicate with others can be more tightly restricted or monitored. Selection bias remains an issue in both the field and the laboratory, but since laboratory experiments are more frequently replicated than field experiments, selection biases may be reduced or mitigated as an experiment is repeatedly conducted by other researchers.

2. **Measurement accuracy.** The control of the laboratory enables better accuracy in the measurement of responses to treatment changes or in the evaluation of overall welfare effects. Consider the "all causes model" of Heckman and Vytlacil (2007), which specifies that the outcome variable of interest,

$$Y = f(X_1, X_2, \ldots, X_N, U),$$

is a function of various X_i causal factors (some of which are the subject of treatment manipulation) and where U represents other exogenous factors for which no explanatory mechanism is posited (e.g., gender). To accurately measure the effects of changes in one casual factor, say a change in factor 1, ΔX_1 on Y, one needs to hold constant all other causal factors (assuming an independent relationship) as well as U. In the field, this can be difficult because other causal or exogenous factors may be unobservable or measured at different intervals of time or across different samples. What is more, participants in treated groups may fail to participate in (or "take-up") the treatment, whereas in laboratory studies, treatment interventions are typically fully enforced such that attrition and other selection biases are greatly reduced. It follows that the measurement of treatment effects is enhanced by the stationarity and control of the laboratory environment. In addition, if one has a structural model that is being tested in the laboratory, the greater accuracy of experimental interventions also provides better measures of the model-specified welfare consequences or of the efficiency of the treatment interventions.

3. **Replicability.** A third advantage of laboratory experiments is replicability. The **replication** of experimental findings is an important element of the scientific process, primarily because it lends greater credence to the original findings. Laboratory experiments are designed in such a way as to foster this replicability. For instance, they often involve written instructions and quizzes that can be administered to other subject pools. Moreover, the experiments are often computerized using software that can be run in other laboratories or online. Increasingly, as researchers have begun to conduct experiments using online workforces such as Amazon's Mechanical Turk, and Prolific, the lines between field and laboratory studies have become blurred. However, the collection of data using computerized programs and online workforces makes replications even easier and more faithful, as they make it possible to replicate a study using the *same* subject pool.

By contrast, field studies are often conducted in collaboration with some private or government sector entity under conditions that may be more difficult to replicate. Field experiment partners may impose restrictions on the type of treatment interventions that can be conducted and on the type of information that can be reported. Moreover, the time, setting, and conditions under which any given field experimental intervention is conducted may also be highly unique, meaning that faithful replications of such interventions can be difficult.

Related to the question of where to conduct an experiment is the question of *who* the subjects are. The two issues are clearly linked in that the choice of where one conducts an experiment often restricts the set of subjects who are available to participate in that experiment.

Given that most experimental laboratories are affiliated with universities, it is not surprising that many (though not all) laboratory studies use the convenience sample of university students.

Convenience samples are samples from a population that are not drawn by a well-defined random method. For example, asking the students in a class that you teach to participate in your experiment does not comprise a random sample of the student population because there could be systematic differences between your students and the student population. For instance, your own students may better understand how you think about issues or what your research interests are relative to a random sample of the student population. Hence, they may try to guess what you want them to do and act accordingly—behavior that is referred to as **experimenter demand effects** (see Zizzo (2010) for a discussion).

Indeed, the entire student population at universities is often referred to as a convenience sample, even though samples from the university student population are a very typical subject pool.[1]

While the use of convenience samples is sometimes criticized, convenience samples can be an acceptable choice if there is no a priori reason to think that there are any systematic differences between the convenience sample and another one drawn from the population of interest.

2.2   Reasons to Conduct Experiments in the Field

The appeal of field experiments is that one can observe the authentic behavioral responses of subjects to treatment interventions in their natural habitat, thus removing the sterility, abstract framing, and monitoring that may alter or adversely impact subject behavior in laboratory experiments. At the same time, the very naturalness of the environment in which field experiments are conducted can often result in some loss of control (e.g., over communication among subjects, the information they have available, their continued participation in the study) and replication can be more difficult.

The main advantage of field experiments is that they are conducted on a population of direct interest to the research question, meaning they can provide greater external validity. For example, development economists have conducted field experiments to evaluate the impact of various policies aimed at improving educational outcomes or lifting people out of poverty. To address whether these policies work, there can be no better population than the one for which those policies were designed.

The field experiments of development economists often involve simple randomized control trial (RCT) methods following the lead of Nobel prize winners Abhijit Banerjee, Esther Duflo, and Michael Kremer. In such

---

[1]Students at western universities have been referred to as "WEIRD", i.e., western, educated, industrialized, rich, and democratic by Henrich *et al.* (2010), which is to say that they may *not* be all that representative of the rest of the world.

studies, one specifies the outcome variable(s) of interest and then randomly assigns participants to a treatment or control group. For example, beginning in the 1990s, RCTs conducted in India by Banerjee and Duflo showed that special needs students who received the treatment of targeted tutoring improved in their educational performance relative to students in the control group who did not receive such treatment. In Kenya, Kremer and his colleagues tested whether students in schools that received extra resources, such as textbooks and free meals, improved in their educational performance and found no difference in performance relative to a control group of students who did not receive those extra resources. These conclusions would not be as strong or convincing if the populations were not ones for which the policy interventions were being evaluated.

Harrison and List (2004) provide a useful typology of field experiments and contrast these with conventional laboratory experiments, which they define as employing "a standard subject pool of students, and abstract framing and an imposed set of rules." The three major types of field experiments are as follows:

1. An **artefactual** (i.e., "fake") field experiment, which is essentially a laboratory experiment but with non-standard subjects. Such experiments do not have to be conducted in a laboratory so long as they use laboratory-like methods that control information flows and involve random assignments. Indeed, one variant of the artefactual field experiment is known as a "lab-in-the-field" design, e.g., where the experiment is conducted on non-student subjects using mobile devices or pen-and-paper.

2. A **framed field** experiment goes beyond the artefactual field experiment and uses some real field context, e.g., in the framing of the task, the items traded, or in the information available.

3. A **natural** field experiment is a fully immersive field experiment where subjects naturally undertake tasks common to their everyday lives and do not know that they are participating in an experiment. A natural field experiment should not be confused with a *natural experiment*, which is an experiment that occurs due to some chance policy change, act of god, or happenstance and was not part of a planned experimental design.

We can provide a clearer sense of the three types of field experiments and their advantages using some examples from the literature.

An example of an artefactual or lab-in-the-field experiment is that of Chakravarty *et al.* (2016), who report on a field experiment conducted in India. They explore how village-level religious identity—either Hindu or Muslim—affects intra- and inter-group cooperation in two-player, one-shot, Stag Hunt, and Prisoner's Dilemma Games. Treatments involved (1) the religious identity of the village (mostly Hindu, mostly Muslim, or fragmented) and (2) the religious identity of the two players. They considered in-group/in-group matches where a Muslim subject played with a fellow Muslim subject or a Hindu subject played with a fellow Hindu subject and in-group/out-group matches where a Hindu subject played with a Muslim subject. In their control treatment, the identity of a subject's match was not known. The two games were presented to subjects in a manner similar to a laboratory setting. The two actions available to the two players (cooperate and defect) and the payoffs earned by each from the four possible outcomes were explained to the subjects. However, the religious identities of the participants and the religious fragmentation of the village were hypothesized to have an impact beyond the strategic considerations of the games. Indeed, they found that cooperation rates among people of the same religious group were higher when subjects were drawn from religiously fragmented villages as compared with the case where they were drawn from religiously homogeneous villages. This is a good example of where the field nature of an experiment—the religious identity of players and the religious fragmentation of the village—would be challenging to replicate in a laboratory setting, yet where laboratory-type games can be easily played in the field.

An example of a framed field experiment is a study by Noussair *et al.* (2015), who explore the tragedy of the commons (over-exploitation of a natural resource subject to regeneration) by using experienced fishers at a recreational fishing facility as subject participants. Groups of 4 fishers could fish for trout in up to 4 sequential periods of 1 hour each. The group catch was limited to 8 fish per period. Initially, in period 1, 2 fish per fisher (8 fish) plus a few extra fish were released. The facility was such that the stock of fish in the lake could be artificially replenished at the start of each subsequent 1-hour period. The fishers were instructed that, at the start of period (hours) 2, 3, and 4, a quantity of new fish would be released that was equal to the number of fish caught in the previous period by groups *who had not exhausted their catch limit of 8 fish*. The experiment explores whether a group of 4 fishers can achieve the social optimum, which here is defined as catching 4 fish in each of the first 3 periods and then 8 fish in the final period (a total of 20 fish) or the non-cooperative Nash equilibrium, where each group catches 8 fish in the first period so that the resource is exhausted and all fishing ends after a single period. Here the field experiment is framed in terms of the number of fish caught, while other field-specific features involve the natural competitiveness of the experienced fishers. Finally, fisher effort is measured by the (average) number of times a fisherman casts his rod per minute. The main finding is that there is no support for the cooperative outcome: there is no difference in effort between the fourth period and the first period and effort does not seem to depend on the stock of fish remaining. Here the framing of the study and the use of experienced fishers help to reinforce the idea that the tragedy of the commons is a real phenomenon.

Finally, an example of a natural field experiment is a study by Karlan and List (2007), who explore how changes in the price of charitable giving affect contributions in a direct mail solicitation of 50,000 supporters of a liberal organization. The supporters (or, in this case, the subjects) were unaware that they were participating in an experiment, which qualifies this study as a natural field experiment. Subjects were sent fundraising letters that differed in terms of whether their contributions would be matched or not (control). Karlan and List randomized their subjects into two main groups: 33% control (no match) and 67% treatment (match). Within the match treatment, 3 different match rates were considered—a 1:1 match, a 2:1 match, and a 3:1 match—where the first number is the dollars matched for every dollar donated. They report that those assigned to a match group treatment contribute 19% more than those in the control treatment and that a match offer significantly increases the probability that an individual donates anything by 22%. On the other hand, the higher match ratios of 2:1 and 3:1 had no additional impact on donations beyond the 1:1 match. This is a good example of how a natural field experiment can make effective use of an existing institutional feature—in this case the fundraising letter—to shed light on a question of economic interest—how the price of charitable contributions affects giving behavior—all within an environment that is so natural that subjects do not know they are participating in an experiment.

2.3   Are Student Subjects Different from Non-student Subjects?

Lurking in the background in the debate as to whether experiments should be conducted in the laboratory or in the field is the question of whether the convenience samples of student subjects used in most laboratory experiments differ from the samples of non-student subjects that are used in most field experiments. Indeed, in a survey of 60 laboratory experimental economics papers published in major economic journals, Danielson and Holm (2007) report that just 4 (6.67%) used non-student subject pools.

Non-student subject pools can be further classified as being (1) a representative sample from the general population or (2) "professionals" who are skilled in the matter at hand, e.g., the fishers in the tragedy of the commons experiment discussed earlier.

In the case where a representative sample from the general population is the target sample, various comparisons suggest that there can be differences. For example, Snowberg and Yariv (2021) compare the outcome of various experimental interventions on university students versus a representative sample of the U.S. population (their non-student population). For the student population, they further consider whether participants complete experimental interventions inside a laboratory or outside a laboratory. While they find some differences in behavior between the student and non-student populations, these differences primarily amount to noisier responses in the non-student subject pool. The noisier responses are attributable to differences in subject attributes that are easy to control with econometric methods. Importantly, they do not find that subjects behave differently inside the laboratory than outside of it. In strategic settings, a common difference between student and non-student subjects is that students are closer to the homo-economicus ideal of money-maximizing behavior, while non-student subjects exhibit more other-regarding social concerns (see, e.g., Belot *et al.* (2015)).

The question of students versus "professionals" has also been studied and has produced mixed results. Perhaps this is because the notion of what constitutes a professional for an experimental study is not always so clear. For instance, financial traders or business people are often thought to be more "professional" in regard to, say, pricing assets or making profit-maximizing decisions. On the other hand, the experimental environments in which they are placed might not precisely capitalize on their experience. Fréchette (2015) reports on 13 experimental papers where a treatment variable hinged on whether the subjects were students or professionals. He categorized the experimental outcomes in terms of how close the two different subject pools were to theoretical predictions. The results are shown in Figure 2.2, from which it can be seen that professionals are sometimes closer and sometimes further from theoretical predictions than students; yet, in 69.2% of the reviewed studies, there were no differences. One reason for

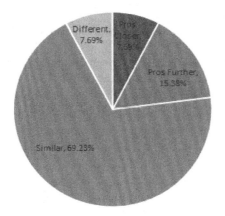

Figure 2.2: Professionals versus students in terms of distance to theoretical predictions.
Source: Data from Fréchette (2015).

this may be that the controlled nature of experimental interventions often leads to settings that are unfamiliar to *all* subjects, even those regarded as professionals.

2.4 Online Workforces

The lines between laboratory and field experiments have become increasingly blurred with the development of **online workforces**. The first online workforce, Amazon's Mechanical Turk or "MTurk," was originally developed to solve a problem related to duplicate products appearing on its website after Amazon found that human workers were better at correcting these errors than were artificial intelligence algorithms. In 2005, this online workforce, devoted to what had become known as Human Intelligence Tasks (HITs), was offered up to the general public for the completion of other tasks, with Amazon collecting administrative fees. Thus, a new subject pool was born. Since then, other online workforces have appeared, including Upwork and Guru, with some specifically aimed at social science researchers such as Prolific.

Online workforces have certain advantages. For instance, they provide a broader demographic sample of subjects than the convenience sample of university students. Moreover, they are considerably cheaper subject pools, perhaps because the subjects are already online, are accustomed to working online, and lack the distractions that student subjects have of needing to attend classes or show up to laboratories. However, they also come with certain disadvantages. These tend to be the disadvantages associated with any field population, such as the lack of monitoring of their activities and the inability to restrict their communication or use of other information. Furthermore, there is also the possibility that an online workforce agent is actually a programmed robot player, although there are ways to check for such subjects by administering comprehension quizzes before the start of an experiment.

To date, the use of online workforce subjects in experimental economics is still rather new, but preliminary results suggest that, like students versus non-students, there are not great differences between the behavior of online workforce subjects and other subject pools. For instance, Arechar *et al.* (2018) compare play of voluntary contribution games with student subjects and MTurkers and report that the same patterns of cooperation and punishment in the laboratory are also observed in the online population. Similarly, Snowberg and Yariv (2021) report that MTurkers are noisier in their behavior than student subjects but more similar in their behavior to subjects drawn from a representative sample of the U.S. population.

Technological developments are also blurring the lines between laboratory and field experiments. For instance, Li *et al.* (2021), after getting student subjects to play a variety of traditional laboratory games on their own mobile phones in their location of choice, find few differences between the data they collected and data sourced from more controlled laboratory settings. Indeed, as the technology for conducting experiments evolves further, the distinction between lab and field experiments may disappear entirely. What is likely to remain are the elements of control that are the hallmark of experimental social science. We turn to these elements in the next chapter.

Chapter 3

How to Experiment: Methods

The advantages of laboratory or field experimentation lie in the **control** that the researcher exerts over the environment in which subjects make choices. Good control over the environment is what enables good internal validity. The various methods of control discussed in this chapter lie at the heart of the experimental methodology; thus, it is important to understand these elements of control before engaging in experimental research.

3.1 Randomization

While *random sampling* from a population is desirable from the perspective of external validity, once one has selected a subject sample, it is the *random assignment* of subjects to the baseline and other treatment conditions that is perhaps the most important element of control used by experimenters in both the laboratory and the field. Indeed, random assignment is the essential element of control in field RCTs and is associated with planned experimental design. The purpose of **random assignment** is to assure that the treatment subgroups are ex-ante identical to one another prior to the experimental intervention. If this were not the case, then any differences observed across treatment subgroups could potentially be attributed to factors other than the treatment itself, leading to confounding variables that could affect the interpretation of causality. Indeed, in field RCTs, it is a common practice to report statistics on the characteristics of subjects (e.g., age, gender) who were randomly assigned to control and treatment groups and establish that there are no systematic differences in these subject characteristics. This is because random assignment is a critical factor for causal inference. One approach to ensuring that this is the case is to use a **matched pairs design**. In this type of design, subjects are paired according to the similarity of their characteristics, such as age, gender, or socioeconomic status. One member of each pair is then randomly assigned to the control group while the other is assigned to the treatment group, thereby ensuring that each group has a similar distribution to the matching variable(s). This approach allows the researcher to more conclusively associate any difference in outcomes to the treatment change rather than to differences in characteristics between the two groups.

Random assignment is not limited to the assignment of subjects to treatment conditions. Indeed, it is often the case that subjects within a treatment are randomly assigned different roles, tasks, or are randomly matched into groups of players. Once again, the logic is that ex-ante, each subject has an equal probability of being assigned to a role or group, so that there are no selection biases that might confound the interpretation of the results.

The type of randomization described thus far is known as complete or **simple random assignment**. An alternative approach, **block random assignment**, randomizes subjects into groups in order to produce equal sample sizes. A variant of block randomization is **stratified randomization**, which is utilized when one needs to control the influence of covariates, e.g., subject characteristics such as cognitive ability, age, or location. To apply this method, one requires knowledge of these covariates and how they might influence outcomes in advance. The stratified random procedure is designed to create separate blocks for each combination of covariates and to then assign subjects to the appropriate block.

3.2 Within versus Between-Subject Designs

Block and stratified random designs are thought of as *error-purifying* randomization methods. Perhaps the ultimate error-purifying method is the "within subjects" experimental design, which is where each subject participates in both the control and *all other* treatment conditions. In this case, the heterogeneity in subject characteristics across treatment conditions is theoretically zero and random assignment is no longer needed as a method of control, though random sampling of the set of subjects from the population is still desirable.

However, such "within subject" designs present other problems. Among these are (1) "order effects," where the order in which subjects face the different treatments of a within subject design can influence the observed outcomes, and (2) "experimenter demand effects," where announced changes in treatment conditions might reveal or signal to subjects that the experimenter wants them to behave differently, and the subjects respond to such "demands." The remedies to these issues are many, but to address order or spillover effects it is common for experimenters to conduct sessions in which all or many of the different possible treatment orders are considered to check for evidence of spillover effects. As for experimenter demand effects, these can be unavoidable in a within subjects experimental design but can be minimized by not announcing in advance the treatment change until the point in the study where the treatment conditions do in fact change.

At the other extreme is the so-called "between-subjects" design, where each subject is confronted with only one treatment.[1] This design is commonly used when the researcher wants to record multiple observations on individual or group behavior over time, but where repeated data collection would limit the amount of time for collecting data or giving instructions for other treatments. In a between-subjects design, subjects should be both randomly sampled from the population and randomly assigned to the different treatments using the complete, block, or stratified randomization methods.

The main advantage of between-subject designs is the lack of order or experimenter demand effects. Subjects experience only a single treatment condition and so they do not have a clear sense of the hypotheses the experimenter is testing. Consequently, there are no spillover or order effects.

Having said this, such spillover effects cannot be ruled out if there *were* different treatments or if subjects come to the experiment in one frame of mind or the other, and so, in a between-subjects design, one is essentially sweeping such concerns under the rug. As Charness *et al.* (2012) note, it is also the case that within subject designs are more consistent with theoretical *comparative statics* exercises, where the researcher imagines certain scenarios, e.g., what happens when the group size increases or the cost of some activity changes. This is more difficult to assess if the subjects

---

[1]The word "between" refers to the fact that the researcher is comparing different conditions between groups. By contrast, "within" means that the researcher is comparing different conditions within the same group.

assigned to two different treatment conditions always reside in separate
experimental sessions.

3.3   Induced Value Theory

A further element of control, especially for use in laboratory studies, is
induced value theory (IVT), as first elaborated upon by Vernon Smith
(Smith (1976),Smith (1982)). The idea of IVT is that if one wants to assign
value to some fictional item that agents trade for or if one wants to induce
subjects to maximize profit, utility, or other payoff functions, then it is
first necessary to consider whether the inducements used to assign values
will properly capture the incentives of the theory, thereby providing a clean
test.

As an illustration of the need for inducing values, consider a standard
first-price sealed-bid auction experiment (to be discussed in greater detail
in Chapter 9). N subjects $i = 1, 2, \ldots, N$ are assigned a private value v_i
for the item being auctioned off. They are each asked to simultaneously
place a bid, b_i for the item, with the understanding that the highest bid
will win the auction. Specifically, they are told that their payoff is given by
the following:

$$\pi_i = \begin{cases} v_i - b_i & \text{if } b_i = \max\{b_1, b_2, \ldots, b_N\}, \\ 0 & \text{otherwise.} \end{cases}$$

By describing subject i's payoff in this manner, their induced value v_i comes
to mean something in payoff terms: subjects learn that their objective is
surplus maximization, and they have to trade off the amount of the surplus
they can possibly get with their bid, $(v_i - b_i)$, against the fact that a higher
bid, b_i (and a lower surplus), increases the probability that they will win
the auction.

Smith (1982) proposes 3 sufficient conditions for inducing values. All
of these conditions concern the *reward* medium used to induce values or
objectives. While there are many possibilities for such rewards—including
gift cards, grades, food, and prestige—experimental economists have largely
settled upon money payments as the most effective reward medium.

The three sufficient conditions are as follows:

1. **Non-satiation (or Monotonicity).** Let $V^i[m, \theta]$ be the unobserved, homegrown utility of subject i over the reward medium, m,
   and everything else, θ. It is asserted that $V_m^i > 0$ for all i and (m, θ)

combinations, where V_m^i is the partial derivative of homegrown utility with respect to m.

For example, suppose a theoretical objective is to maximize $\pi(x) - cx$ by choice of x, where $\pi(x)$ is a profit function and c is a variable cost, and rewards m are proportional to the π function. Then the profit-maximizing choice of x^* is unaffected by V^i, i.e., subject i maximizes $V^i[m, \theta] = V^i[\pi(x) - cx]$. The first-order conditions imply that $V_m^i[\pi_x(x) - c] = 0$, or $x^* = \pi_x^{-1}c$ since $V_m^i > 0$.

As noted, it is generally believed that monetary rewards (specifically *cash* or electronic money transfers) satisfy nonsatiation.

2. **Salience.** This condition requires that changes in the rewards offered, Δm, are determined by the individual's actions (and possibly by the actions of others or by Nature/chance) in a precise fashion that is in accordance with the environment/institution/theory being induced. For example, suppose that, in theory, the objective is to maximize $U(x) = \log(x)$. Then suppose a choice of x in the experiment yields a monetary reward of $m(x)$. Salience requires that $m(x') - m(x) \sim \log(x') - \log(x)$.

Salience also requires that changes in monetary rewards are sufficiently *perceptible* to subjects. On this point, Harrison (1989) criticized some early auction experiments, arguing that departures from Nash bidding behavior could be rationalized by the flatness of the payoff function near the equilibrium. In such cases, subjects may not be properly incentivized to achieve the optimal policy. Experimenters should remain cognizant of this potential issue and make efforts to emphasize the optimality of the reward mechanism, particularly in monetary terms, to ensure subjects are sufficiently incentivized.

3. **Dominance.** The third condition of dominance is that changes in subjects' utility depend primarily on changes in the reward mechanism, m, and *not* on other factors, θ. Such additional factors may include the payments earned by other subjects, the experimenter's own preferences, transaction/decision costs associated with the complexity of the experimental design, and, finally, the opportunity cost of participating in the experiment. These other factors should all be minimized, but how?

The standard solutions are as follows: (1) Not revealing other subjects' payoffs. Smith calls this privacy, and it is done to avoid other-regarding concerns; (2) Not revealing the aims of the experiment.

This is done to avoid experimenter demand effects (see Zizzo (2010)). Relatedly, researchers should minimize any contextual cues that may trigger normative behavior. For example, experimenters should avoid the use of any loaded terminology. That is to say, if the context or framing seem as though they may be important, then consider context/framing as a treatment variable and compare the outcomes with context/framing versus with a neutral framing. (3) Making decisions as clear/simple as possible. This minimizes decision-cost concerns. A good maxim to remember is: KISS—keep it simple stupid! One should make all decision screens as simple as possible. Provide figures and sliders/calculators as needed. To the extent that decision-making cannot be simplified, increase the rewards, m. (4) In order to maintain the subjects' attention on the experiment itself and prevent them from being preoccupied with alternative uses of their time, it is essential that the researchers offer sufficiently attractive compensation in the chosen reward medium. Determining the precise amount can be somewhat subjective, but Smith suggests "[using] payoff levels that are high for the subject population" (p. 934).

Smith argues that non-satiation, salience, and dominance are *sufficient conditions* for conducting a controlled experiment with parallel implications for behavior in actual economies and that these three conditions continue to guide the experimental designs of experimental social science researchers.

If one has set up a proper controlled experiment using IVT, then Smith argues that one may claim **parallelism** with regard to the inferences that can be made, which is related to the notion of external validity. By parallelism, (Smith, 1982, p. 936) means the following: "Propositions about the behavior of individuals and the performance of institutions that have been tested in laboratory microeconomies apply also to nonlaboratory microeconomies where similar ceteris paribus assumptions hold."

3.4   Extrinsic versus Intrinsic Rewards

While experimental economists typically assume that variations in monetary rewards are the chief factors motivating an individual's choices, this may not always be the case. Psychologists often distinguish such "extrinsic" rewards from "intrinsic" rewards, which are rewards that are intrinsic to the activity itself, e.g., the feeling of pride in a job well done or the warm glow feeling one gets from altruistically giving to another.

It is possible that extrinsic rewards like money, which are typically offered in economics experiments, may "crowd out" these intrinsic motivations. For this reason, Gneezy and Rustichini (2000) advise researchers to "pay enough or don't pay at all," which can be interpreted as making the reward medium money, the dominant concern.

But what is enough? As noted above, Smith (1982) suggested paying subjects amounts that are high for the subject population. However, what constitutes a high payoff can be very subjective—thus, what one individual may deem a high payoff, another individual may see as too low or even insulting. Hence, an appropriate balance must be struck.

As an illustration of this, consider one of the studies reported on by Gneezy and Rustichini (2000). They recruited 160 undergraduates students at the University of Haifa for this study and offered them a fixed payment of 60 NIS for answering 50 IQ questions in a 45-minute period.[2] There were four treatments, and so 1/4 of the subjects, 40, were randomly assigned to each treatment which varied the variable incentives for answering the 50 IQ questions. The treatments were as follows:

- Treatment 1: No additional payment (beyond the fixed show-up payment).

- Treatment 2: 0.10 NIS per correct IQ quiz answer.

- Treatment 3: 1 NIS per correct IQ quiz answer.

- Treatment 4: 3 NIS per correct IQ quiz answer.

The results of these 4 treatments, in terms of the number of correct answers (the outcome variable), are shown in Figure 3.1.

The means suggest that the payment of a small amount, 0.10 NIS, might *crowd out* the intrinsic desire to perform well on the IQ test, as evidenced by the difference in mean scores between no payment and the 10 cent treatment. In statistical tests, however, there is no statistically significant difference in IQ scores between the 0 and 10 cent treatments, or between the 1 and 3 NIS treatments, but there *is* a significant difference between the latter two treatments (1 and 3) and the first two treatments (0 and 0.1), which underscores the notion that one should pay "enough," otherwise there will be no reason to use money as an incentive in the first place. It further follows from these results that one can pay too much as well!

---

[2] At the time of the experiment, $1 USD = 3.5 NIS.

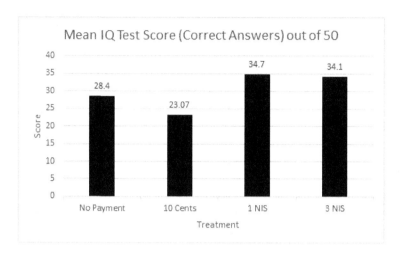

Figure 3.1: Mean IQ scores across different payment treatments in the study by Gneezy and Rustichini (2000).
Source: Data from Gneezy and Rustichini (2000).

3.5 Payment Protocols

The example above nicely illustrates the convention that experimental economists have adopted of providing a fixed show-up payment to induce subjects to participate coupled with variable payments that depend on their performance in the experiment in a manner that conforms to theory or some desirable outcome, like getting a good score on a test.

As a general practice, most experimentalists typically set the mean of subjects' variable earnings to be a multiple (usually greater than 1) of the fixed show-up payment. The idea behind this approach is to emphasize the power of the reward medium on the decisions that subjects make in the experimental study, and not for merely participating in the study. Thus, in practice, one should first set the fixed payment for participation and then parameterize the variable payment in such a way that the bulk of the expected monetary earnings come from the variable component.

Regarding this variable component of earnings, there are several different payment protocols that experimentalists use.

1. Pay every round/task. In experiments where subjects make decisions repeatedly or complete multiple tasks, the pay every round/task protocol is used to reflect this: subjects are paid their earnings for every round or task completed. This approach would seem to have

the advantage of being simple to explain and ensuring that money rewards are an ever-present concern, but there are also some potential problems to consider. First, as subjects are usually informed of the state of their earnings, or "wealth," this information might affect their behavior, depending on their attitudes toward risk. For instance, subjects might behave in a more risk-seeking manner if their earnings/wealth is low and might behave in a more risk-averse manner as their wealth increases. For instance, in auction experiments, Kagel and Levin (1986) and Ham *et al.* (2005) report that bidders who have won in previous rounds bid less aggressively in later rounds. There is also evidence of hedging behavior from paying for all tasks. For example, consider a two-player binary-choice (X or Y) game where subjects are asked to provide incentivized beliefs regarding what they think their opponent will choose in the game (mechanisms for eliciting such beliefs are discussed in the next section). If subjects are also incentivized to make a certain choice in the game, then they might follow a simple hedging strategy where they state their belief regarding what their opponent will do and choose an action that is the opposite of a strategic best response to their reported belief, thereby maximizing the chance of earning *some* payoff (see, e.g., Blanco *et al.* (2010) and Armantier and Treich (2013)).

2. Pay just one round randomly chosen from all rounds played. To avoid "wealth effects" or hedging opportunities, many experimentalists choose to pay just one round of a repeated task, randomly chosen at the end. If there are hedging opportunities among two or more tasks, then, under this protocol, one pays for just one of the tasks, randomly chosen. This pay-one approach has the advantage of minimizing wealth effects and hedging behavior. Furthermore, it enables the researcher to raise the monetary stakes by a considerable amount each round. Finally, Azrieli *et al.* (2018) show that, under certain conditions, the pay-one round/task is the optimal payment protocol.

Common concerns regarding the pay-one approach are that it might dilute subjects' incentives to perform well in every round or confuse subjects about their expected payoffs, e.g., in tasks where subjects are making choices about lotteries. For instance, Harrison *et al.* (2015) find violations of the reduction of compound lotteries axiom if subjects have to make a series of choices between lotteries and then one of those lottery choices is randomly paid. They do not find such violations if subjects face just one choice and are paid for it.

More generally, the experimental evidence for whether pay-one or pay-all affects experimental findings is mixed, though both the consensus and theoretical arguments seem to favor the pay-one approach (see, e.g., Charness *et al.* (2016), Voslinsky and Azar (2021)).

3. Choose a subset of subjects for payment of their variable earnings. Under this protocol, just one or a subset of subjects (e.g., 10%) are randomly chosen to receive their earnings from the experiment. This approach can be viewed as weaponizing the advantages of the pay-one protocol to the entire subject pool: if randomly selecting one round/task enables the researcher to pay more, then randomly selecting one or a subset of subjects for payment enables even greater payments.

   Evidence regarding the effects of paying a subset of subjects is also mixed. Charness *et al.* (2016) report that in the few studies comparing treatments where all subjects are paid something versus treatments where only some subjects get paid, the evidence seems to suggest only minor differences in behavior. In practice, this approach is typically adopted when there are logistical difficulties involved in paying each subject, as in certain field experiments. A potential concern, though, is that if this payment protocol is repeatedly used, it could lead to undue effects on subjects' motivation to participate in future studies.

3.6   Control of Risk Preferences

Economic theories often presume that agents are risk-neutral with respect to uncertain money earnings. If applied to the experimental setting, then subjects are assumed to be indifferent to risk, basing their choices solely on the expected values or payoffs of the different outcomes. However, subjects often come to experimental studies with "homegrown" preferences that are *not* risk-neutral. One solution, discussed in the next section, is to elicit subjects' **risk preferences** using pretests/surveys during the experiment, so that one can examine the extent to which risk preferences differ from assumptions and how those risk preferences might alter predictions for individual participants.

An alternative approach, which is related to the discussion of payment protocols in the previous section, is to use the binary lottery transformation of payoffs originally developed by Roth and Malouf (1979) and generalized by Berg *et al.* (1986). This method amounts to inducing a particular attitude toward risk, regardless of the subjects' innate, or homegrown, preferences regarding uncertain payoffs and is similar in aim to inducing values, as discussed earlier.

The original idea of the binary lottery (Roth and Malouf (1979)) was to induce *risk-neutral* behavior by converting payoffs into points (or lottery tickets), which could then by used to win a large fixed prize as opposed to earning only a small fixed prize—i.e confronting subjects with a binary lottery payoff. Specifically, suppose we pick two fixed monetary prize amounts, $x_h > x_\ell$, and suppose further that subjects' payoffs in the study are expressed in terms of points, $q \in [0, Q]$, where higher payoffs = more points. Suppose, too, that after points have been determined, the subject earns the high monetary prize x_h with probability q/Q and the low monetary prize x_ℓ with probability $(1 - q/Q)$. The subject's expected utility is thus: $q/Q(U(x_h)) + (1 - q/Q)(U(x_\ell))$ where U is the subject's unknown utility function over monetary amounts. Without loss of generality, we may normalize $U(x_h) = 1, U(x_\ell) = 0$. In this case, expected utility reduces to q/Q, i.e., it is linear in points! A subject with a concave (risk-averse) U function who is paid in points (lottery tickets) should act as a risk-neutral agent in decisions where payoffs come in the form of points (lottery tickets) toward winning the high prize. As an example of the implementation of this binary procedure, consider the two-player coordination game studied by Duffy and Feltovich (2002, 2006), as shown in Figure 3.2: In their design,

	C	D
C	70,70	10,80
D	80,10	40,40

Figure 3.2: Coordination game payoff matrix from Duffy and Feltovich (2002, 2006).

$x_h = \$1$ and $x_\ell = \$0$. Suppose the row player plays C and the column plays D. The row player then has a 10% chance of earning \$1 (90% chance of earning \$0), while the column player has an 80% chance of earning \$1 (and a 20% chance of earning 0) (Q max was set at 100, even though this number of points is not attainable). The experimenters had subjects take turns drawing a random number between 1 and 100 to determine earnings.

Berg *et al.* (1986) show that one can use the same binary lottery design to induce *any* risk preference specification, not just risk neutrality, using a variety of spinners, as shown in Figure 3.3. If the spinner stops in the

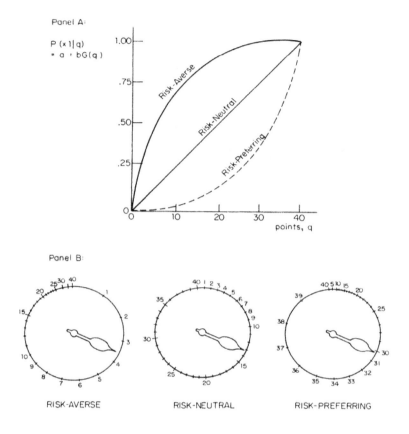

Figure 3.3: Panel A: Probability of winning the larger prize (vertical axis) as a function of points earned (horizontal axis) across three inducements (risk-averse, risk-neutral, and risk-loving). Panel B: Spinners used to induce these three types of preferences assuming $Q = 40$.
Source: Berg *et al.* (1986), copyrighted material reproduced with the permission of Oxford University Press.

area between 0 and the number of points the subject has received, the subject wins the larger prize x_h; otherwise they win the lower prize x_ℓ. By adjusting the area assigned to numbers on the spinner, one can, in practice, use the binary lottery design to induce risk-averse, risk-neutral, or risk-loving preferences.

In practice, binary lotteries are not used very often because, as Selten *et al.* (1999) reports, they can result in significantly greater deviations from risk-neutral behavior as compared with the case where they are not used and subjects are paid based solely on the points they earned in the experiment.[3] The difficulty with such lotteries is that they add an extra layer of complexity/time to payoff determination that takes away from data collection. Furthermore, laboratory payoffs are often so small that, even for risk-averse subjects, the curvature over experimental payoff possibilities should be viewed as approximately linear (though in practice this does not seem to be the case). As a consequence, many experimenters ignore homegrown risk attitudes and assume that subjects act as though they were risk-neutral with respect to uncertain payoffs, or they elicit subjects' risk preferences separately from trying to induce them, as discussed in the next section, and attempt to reconcile their theories to allow for departures from risk-neutral preferences.

3.7   Elicitation Mechanisms

While it is standard practice to pay subjects based on the *choices* they make in combination with payoff incentives, induced values, or profit or utility functions, the collection of certain types of experimental data require more specialized techniques. This is especially the case when there is no clear objective function against which to measure a subjects' payoffs (e.g., subjects' willingness to pay or their attitudes toward risk, which can vary from subject to subject). Even when there does exist a clear objective function for calculating payoffs, it may be possible and desirable to collect experimentally relevant data beyond the choices that subjects make with the aim of better understanding subjects' decision-making. To collect such data, experimentalists have devised a variety of different elicitation mechanisms, some of which we discuss in this section.

1. **Strategies (Strategy Method)**

   Instead of simply collecting incentivized choice data, it may be possible, in many controlled settings, to collect information on subjects' *strategies*, which would indicate their choice in a given setting.

---

[3] For an alternative perspective, see Prasnikar (2002), who produces evidence that binary lotteries may not have such a negative impact. Harrison *et al.* (2013), meanwhile, find that the binary lottery procedure does seem to move risk preferences in the direction of risk neutrality, even if they do not move all the way there.

This experimental method is known as the **strategy method** and it was first proposed by Selten (1965). Instead of making a choice, subjects specify the *strategy* they would apply to make their choice. Since a strategy in game theory is a complete contingent plan of action, the subject's strategy has to explain what choices they would make in all possible states of the world and for all past histories of play. As the strategy space can be relatively large, in practice the space is limited to some degree so that subjects are not overwhelmed with too many contingencies. Once the strategy is given, then the subject's strategy is played out for them (their choice is made based on the strategy they supply) and they are paid based on choice outcomes in the usual manner. With a player's strategy, the researcher is able to observe all possible choices a subject can make, not just those that arise at information sets actually reached.

As an illustrative example, consider Seale and Rapoport (2000)'s application of the strategy method to the n-player market entry game studied at the end of Chapter 1. Suppose the payoff for not entering the market is 1 while the payoff for entering is $1 + 2(c - m)$, where m is the number of the n subjects choosing to enter and c is a capacity constraint variable, varied by the experimenter. Recall that, in any equilibrium, $m = c$. In the strategy method adopted by Seale and Rapoport, in each of 50 periods the $n = 20$ subjects were asked to state their decision—either to enter or not enter—for a list of different capacity values, i.e., $c = 1, 3, 5, \ldots, 19$. Next, a random odd number c-value was drawn. Subjects' strategies were used to determine their actions for that c value. The procedure of strategy elicitation was then repeated (50 periods total). The aggregate results using the strategy method are similar to those found using choice decisions. However, the strategy profiles revealed that subjects were not employing mixed strategies. Rather, they were using various cutoff strategies, e.g., enter if $c > 8$ and don't enter otherwise. This example illustrates the value of the strategy method.

Another advantage of using this method is that, after one has gathered data on the subjects' strategies, it becomes possible to simulate them over long periods of time. For instance, Axelrod (1984) conducted a repeated Prisoner's Dilemma tournament using this approach. Selten *et al.* (1997) study the play of experienced subjects' strategies in repeated duopoly games. Romero and Rosokha (2019) have further refined this approach by simulating long-horizon repeated games with subject-supplied strategies and allowing subjects to make periodic revisions to those strategies. These methods combine human subject innovation with computational simulations that enable the study of long-horizon outcomes that would not generally be feasible in the short horizons of most human subject experiments.

One notable drawback of the strategy method is that the mere act of eliciting a strategy from subjects may potentially influence the decision-making process. Consequently, the choices obtained through strategy elicitation might not be directly comparable to their actual choices. A potential solution to this problem is to have subjects make unconditional choices in one setting and specify a strategy for making choices in another and then randomly implement one or the other elicitation, which should incentivize the subjects to be truthful in both (see, e.g., Falk and Fischbacher (2001)) or to look for consistency between the two approaches Duffy and Ochs (2012).

2. Belief Elicitation

Sometimes a researcher is interested in gathering data about beliefs, e.g., with regard to the actions that one's opponent(s) in a game might take. A simple way to do this is to just ask subjects about their beliefs—the stated belief approach—but if this is not incentivized, subjects may not feel the need to express their true subjective beliefs.

To elicit subjective beliefs or probabilities over binary events, experimentalists often use **scoring rules** (originally developed for weather forecasting) that provide (additional) payoffs as a function of the submitted n-dimensional forecast vector (p) and n-dimensional set of (binary) realizations. In this case, subjects' total variable payoff might include their belief elicitation payoff plus their choice payoff; as noted above, the experimenter now has to be concerned about "hedging" behavior and might want to choose to randomly determine whether the belief or action choice payoff is paid. One scoring rule is the linear scoring rule: $s^i(p) = a + b\sum_{j=1}^{n} p_j I_j$, where I_j is an indicator function equal to 1 if event j occurs and 0 otherwise. An alternative is the quadratic scoring rule: $s^i(p) = a - b\sum_{j=1}^{n}(p_j - I_j)^2$.

A scoring rule is labeled "proper" if it is incentive-compatible for the subject to reveal his/her true belief. It transpires that the linear rule is not "proper" because subjects maximize their expected linear score by attributing maximum weight to the more likely event. By contrast, quadratic and some other rules (e.g., the logarithmic scoring rule) are proper scoring rules (see, e.g., Palfrey and Wang (2009) for a detailed discussion). We can illustrate the incentive issue using an example for the binary $n = 2$ case. To do this, we use $p_1 = p$ to denote the belief that outcome 1 will occur and $p_2 = 1 - p$ to denote the belief that outcome 2 will occur. For the $n = 2$ case, the quadratic scoring rule is given by the following:

$$s^i(p) = a - b[(p - I_1)^2 + (1 - p - I_2)^2], \quad I_2 = 1 - I_1,$$

where the max value is a and the minimum value is $a - 2b$, so, as a normalization, we can set $a = 1$, $b = 1/2$. Under this normalization, the experimenter pays the subject $2p - p^2$ if $I_1 = 1$, and pays $1 - p^2$ otherwise, if $I_2 = 1$. It is easy to demonstrate that this scoring rule is proper by showing that deviations from the subject's true belief are unprofitable. For instance, suppose the subject thinks the probability of outcome 1 is $p = 0.25$. If that event occurs, the subject's payoff is $2p - p^2 = \$0.44$, and if it does not occur, the payoff is $1 - p^2 = \$0.94$. Alternatively, a $p = 0.4$ earns $\$0.64$ if the event occurs and $\$0.84$ otherwise. Thus, if the subject thinks that the true probability is 0.4, then reporting $p = 0.4$ yields the subject $0.4(\$0.64) + 0.6(\$84) = \$0.77$. Similarly, reporting $p = 0.25$ when the subject's true belief is 0.4 yields the subject $0.4(\$0.44) + 0.6(\$0.94) = \$0.74$. Hence, a risk-neutral subject (i.e., an individual who is insensitive to risk and concerned only with expected returns) would be incentivized to report their true belief that $p = 0.4$. This is the sense in which the quadratic scoring rule is proper.

Palfrey and Wang (2009) compare the linear and quadratic scoring rules along with another proper scoring rule—the logarithmic rule—and show that properness matters in the sense that beliefs are less dispersed and better matched to other features of the data. However, other researchers, such as Offerman and Sonnemans (2004), have found there to be no difference between using a quadratic scoring rule and paying a flat fee based on whether the belief is correct or not.

More generally, the assumption of risk neutrality required for proper scoring rules may not hold and, in such a case, more sophisticated belief elicitation methods involving stochastic payments to elicit beliefs may be appropriate (see Karni (2009) and Holt and Smith (2009) for a more in-depth discussion). These methods use a version of the Becker–DeGroot–Marschak mechanism, which is discussed below.

3. Risk and Time Preferences

Researchers sometimes find it useful to evaluate subjects' risk preferences with regard to uncertain money amounts and/or **time preferences** for early versus late rewards. For instance, such data might be helpful for rationalizing departures of behavior from, say, a modeling assumption that agents are risk-neutral with regard to uncertain money payments. A risk-neutral individual evaluates decisions based solely on expected values. By contrast, a risk-averse individual prefers to make lower-risk decisions and may be willing to sacrifice potential gains for predictability, while a risk-loving person seeks higher potential rewards even if it comes with a greater risk of losses.

There are a variety of methods for eliciting risk and time preferences, ranging from simple survey questions to fully incentivized measures. Here we focus on incentivized measures of risk and time preferences, where there is some money at stake.[4]

In one early incentivized approach, proposed by Gneezy and Potters (1997), subjects are given an endowment of money W and asked to allocate any amount of that endowment, X, to a risky investment, while keeping the rest for certain. With probability p, the risky investment pays $\lambda \times X$; or, alternatively, it pays 0. Thus, the expected payoff from this choice is $p(W - X + \lambda X) + (1 - p)(W - X) = W + X(p\lambda - 1)$. So long as $p\lambda > 1$, then risk-neutral (and risk-loving) individuals should choose to invest everything, i.e., $X = W$, while those who are risk-averse might choose to invest less than W or even 0. In cases where $p\lambda > 1$, investments X typically average around 50% of W, reflecting risk aversion. While this measure provides a straightforward means by which to identify the risk-averse, it is a somewhat crude measure of the degree to which subjects are risk-averse and cannot distinguish between the risk-neutral and the risk-loving.

Another incentivized mechanism for gathering information on subjects' risk preferences is the gamified bomb risk elicitation task

---

[4]Nevertheless, simple unincentivized survey elicitations are often highly correlated with these same types of incentivized measures and can be less time-consuming (and cheaper) to use—for an example of empirically validated survey questions, see, e.g., Falk *et al.* (2023).

(BRET), introduced by Crosetto and Filippin (2013). This task is often visualized using a 10×10 matrix, where 99 elements of the matrix are empty and 1 element contains a "bomb." Subjects are asked to choose how many elements of the matrix, $e \in [0, 100]$, they wish to reveal, starting from the first element. After they have made this choice, the location where the bomb is placed within the matrix is randomly determined by a uniform draw over [1, 100]. If subject i's choice $e \geq b$, they collect the bomb and earn 0, while if $e < b$, then they earn a payoff amount, γ, for each of e matrix elements they chose to reveal, for a total payoff of γe. Effectively, this amounts to the subject's favorite choice of lotteries as indexed by e each paying 0 with probability $e/100$ and γe with probability $(100 - e)/100$. The expected payoff of lottery e is $\gamma(e - 0.01e^2)$, which is maximized at $e = 50$, and is thus the choice of a risk-neutral expected utility maximizer.[5] Those choosing $e \leq 49$ are considered risk-averse, while those choosing $e > 50$ are considered risk-loving. Crosetto and Filippin (2013) report that the majority of subjects are risk-averse.

Yet another approach to eliciting risk preferences is to present subjects with a list of multiple pairs of binary lottery choices and to ask them to make a choice for each pair. This approach, known as the **multiple price list** (MPL) approach, was first developed by Binswanger (1981), who used it to elicit the risk preferences of farmers in rural India. A commonly used MPL for risk preference elicitation is the MPL risk elicitation task of Holt and Laury (2002), which is illustrated in Table 3.1. Each lottery option, A or B, involves two amounts of money, with subjects being informed of the probability of receiving each amount. For instance, in choice 1, option A pays $2 with probability 0.10 and $1.60 with probability 0.90 (expected value $1.64), while option B pays $3.85 with probability 0.10 and $0.10 with probability 0.90 (expected value $0.475). The expected payoff difference between A and B for choice 1 is thus $1.17, as reported in the final column, but this calculation is *not* shown to subjects.

For each of the 10 choices, a subject selects either option A or B. This risk elicitation is typically incentivized by having subjects make all 10 choices and then randomly choosing one of the 10 choices and playing out each subject's selected lottery for that choice. For instance,

---

[5]A risk-neutral expected utility maximizer treats expected payoffs as if they were certain.

Table 3.1: Paired lottery choice table.

Choice Number	Option A	Option B	Expected Payoff Difference*
1	1/10 of \$2.00, 9/10 of \$1.60	1/10 of \$3.85, 9/10 of \$0.10,	\$1.17
2	2/10 of \$2.00, 8/10 of \$1.60	2/10 of \$3.85, 8/10 of \$0.10,	\$0.83
3	3/10 of \$2.00, 7/10 of \$1.60	3/10 of \$3.85, 7/10 of \$0.10,	\$0.50
4	4/10 of \$2.00, 6/10 of \$1.60	4/10 of \$3.85, 6/10 of \$0.10,	\$0.16
5	5/10 of \$2.00, 5/10 of \$1.60	5/10 of \$3.85, 5/10 of \$0.10,	−\$0.18
6	6/10 of \$2.00, 5/10 of \$1.60	6/10 of \$3.85, 4/10 of \$0.10,	−\$0.51
7	7/10 of \$2.00, 3/10 of \$1.60	7/10 of \$3.85, 3/10 of \$0.10,	−\$0.85
8	8/10 of \$2.00, 2/10 of \$1.60	8/10 of \$3.85, 2/10 of \$0.10,	−\$1.18
9	9/10 of \$2.00, 1/10 of \$1.60	9/10 of \$3.85, 1/10 of \$0.10,	−\$1.52
10	10/10 of \$2.00, 0/10 of \$1.60	10/10 of \$3.85, 0/10 of \$0.10,	−\$1.85

Source: Holt and Laury (2002).

if choice 7 is chosen and the subject chose option B, then the subject earns \$3.85 with probability 0.7 and \$0.10 with probability 0.3.[6] Since the expected payoff for lottery A is higher than that for lottery B for the first four choices, while the expected payoff from lottery B is higher than the expected payoff for lottery A for the last six choices, a *risk-neutral* expected utility maximizer would select lottery A for the first 4 choices and then switch to lottery B for the last 6 choices, since risk-neutral expected utility maximizers treat expected payoffs as if they were certain.

[6]The expected payoff difference calculation shown in the table is not typically present in the MPL elicitation task; it is included here only for reference purposes.

However, more generally, if we assume that agents have constant relative risk aversion (CRRA) utility functions of the form

$$u(x) = \frac{x^r}{1-r},$$

then it is possible to use the Holt-Laury MPL approach to develop measures (bins) for each individual's preference parameter r, i.e., the individual's coefficient of relative risk aversion. For instance, if one chose A for the first 6 choices and then switched to B for the last 4 choices, this could be rationalized, using expected utility calculations, by an r in the interval (0.41, 0.68), which is approximately symmetric around a coefficient of 0.5, representing moderate risk aversion. Similarly, if one chose A for the first 2 choices and B for the last 8 choices, this could be rationalized by an r in $(-0.95, -0.49)$, representing highly risk-loving behavior.

The MPL approach has also been used to elicit subjects' time preferences, as is done, e.g., in a study by Coller and Williams (1999). In their design, subjects choose between a fixed amount of money to be earned one month from now versus various larger amounts of money to be earned three months from now. Table 3.2 shows the MPL table they used in their study. In line with the Holt and Laury risk elicitation, many subjects will start out choosing option A before eventually switching over to option B. The point at which they switch over reflects their subjective *discount rate*, which is the rate at which the value of their discount function declines. For this purpose, one uses the annual effective interest rate, which includes the effects of daily compounding of interest. For instance, if a subject chooses option A for the first 10 choices and then switches to option B, one may infer that their subjective discount rate must lie above 19.12% but below 22.13%.

Meanwhile, Coller and Williams' employed the "choose a subset of subjects" payment protocol, in which just one subject was chosen from sessions involving around 35 subjects each. For the chosen subject, just one of their 15 choices was implemented and paid out. An important aspect of their design is that there is always a delay in the receipt of any payment, known as a "front-end" delay. This design eliminates any biases in favor of receiving immediate payments versus delayed payments.

Coller and Williams assume that preferences are linear (i.e., subjects are risk-neutral with respect to uncertain monetary payments). If

Table 3.2: Multiple price list for time preference elicitation.

Choice Number	Option A Paid in 1 Month	Option B Paid in 3 Months	Annual Interest Rate	Effective Annual Int. Rate
1	$500	$501.67	2.00%	2.02%
2	$500	$502.51	3.00%	3.05%
3	$500	$503.34	4.00%	4.08%
4	$500	$504.18	5.00%	5.13%
5	$500	$506.29	7.50%	7.79%
6	$500	$508.40	10.00%	10.52%
7	$500	$510.52	12.50%	13.31%
8	$500	$512.65	15.00%	16.18%
9	$500	$514.79	17.50%	19.12%
10	$500	$516.94	20.00%	22.13%
11	$500	$521.27	25.00%	28.39%
12	$500	$530.02	35.00%	41.88%
13	$500	$543.42	50.00%	64.81%
14	$500	$566.50	75.00%	111.53%
15	$500	$590.54	100.00%	171.45%

Source: Coller and Williams (1999).

preferences are in fact concave rather than linear, then the MPL approach of Coller and Williams will result in a positive bias in estimated discount rates. A solution, proposed by Andersen *et al.* (2008), is to jointly elicit both risk and time preferences using the approaches laid out by Holt and Laury and Coller and Williams, respectively, and then to correct the discount rate measure for each subject's degree of risk aversion. Alternatives to this approach include the Andreoni and Sprenger (2012) convex budget set approach and the binary lottery approach of Laury *et al.* (2012).

4. **Becker–DeGroot–Marschak mechanism for Willingness to Pay/Willingness to Accept**

Another common elicitation method concerns a seller's **willingness to accept** (WTA) or a buyer's **willingness to pay** (WTP). The most commonly used incentive-compatible method for obtaining such elicitations is the Becker–DeGroot–Marschak (BDM) mechanism of Becker *et al.* (1964). Consider the case of a seller who possesses an item and attributes a private (unobservable) value of V to that item. Under the BDM approach, the individual first submits a price they are willing to accept to give up the object, P_A. A price is then randomly drawn from some interval, say, from 0 to $\overline{V}$, where the upper bound, $\overline{V}$, is typically much higher than most individuals' valuations for the item. If the randomly drawn price, $p \geq P_A$ (which occurs with probability $\overline{V} - P_A)/\overline{V})$, then the seller gives up the item in exchange for the price p. In this case, the seller's payoff is $p - V$. By contrast, if $p < P_A$ (which occurs with probability $P_A/\overline{V})$, then the seller keeps the item and no exchange occurs. In this case the seller's payoff is V—her private value for the item that remains in her possession.

The same approach works for eliciting willingness to pay, but the implementation is reversed. A buyer with valuation V for an item states a willingness to pay (buy) price P_B for that item. A price is then randomly drawn from some interval, say again from 0 to $\overline{V}$. If $p \leq P_B$ (which occurs with probability $V_B/\overline{V})$, then the buyer buys the item at price p and earns a payoff of $V - p$. Otherwise, if $p > P_B$, (which occurs with probability $\overline{V} - P_B)/\overline{V})$, then the buyer does not receive the item and earns a payoff of 0.

The BDM is incentive-compatible under the assumptions of expected utility theory. A seller maximizes the probability of selling the item by stating a WTA price (P_A) that is as low as possible. Equally, a buyer maximizes the probability of buying an item by stating a WTA price (P_B) that is as high as possible. The incentive compatibility logic follows that of Vickrey (1961) for second-price auctions.

A drawback of the BDM mechanism is that, while it is incentive-compatible, participants may not be accustomed to stating a WTP or a WTA or fully understand the BDM procedures. Indeed, there is evidence that the BDM mechanism generates a WTA-WTP "gap." For instance, Kahneman *et al.* (1990) (KKT) studied WTA/WTP for Cornell coffee mugs using the Becker–DeGroot–Marschak mechanism. Subjects were randomly divided into buyers and sellers. Sellers were given a Cornell coffee mug and asked to state their WTA for their mug. Buyers, who were not endowed with a mug, were asked to state their WTP for such a mug. After that, sellers sold their mug if the randomly drawn market price exceeded their willingness to accept, while buyers bought a mug using their own money if the randomly generated price was less than their willingness to pay. The researchers repeated this process several times to allow for subject learning. The experiment yielded a median seller reservation price

(WTA) of $5.25 and a median buyer reservation price (WTP) of $2.25 for the *same* Cornell coffee mug. While, theoretically speaking, there should be no difference between WTA and WTP, a noticeable gap emerged. Explanations for this gap have primarily revolved around seller behavior, highlighting factors such as loss aversion and the so called "endowment effect." Plott and Zeiler (2005), however, showed that the WTA-WTP gap can effectively be eradicated if subjects are provided with extensive training on the elicitation mechanism before submitting their WTA and WTP responses.

5. **Cognitive and Non-Cognitive Measures**

In addition to risk and time preferences, experimenters sometimes elicit **cognitive** and/or **non-cognitive (personality) measures**. These measures can be helpful in understanding the ways in which subjects depart from theoretical predictions.

To measure cognitive abilities, a common instrument is the cognitive reflection test (CRT), devised by Frederick (2005). The questions in this test evaluate subjects' abilities to reflect on the problem at hand. Each question has an intuitive and immediate answer that is incorrect; by contrast, the correct answer, which requires a certain amount of reflection, thereby providing a measure of cognitive abilities. Thus, the questions capture the degree to which individuals employ what psychologists call "system 1" and "system 2" thinking (see, e.g. Kahneman (2011)).

The original 3 questions, along with the right and wrong answers, are provided below.

1. A bat and a ball cost $1.10 in total. The bat costs a dollar more than the ball. How much does the ball cost? (Intuitive answer 10 cents; correct answer 5 cents).

2. If it takes 5 machines 5 minutes to make 5 widgets, how long would it take 100 machines to make 100 widgets? (Intuitive answer 100 minutes; correct answer 5 minutes).

3. In a lake, there is a patch of lily pads. Every day, the patch doubles in size. If it takes 48 days for the patch to cover the entire lake, how long would it take for the patch to cover half the lake? (Intuitive answer 24 days; correct answer 47 days).

These questions have been used so often that there is some concern that many subjects may have already encountered them and/or already heard the correct answers. To mitigate such concerns, researchers have developed variants of these questions as well as other similar questions with the system 1/system 2 tradeoff.[7]

Another measure of cognitive abilities is the Ravens progressive matrices (RPM) test (Raven (1936). The RPM has the advantage of being a non-verbal measure of cognitive ability. The test has a multiple-choice format and requires subjects to choose the missing element in a matrix of patterns from among a set of options that exhibit different patterns. The test becomes more challenging with each step (the progressive part) and subjects can be incentivized according to the number of answers they get right. Burks *et al.* (2009) show, for instance, that RPM performance is correlated with calculated risk-taking and job perseverance.

In addition to task-based measures of cognitive performance, it is also possible to collect data on cognitive abilities in other ways. For instance, one can simply ask subjects to report their grade point average or their university major program of study. University major can be quantified in terms of cognitive ability using various classification schemes (see Duffy *et al.* (2021) for one example). Finally, one can keep track of the number of answers that subjects answer correctly or incorrectly on comprehension quizzes about the instructions for the experiment they are about to participate in.

To measure non-cognitive abilities, a commonly used instrument is the big five personality test (see, e.g. John (2021). This test assesses five universal major personality traits: conscientiousness, agreeableness, neuroticism, extroversion, and openness. An online link to the test can be found at: www.truity.com/test/big-five-personality-test).

To explore social attitudes, the social value orientation task of Murphy *et al.* (2011) can be used. This task matches subjects in pairs, say around a circle network where each player interacts with the player to his or her right on the circle. Players are asked how much they would be willing to sacrifice in order to make their matched player better off or perhaps worse off. Based on the answers to 6 decisions which vary the amounts received for the player and the match, it is possible to classify subjects as Prosocial, Individualistic, Competitive, or Unclassifiable.

---

[7]See, for example the discussion at: https://absolutedecisionsblog.wordpress.com/tag/cognitive-reflection-test/.

The track record of such personality measures correlating with choices in incentivized experiments is mixed (see, e.g., Müller and Schwieren (2020) for a review and some tests). Thus, the researchers should only collect such data if there is a strong indication that personality is likely to play a major role in the decisions made in the study.

3.8 Robot Players

A further method of control that experimental economists have employed is the use of computerized **robot players** who interact with human subjects. The use of such robot players is typically done in computerized experiments, though it is possible for the experimenter to implement algorithmic strategies in other settings as well. For a survey of the use of robot players in experimental economics, see March (2021).

There are three main reasons to use such robot players.

One aim in game theory experiments is to reduce the strategic uncertainty that players feel regarding what their opponents will do. This reduction in noise enables the researcher to determine whether players are in fact producing their best responses to the strategies of the robot players.

A second and related aim is to distinguish between explanations for anomalous behavior in group decision-making experiments. For instance, in social dilemma experiments, where the dominant strategy involves free-riding behavior, it may not be clear whether the absence of free-riding behavior is caused by social, other-regarding concerns for the payoffs of the other players in the room or by confusion with the payoff incentives to free-ride. The addition of free-riding robot players, whose payoffs should, presumably, be of no concern to the other human subject players, can help to address whether outcomes are the result of other-regarding social concerns or confusion about whether free-riding is a best response. For instance, Houser and Kurzban (2002) find that subjects' decisions move closer, but not completely towards, free-riding behavior in social dilemmas when they play against robot players, which suggests that other-regarding concerns for others plays a greater role in settings where only human players are involved.

A third reason to employ robot players may be that the behavior of one type of player is not particularly interesting. For example, if it is assumed that workers always supply labor inelastically, then it might be better, not to mention cheaper, to have robot players fulfill that role.

Finally, given that human-computer interaction is becoming more common in everyday life, particularly in financial markets, experiments where subjects interact with robot players that are trying to manipulate market conditions are becoming increasingly popular. See Bao *et al.* (2022) for a review. Furthermore, as these robots are programmed by human subjects, it could be interesting to have subjects program robot strategies to play on their behalf as in a strategy method. The subject-programmed robot strategies can then be played out quickly, enabling longer repetitions of strategic behavior than would typically be possible in human-to-human-subject experiments.

3.9   Time Horizons and Discounting

The length of an experimental session is also an important element of control. If the theory that is being tested is a one-shot game/decision, then it may not be necessary to have subjects repeat the game/task more than once. However, it is generally a good practice to consider that subjects may only learn a game or solve a task if they have had sufficient experience with it. For instance, if one is studying games with a unique mixed strategy Nash equilibrium (e.g., Rock, Paper, Scissors), then a single play of that game would not be particularly informative as to whether subjects are playing according to the unique mixed strategy prediction for the game. Thus, the length of the repeated play of a game or task is an important consideration.

If a game is repeated a finite and known number of times, then one may be able to rely on backward induction arguments to arrive at a solution and predict behavior in the finitely repeated game.

A more difficult setting arises, however, if the theory being tested requires subjects to make decisions over an *infinite horizon*. For instance, suppose the theory being tested imagines that agents make repeated decisions about some variable x affecting their payoff π over an infinite horizon:

$$\max_{x_t} E \sum_{t=1}^{\infty} \delta \pi(x_t),$$

where $\delta \in (0, 1]$ is the period discount factor, and E is the expectation operator. While it is not possible to implement infinite horizons in the laboratory, an alternative approach (assuming that subjects are risk-neutral expected utility maximizers) is to suppose that they make decisions over an *indefinitely repeated* horizon. The **random termination method** developed by Roth and Murnighan (1978) imagines that the discount factor, δ, can be reinterpreted as the probability that a game or task continues from one round to the next; the game ends with probability $1 - \delta$, in which case payoffs are finalized. Since subjects do not know when a repeated game or task will end, this random termination method induces the stationarity associated with an infinite horizon, not to mention the discounting of future payoffs at rate δ per period. In such a case, the expected duration of a sequence of periods (also known as a "supergame") is $\frac{1}{1-\delta}$ periods at the start of any round reached. One concern with this approach, though, is that, depending on the discount factor, the length of the supergames can be shorter than is desirable for data collection. To address this issue, Fréchette and Yuksel (2017) propose a **block random termination method** that collects data in blocks while still ending the game in the random termination manner. This approach allows for the collection of more data than is possible using the standard random termination method. Whether random termination effectively implements an infinite horizon has been the subject of some debate. It does seem to be useful for eliminating so-called end-game effects that occur in finitely repeated games when players adjust their behavior to the knowledge that the game will soon end (see Normann and Wallace (2012) for a more detailed discussion of this topic).

An alternative approach to the random termination method of implementing discounting (which is used in the bargaining literature), is to physically shrink the value of payoffs earned in each period of a game or task as it progresses (see, e.g., Binmore *et al.* (1985)). That is, in period $t = 1, 2, \ldots,$ the player earns $\delta^{t-1}\pi(x_t)$, where δ is the rate of shrinkage of the payoffs per period. This method implements discounting but is perhaps better suited to finite horizon games because indefinite horizon payoffs will decline geometrically, and, for longer supergames, the payoff differences across available choices will quickly lose salience.

3.10 Matching

In game theory experiments, the manner in which subjects are *matched* to play a repeated game can have an influence on the outcome. Experimental economists distinguish between **partner matchings** and **stranger matchings**.

Under a *partner matching* design, players are matched with the same opponent(s) in the repeated game or task. This approach has the advantage of facilitating learning because experience playing with the same player(s) reduces strategic uncertainty. Furthermore, partner matching may be empirically relevant to the question of interest. At the same time, partner matching can enable *collusive* or reputational dynamic game behaviors that may be at odds with the theory being tested.

Meanwhile, under a *stranger matching* protocol, players are randomly (and typically anonymously) matched with one or more other player(s) in each repetition of the game and this fact is made known to the subjects. If the experiment tests the predictions of a one-shot interaction, then a random stranger matching protocol is a good way to proceed. The downside of the random matching protocol is that the researcher will need to recruit a sufficient number of subjects to make the likelihood of repeat re-matching with the same player sufficiently small to avoid contagion or teaching effects.

At the extreme, one can implement **perfect stranger matching**, where players meet, for example, in pairs, only once per session using what is known as a "zipper" (or turnpike) matching protocol (see, e.g., Cooper *et al.* (1996)). For instance, consider a scenario where there are N participants in a session. In the context of perfect stranger matching, which aims to create one-time pairings, there are $m = N/2$ potential pairings. Prior to the first interaction in the session, the N subjects can be randomly divided into two equal-sized groups, A and B of m subjects each. Then, under the zipper matching protocol, each member of group A plays each member of group B exactly once. More specifically, suppose we index the members of the A and B groups by $i \in 1, 2, \ldots, m$. In the first interaction or period, each player A_i meets the corresponding player B_i, where both share the same index number i. Thereafter, one can imagine that the B_i players are rotated cyclically, resembling positions on a circle, to meet different A_i players. Figure 3.4 provides an illustration of this rotation scheme for the case of $m = 4$: Thus, in the first period, A_1 meets B_1. In the second period

	Time Period			
	1	2	3	4
A_1	B_1	B_2	B_3	B_4
A_2	B_2	B_3	B_4	B_1
A_3	B_3	B_4	B_1	B_2
A_4	B_4	B_1	B_2	B_3

Figure 3.4: Illustration of perfect stranger matching: Matchings of players A_i to players B_i, $i = 1, 2, 3, 4$ in each of 4 periods.

A_1 meets B_2, and so on . . . An important property of this zipper matching model is that the actions taken by a pair in each period cannot influence the behavior of other participants that these players will be matched with in the future, thereby avoiding "contagion" effects.[8] However, while contagion may be avoided, this approach requires more subjects to generate more unique matched pairings.

As one can see, it is important for experimental researchers to carefully assess and choose the methods by which they collect the data relevant to the hypotheses they wish to test.

---

[8]This matching protocol uses the notion of Latin squares from combinatorial mathematics (see Aliprantis *et al.* (2007) for details).

Chapter 4

How to Experiment: Implementation

Understanding the various methods of control enables experimenters to harness the power of the experimental method. However, the power of the experimental method also requires proper *implementation* of the experimental design, which is the subject of this chapter. Implementation issues range from obtaining human subjects' approval to pre-registration of hypotheses and power analyses, the writing of instructions, and the recruitment of subjects. We discuss each of these implementation issues in turn.

4.1 Institutional Review Board Approval

Prior to conducting experimental interventions with human subjects, it may be necessary to obtain approval for such interventions from an administrative body known as an **institutional review board** (IRB), or, in some countries, as a **research ethics committee** (REC). The aim of an IRB (or REC) is to protect the rights and welfare of human research subjects participating in studies conducted by researchers affiliated with the institution overseen by the IRB.

The need for IRB oversight of human subject research is the result of the field's chequered history prior to such IRB oversight. For instance, evidence brought to light during the Nuremberg trials regarding the medical experimentation abuses of World War II Nazi doctors led to the creation of

the Nuremberg Code in 1945. This code enshrined the fundamental principle that human subject participation in research studies must be voluntary.
Similarly, the 1972 disclosure of the Tuskegee Syphilis Study, a study supported by the U.S. government for three decades, where 300 black rural men
were left untreated for syphilis despite the availability of effective antibi-
otics, triggered significant developments in ethical considerations. This
disclosure prompted the articulation of three essential ethical principles by
National Commission for the Protection of Human Services of Biomedical
and Behavioral Research in its "Belmont Report" of 1979:

1. **Respect for Persons.** This principle has two dimensions: first,
   that individuals should be treated as autonomous agents who are free
   to decide whether or not they want to participate in any study (as
   in the Nuremberg code) and, second, that persons with diminished
   autonomy (e.g., children) are entitled to protection.

2. **Beneficence.** This principle includes both the Hippocratic oath of
   medical ethics to "do no harm" but also adds the goal of maximizing
   the potential benefits to research participants, science, and humanity
   while minimizing any harms. In practice, any benefits from a research
   study should outweigh any risks.

3. **Justice.** This principle asserts that the benefits and burdens of
   research interventions should be shared equally or, put another way,
   that all subjects should be treated fairly.

Institutional review boards were created to ensure that researchers adhere
to these important principles in their study interventions and that there is
a disciplinary process in place for researchers who violate these principles.

In practice, obtaining IRB approval requires submission of a research
protocol to the IRB that oversees the institution where the research will be
carried out. The protocol should explain the research questions, the experimental interventions/treatments, the number of subjects intended for each
treatment/intervention, the process by which subjects will be recruited, the
process by which subjects will provide voluntary consent to participate in
the study, and the risks and benefits of subject participation.

IRB approval is required in advance of collecting any data, and so
obtaining such approval should be your first step in implementing any
experiment. As an additional incentive to obtain such approval, many
granting agencies and journals require IRB approval before the disburse-
ment of funds or before it has been officially agreed that your work will be

published. While IRBs/RECs are still not a universal phenomenon, they are now present in 113 countries around the world (Bartlett (2008)) and the growth in IRB governance over human subject research is likely to continue.

4.2 Planned Experimental Design

Prior to running your experiment, it is a good practice to *plan* the design of your experiment—that is, the set of treatment conditions and associated hypotheses that you will explore in your experiment. Such planning is also useful in preparing your IRB protocol (if required).

The simplest RCT experiments have treatment variations along a *single* dimension, e.g., the random assignment of a subject to receive a placebo or a new drug. More challenging experiments have variations between 2 or more independent variables (sometimes called "factors"). In a **full factorial design**, the experimental plan calls for investigation of each level of one independent variable in combination with each level of the other independent variables.

For example, consider a 2×2, full factorial design. This refers to a design where there are two independent treatment variables, T_1 and T_2, each of which can take on two different values or conditions, V_{11}, V_{12} for T_1 and V_{21}, V_{22} for T_2. The 2×2 design is illustrated in Figure 4.1. For

		T_2	
		V_{21}	V_{22}
T_1	V_{11}	Cell 1	Cell 3
	V_{12}	Cell 2	Cell 4

Figure 4.1: A 2×2 experimental design.

an experimental economics example, T_1 could be the auction format; V_{11}: First-price auction rules (the highest bidder wins and pays his/her bid) V_{22}: Second-price auction rules (the highest bidder wins and pays the second-highest amount bid (or price). T_2 could be the number of bidders, N; V_{21}: $N = 4$, V_{22}: $N = 10$. The experiment involves recording observations on one or more **outcome variables** in all four cells of the design in order to evaluate various hypotheses. For instance, using the experimental design of Figure 4.1, the experimenter can evaluate the effect on an outcome variable, such as the mean amount bid or market efficiency, on the choice of the auction rule, holding constant the group size (4 or 10). Furthermore, the experimenter can investigate whether the number of bidders N matters given a particular auction format. Finally, in a full factorial design, the experimenter can also study the effects of *interactions* between (or among) treatment variables on the outcome variable, e.g., how bids change as the auction changes from first-price rules with 4 bidders to second-price rules with 10 bidders. Other designs are constructed similarly. If you have k factors each at 2 levels then you have a $k \times 2$ experimental design and 2^k cells; k factors at 3 levels is a $k \times 3$ design with 3^k cells, etc.

Sometimes, a full factorial design may *not* be warranted. Indeed, the **sparsity of effects** principle asserts that certain effects are likely to be more influential than others, meaning that, in many cases, main effects (individual factors) and low-order interactions (those interactions involving only a small number of factors) are more significant and have a larger impact on the outcomes of an experiment as compared with higher-order interactions. In cases where some interactions are unlikely to have appreciable effects (e.g., according to theory) and/or when the noise in the data is not excessive, then the researcher might reasonably choose to use a **fractional factorial design**, wherein only a selected subset or "fraction" of the cells of the full factorial design are studied. For example, in Figure 4.1, it might be the case that the interaction between conditions V_{12} and V_{22} (Cell 4) is not particularly interesting because the main effect of treatment variable 1 is better captured by the difference between cells 1 and 2, while the main effect of treatment variable 2 is better captured by the difference between cells 1 and 3. In such cases, one could choose to conduct the *fractional* factorial design involving cells 1 3 only.

Once one has planned the experimental design, conducting the **experiment** involves collecting data on relevant outcome variables in all of the cells of that design. Precisely how many observations is needed per cell is discussed below in Section 4.4.[1] There are many advantages to planning your experiment. First, it aids in the precise formulation of hypotheses. Second, it may help to optimize resource allocation, such as for financial resources; for instance, if a theory can be evaluated using only 2 different values for a treatment variable, there might be no need to allocate resources for additional treatment values of that variable. Finally, a well-planned

---

[1]Note here the use of the *singular* "experiment" and *not* "experiments"; experimentalists refer to the collection of data in *all* treatment conditions or cells of their planned design as the *experiment*.

experimental design makes for good science in the sense of pre-committing the researcher to a plan of investigation as opposed to the unplanned alternative of simply trying one different treatment after another.

4.3 Pre-analysis Plans and Pre-registration of Hypotheses

Related to the pre-commitment afforded by planned experimental design, it is good practice to **pre-register** an experimental design, the hypotheses to be tested and the data collection plan. Pre-registration of designs, hypotheses, and data collection plans is rapidly growing in popularity, although, at the time of writing, the practice is not yet universal among social science experimenters.[2]

There are a number of free and open-source registries where researchers can pre-register their social science experiment. The American Economic Association's RCT registry is perhaps the most relevant to researchers conducting field RCT experiments. Other pre-registration sites for experimental social science researchers are administered by the Center for Open Science and The Penn Wharton Credibility Lab. Pre-registration involves stating the hypotheses to be tested, the outcome variables that will be collected, the number of observations per treatment cell, and the data methods by which the hypotheses will be evaluated. Pre-registration sites provide time stamps as to when data plans and hypotheses were first registered and enable real-time updates, which can be useful in addressing any challenges that may arise during the execution of the experimental design.

There are three main advantages to pre-registering hypotheses and data plans using such registries (see Dal-Ré *et al.* (2014) for a further discussion.)

First, by pre-registering, the researcher credibly fixes the set of hypotheses and data analysis that will be conducted. By construction, this should have the benefit of improving confidence in a study's reported outcomes. In particular, "*p*-hacking," the practice of slicing the data or running many different regression analyses so as to obtain statistically significant results (low probability or *p*-values), may be reduced if the data sample and econometric methods are declared in advance. Furthermore, this practice helps curb the tendency to cherry-pick hypotheses for evaluation, ensuring a more impartial approach to hypothesis testing. Lastly, pre-registration

---

[2] The first pre-analysis plan in economics is credited to Casey *et al.* (2012), who provide further details regarding the merits of their approach.

is thought to reduce the incidence of HARKING, or "hypothesizing after results are known" which is the practice of forming or modifying hypotheses after observing research findings, but presenting those hypotheses as if they were a priori rather than post hoc hypothesis. This practice is generally regarded as bad science, since tailoring hypotheses to outcomes from a specific experiment increases the likelihood that the results are not reproducible or generalizable.

A second and related aim of such pre-registrations is to combat the "file-drawer" problem. The latter is the notion that authors are more likely to file away in a drawer any results that are inconclusive or that undermine their experimental hypotheses and are more likely to submit for publication only positive results confirming hypotheses. The file drawer problem results in a publication bias that skews scientific knowledge toward studies with more positive results.

Finally, a third advantage of pre-registration is that it provides a public record of the experiments that are being carried out by researchers, enabling other researchers to get a clearer picture of what studies have or have not yet been conducted on a particular topic.

On the other hand, some experimental economists (e.g., Coffman and Niederle (2015)) argue that pre-analysis plans and hypotheses registrations may not be desirable for several reasons. First, while pre-analysis plans may be valuable for very large-scale and unique studies that are unlikely to ever be replicated, the advantages of pre-registrations are much smaller for lower-cost studies that are more likely to be replicated by others. Thus, the potential costs of such plans should be weighed against any benefits.

Second, the requirement of a pre-analysis plan might discourage exploratory research involving risky research with unknown outcomes. Instead, researchers might engage in only very incremental research with low risks and higher predictability. Relatedly, it might also inhibit follow-up analyses that make better sense of the data including add-on or expository treatments that condition on the experimental data. If one chooses to engage in such expository follow-up hypotheses, then it is good practice to declare that the hypotheses were developed ex-post, that is *after* the data were collected and observed, a process sometimes referred to as "transparent hypothesizing after results are known" (or THARKING).

Finally, some argue that the problems that pre-analysis and pre-registration plans are designed to reduce are not a pervasive problem in experimental economics; in particular, the evidence of p-hacking in experimental economics is not very strong.

In deciding whether and how much to pre-register, there are some practical considerations that one might take into account. For instance, if one has an experiment that is specifically designed to test, say, the comparative statics predictions of rational choice theory as applied to some setting, then the design by itself will provide a type of pre-commitment. If the experimental data do not support the hypotheses being tested, then one can always "blame the theory" for this outcome. On the other hand, if one is testing a hypothesis for which there is no theory, or one for which the relevant theory predicts no treatment differences, then it might be preferable to pre-register the behavioral hypotheses you are testing in advance of conducting such a study. In essence, in the latter case, you are shifting blame for any null outcome to your pre-registered hypothesis.

4.4 Power Analysis to Determine Sample Size

Assuming you cannot conduct your experiment on the entire population of interest, your choice of the **sample size** for each cell of your experiment will be an important consideration that you might also incorporate into any pre-registration or data plan. While many experimenters do not provide any justification for the sample sizes they use, it is generally a good practice to provide *some* justification, if possible. One justification is resource constraints, e.g., there are limits to the money needed to pay subjects or the time interval for which access to a population of subjects was available, e.g., in the field. Another common justification is to follow the sample sizes chosen by other researchers in earlier, related studies, which facilitates comparisons. These are admittedly weak justifications, but they are preferable to no justification at all. Perhaps the best justification comes from conducting an analysis of statistical power, known as a **power analysis**. Here the aim is to choose a sample size that enables you to reliably detect a given **effect size** across treatment conditions, thus providing a quantitative measure of the impact of a treatment change.

Statistical power is defined as the probability of observing a statistically significant effect for a given significance level, α, sample size, n, and desired effect size. The aim of conducting a power analysis is to minimize the possibility of a false negative result, given your desired effect size.

Statistical significance concerns the probability of committing a type 1 error or a false positive. This error occurs when one falsely rejects the null hypotheses, H_0, in favor of the alternative, H_A, i.e., when the null hypothesis is in fact true. The probability of committing a type I error, denoted by α, is defined as follows:

$$\alpha = \Pr\left(\text{Reject } H_0 \mid H_0 \text{ is true}\right).$$

Generally, α represents the threshold for statistical significance chosen by a researcher to assess the likelihood of making type I errors. Conventional values for α are $\{0.10, 0.05, 0.01\}$. In experimental economics, the current convention is to set $\alpha = .05$ or lower (0.10 is considered "marginal"). Some researchers (e.g., Benjamin *et al.* (2018)) have called for even lower values, e.g., $\alpha = 0.005$.

Statistical power is related to the probability of a type II error or a false negative. This type of error arises when one fails to reject the null hypothesis even though the alternative is in fact true. A type II error, denoted by β, is defined as:

$$\beta = \Pr\left(\text{Do not reject } H_0 \mid H_A \text{ is true}\right).$$

Statistical power is the probability of detecting an effect, if there is truly an effect to detect, i.e.,

$$\begin{aligned}
\text{power} &= \Pr\left(\text{Reject} H_0 \mid H_A \text{ is true}\right) \\
&= 1 - \Pr\left(\text{Do not reject } H_0 \mid H_A \text{ is true}\right) \\
&= 1 - \beta.
\end{aligned}$$

The goal of a power analysis is to design an experiment such that the chosen statistical method has a strong chance of detecting the effect of interest if that effect in fact exists. A power analysis involves four components, all of which are all interrelated; if we have three, we can compute the fourth.

1. The effect size, which is the magnitude of a treatment effect relative to the noise in measurement; the latter will be measured using the standard deviation.

2. The significance level used in the statistical test, e.g. α; as noted, 0.05 is the current convention.

3. Statistical power, $1 - \beta$, or the probability of accepting the alternative hypothesis if it is true. The current convention is to set $1 - \beta = 0.8$, i.e., $\beta = 0.2$ (see e.g., Cohen (1992)), though higher power levels are also commonly used, e.g., setting $\beta = \alpha = 0.05$, so that power is 0.95.

4. The number of observations from the experimental interventions.

Changing any one of these four variables will affect the other—for instance, statistical power can be increased by raising the significance level or by increasing the number of observations.

The effect size is the most problematic aspect of a power analysis, often because an experiment has not yet been run and therefore, the researcher does not know what effect size to expect. Here, there are advantages to having a theory-based experiment, particularly if the theory involves a precise prediction regarding the effect that a change in a treatment variable should have on a choice variable. For instance, if one is conducting an auction experiment, a good candidate for the effect size might be the predicted difference in the bid amount in a treatment condition relative to the control. If one does not know the effect size, then one should specify the smallest effect size that is of scientific interest. See Cohen (1992) for an elaboration of this approach.

Here we discuss how to use a power analysis to decide on the sample size, though this is just one possible use of a power analysis. One can also ask, for a given sample size, effect size, and significance level, what is the power of a statistical test?

Specifically, consider an experiment where a researcher is studying the effect of adding an entry fee to a two-player contest for a prize. In the control treatment there is no entry fee, whereas in the treatment there is an entry fee that players have to agree to pay before they can bid to win the contest prize (without knowing if their opponent has paid the fee). Suppose that a two independent sample, between-subjects design is chosen where the theory predicts that the control group should bid 25 while the treatment group should bid only 15, on account of having to pay an entry fee. Thus, $\mu_0 = 25$ and $\mu_1 = 15$. Assume further that the standard deviation of bids in a similar setting from prior research is $\sigma = 8$.[3] Then, the effect size the researcher is hoping to detect, $d = \mu_1 - \mu_0 = -10$; the *standardized* effect size is $(\mu_1 - \mu_0)/\sigma$, in this case, -1.25. If we use a t-test to evaluate $H_0 : d = 0$ against $H_A : d < 0$, i.e., if we assume Gaussian errors (as is typical) then we can use a number of statistical packages to compute the sample size needed for a significance level of $\alpha = 0.5$ and power of $1 - \beta = 0.8$. Below we report output from the STATA statistical package using the command, power:

We see that the total number of observations needed to detect the effect size of -10 (delta in Stata) is 24—or 12 observations each for treatment

---

[3]A reliable measure of measurement dispersion is essential, and, often, prior experimental studies on the same or related topics serve as the primary source of such information; theory, after all, often predicts a standard deviation of 0!

```
. power twomeans 25 15, sd(8) alpha(0.05) power(0.80)

Performing iteration ...

Estimated sample sizes for a two-sample means test
t test assuming sd1 = sd2 = sd
H0: m2 = m1   versus   Ha: m2 != m1

Study parameters:

           alpha =      0.0500
           power =      0.8000
           delta =    -10.0000
              m1 =     25.0000
              m2 =     15.0000
              sd =      8.0000

Estimated sample sizes:

               N =          24
   N per group =          12
```

and control. The advantage of this approach for determining the number of observations is that it provides the minimum sample size needed to detect an effect while maintaining sufficient power and avoiding the cost of acquiring a needlessly high number of observations. The main disadvantage is that the elements needed to conduct a proper power analysis may involve some amount of guesswork.

4.5   Writing Instructions and Control Questions

Prior to any experimental intervention, you will want to compose a set of **instructions** that will be given to the experimental participants in advance of their participation in your experiment. It is important to write these instructions clearly and precisely so that if subjects make errors or do not behave as predicted, such behavior cannot be attributed to a misunderstanding of the instructions. To that end, after the instructions have been read (aloud or privately), many researchers proceed to test subjects on their comprehension of the instructions and some do not permit subjects to proceed with the experimental interventions until they have answered all comprehension **control test questions** correctly.[4] Requiring that subjects pass a set of control test questions is not only useful for validating subjects' comprehension of the instructions; it can also be a particularly useful filter for excluding the programmed robot traders that are often found in online subject pools.

Instructions should include the following three items:

1. A description of the tasks to be completed, including the choice(s) to be made, any information that subjects will have available to them (e.g., the number of other subjects they are interacting with), any time and or budget constraints on their choices, and the feedback that will be provided to them following the completion of each task.

2. A clear description of how subjects earn points or money from the choices they make in each task.

3. How subjects will be paid at the end of the experiment. Recall from our earlier discussion that one can pay subjects for all tasks completed or randomly choose a subset of tasks for payment, but this procedure should be made clear in the instructions so that subjects can evaluate the payoff consequences of their choices. Subjects should also be informed of any fixed show-up payment.

Following the reading of instructions, control test questions can be used to evaluate or check subjects' comprehension of the instructions. These test questions can also be used to further elaborate on the instructions, for example by having subjects work out specific examples, and calculate their earnings.

In field experiments, it can be necessary to forego written instructions as the subjects may not be literate or may be unaware that they are even participating in an experimental intervention. In such cases, in place of written instructions, the researchers should write down the experimental procedures they follow in the control and treatment arms and repeatedly follow these same procedures in the implementation of the experiment. If instructions are provided orally, then a video can be made as a record of the instruction process.

---

[4]Some researchers use the score on the instructions test as a measure of subjects' comprehension skills, which may correlate with their behavior in the experiment.

4.6   Deception

Deception in experimental research is the act of explicitly inducing subjects to believe something that is not true. For example, instructing subjects that they will be making strategic decisions with other subjects when, in fact, some or all of these "other subjects" are confederates of the experimenter, or are robot players, or are the experimenter him/herself! For another example, providing subjects with misleading information about what other subjects have done, so as to induce some kind of norm, when in fact the information regarding other subjects' actions was made up by the experimenter.

In experimental social science research, such *deception of subjects is not allowed*. The rationale for this prohibition is that the trust that experimental subjects place in what experimenters tell them is viewed as a *public good*. If some experimenters were known to break this trust by deceiving their subjects, this could have spillover effects to other experimenters using the same subject pool, and subjects might then not believe any instruction that they are given. The result is a loss of control over what subjects believe—and control, as we have seen, is an important element of the internal validity of the experimental method. For this reason, social science experimenters who deceive their subjects are at risk of having their research rejected for publication.

While the "no deception" *taboo* is strong in experimental social science, whether and when deception occurs is still the subject of some debate (see, e.g., Hertwig and Ortmann (2008); Ortmann (2019)). A distinction is sometimes made between "acts of commission" and "acts of omission." The former refers to deliberate deception, such as telling subjects false information about other subjects. The latter refers to the practice of not telling subjects information that may be germane to the decisions the subjects make (e.g., that subjects are randomly matched every period to another subject in the room, so that they are not repeatedly interacting with the same other subjects(s)). While acts of commission are generally forbidden, acts of omission are generally less frowned upon since most experimenters are guilty of concealing some details about their experiment from the subjects, and often for good reasons. For example, the hypotheses the experiment is designed to test and whether subjects are in a control or treatment group are generally not divulged because the knowledge of such information may affect subjects' behavior (e.g., experimenter demand effects).

One class of studies related to this discussion are field "audit" studies used by labor and urban economists to detect discrimination. Consider, for example, the audit study experiment by Bertrand and Mullainathan (2004). In this study, fictitious resumes were sent in response to help-wanted ads in two large American cities. The treatment involved randomly changing the name on the resume to either an African-American- or a White-sounding name. The outcome variable was the rate of callbacks for real job interviews. The major finding from this study was that the White names callback rate was 50% greater than for the African-American names, even though the resumes were otherwise identical. While this finding is quite interesting, it nevertheless involves a deliberative act of commission (falsely claiming to be a job applicant) that resulted in wasted effort in resume review by real firms, since the resumes were all fictional. The authors of such audit studies would claim that the benefits of documenting discriminatory behavior outweigh the costs of deception, but this claim is difficult to substantiate.

As a potential solution to this problem, Kessler *et al.* (2019) introduced a new design that they called **incentivized resume rating** (IRR). Under IRR, real human resource professionals are asked to evaluate resumes they *know* to be fictional and their reward for doing so is that they are subsequently presented with real job candidates whose resumes most closely matched the features the professionals claimed to like the most when reviewing the fictional resumes. Using IIR, Kessler *et al.* (2019) find only small amounts of discrimination against under-represented job applicants. The advantage of this approach is that it avoids deception. A disadvantage, however, is that subjects (in this case human resource professionals) might not be acting in the same manner when they know their actions are being viewed by experimenters. Still, for the reasons outlined above, it is best to avoid deception, particularly acts of commission.

4.7 Data Collection Methods

Experimental data can be collected in a variety of different ways. Here we discuss the four most common methods.

1. **Paper and pencil.** Many of the original social science experiments were conducted using paper and pencil. In this approach, one can ask the subjects to perform simple mathematical calculations and keep track of items such as their choices and payoffs using paper "record sheets." At the end of the experiment these record sheets can be collected and can serve as an additional means of data collection.

2. **Survey software.** Many interesting experimental data can be collected using specially designed survey software such as Qualtrics or SurveyMonkey. For instance, if one is interested in conducting multiple price list data on risk or time preferences, such price lists can be easily programmed using survey software. However, paying subjects may still have to be manually determined based on the data collected by the survey programs, as these programs are not (yet) set up to make subject payments.

3. **Computer programs.** Perhaps the best and most thorough method of data collection is to write a computer program to collect data and compute subject earnings. The program may also include the instructions and instruction comprehension quizzes. The advantages of programming an experiment are speed, consistency of the decision-making environment, and accuracy of data collection and payoff calculations. While one can develop from scratch computer programs to implement a variety of different types of experiments, there are already several software packages that enable quick programming of experiments. One widely used package at the time of this writing is z-Tree (Fischbacher, 2007). Another widely used and Python-based package is oTree (Chen *et al.*, 2016). Both are freely available.

A further advantage of using such ready-made platforms is that, if you intend only to modify already-existing experiments, then you can try to borrow the researcher's code (with proper attribution, of course). Moreover, market trading institutions such as continuous double auction mechanisms (discussed in Chapter 10) which can be quite tricky to program have already been programmed (and debugged!) by others, and again you can include this part of the code in your own experimental programs.

4. **Other methods.** In field experiments, it is often desirable if the subjects do not know they are participating in an experiment, as this helps to preserve the natural field elements of the experiment. To accomplish this goal, the data collection methods can be quite varied. For example, consider the field experiment conducted by Karlan and List (2007) (discussed earlier), which examined how changes in the price of charitable giving affected contributions to a non-profit organization using a direct mail solicitation of 50,000 supporters. In this experiment, the data collected was the amount that supporters

donated in response to different solicitation letters received, which varied the matching amount for a donation (the treatment variable).

4.8 Recruitment of Subjects

Subject **recruitment** is an important task in implementing any experiment. Before recruiting subjects, the experimenter has presumably made a choice regarding the population of subjects that he/she will sample from. Recruitment of subjects can be done in a variety of ways ranging from using flyers, electronic notices, email messages, social media, or, if one is working with a dedicated subject pool, recruitment software. Several recruitment software systems are presently available, including the Online System for Economic Experiments (ORSEE) Greiner (2015), the Hamburg Registration and Organization Online Tool (hRoot) Bock *et al.* (2014), and the commercial cloud software SONA systems www.sona-systems.com. Online workplaces such as Amazon's Mechanical Turk www.mturk.com and Prolific www.prolific.com also provide recruitment services (for a fee). In recruiting subjects, the experimenter will want to keep track of *who* has participated in the same or related studies in the past. Recruitment software programs can do this for you. The reason to keep track of this information is that subjects with different levels of experience may affect your results. A typical practice is to restrict subjects' participation to a single session of your experiment so that all subjects have the *same* level of experience with your experimental interventions.

On the other hand, some experimenters have also studied the experience level of subjects as a treatment variable, and for this purpose it can be necessary to recruit "experienced subjects," defined as those who have already participated in the experiment at least once. Again, recruitment software can be useful for ascertaining who is experienced with a particular experimental intervention and who is not.

4.9 How Much to Pay?

The question of how much to pay subjects is an important design question. A good experimental design uses both a power analysis to efficiently determine the number of subjects needed to detect a treatment effect relative to some baseline control and, in consideration of the budget the researcher has available, next decides how many treatments can be implemented given a certain expected cost per subject. Note that the answer to this question might be zero, i.e., the researcher's budget might not be large enough to run a sufficiently high-powered experiment.

The general rule on payment per subject is that subjects should earn at least their **opportunity cost** for participating in the experimental intervention(s) and, ideally, even more.

This opportunity cost will of course depend on the subject population that one is recruiting from. In developed industrialized countries with minimum hourly wages, those minimums tend to provide a good lower bound for these opportunity costs, particularly if one is using unemployed student subjects. However, each subject pool is different; as members of the "gig economy" working remotely from home, online workers tend to require less than mandated minimum wages for their hourly compensation and certainly a lower "show-up" payment as they choose by themselves when to show up for online work.

Subjects in laboratory social science experiments are generally guaranteed a fixed **show-up** or **completion payment** for showing up and completing a study. In addition, subjects in economic decision-making experiments are provided **variable payments** that depend on the choices they make in the experiment in accordance with the incentives of the theory being tested.

By contrast, paying subjects in field experiments may not be required, particularly if the subjects are not aware that they are participating in a field experiment. However, for lab-in-the-field-type experiments, some type of fixed and variable payment scheme is also commonly used.

Thus, in settings where the experimental intervention is known to subjects, the total payment will consist of a fixed (show-up/completion) component and a variable component that is based on decisions made in the experimental tasks. As a general rule, the variable payment component of a subject's total payment should comprise the *bulk* of their payment, perhaps by a ratio of 2 or 3 to 1. Thus, in practice, one can fix the show-up payment first and then determine the mean or expected variable component as some multiple of that fixed component.

A final point about subject payment is that researchers should be careful to avoid the possibility that subjects earn *negative* payoffs from their participation in a study. There are two reasons to avoid negative payoffs. First, it may be de-motivating for subjects' behavior—in other words, once they start earning negative payoffs, subjects may lose interest, make poor decisions, or even drop out. Second, it is not credible that a subject who has volunteered their time to participate in a researcher's study will agree to pay the researcher the negative earnings owed; in practice, many experimenters would truncate the payoff to 0, but such a truncation would render the controlled incentive scheme of the experiment not fully operational, and such events will have to be reported by the experimenter in the data analysis. To avoid the possibility of negative payoffs, then, one can either design the experiment in such a way as to eliminate such a possibility (e.g., by giving subjects a sufficiently large endowment of points or money at the outset of the study) or warn subjects that if their payoffs are trending below a certain level that they might be removed from the experiment. The aim in paying subjects is to keep them sufficiently interested to complete the study and motivated enough to think carefully about the choices they make.

As this chapter has emphasized, there is significant groundwork that has to be covered *before* an experiment can be conducted. Implementation of an experiment involves the careful design of treatments; the acquiring of any necessary human subject research approvals; the development of hypotheses, data plans, and pre-registrations; and, finally, the programming of the experiment, the writing of instructions (if necessary), and the recruitment of subjects. The reward for this large amount of preparation is that the researcher will end up with a unique dataset, where the data have been "baked" to specifically address the hypotheses and treatment variable variations that the researcher finds interesting.

Chapter 5

Data Analysis

Once you have gathered all of your experimental data, the next step is to analyze it and present it in a manner that enables your readers to clearly understand the results of your experiment. In this chapter we review some of the basics of experimental data analysis and presentation of data. As a first preparatory step, a good practice is to save all original data files with time stamps for the date collected in a secure location (e.g., on a cloud server or other online data repository that is subject to regular backup) and to conduct your data analysis on *copies* of these original files (and not on the original versions themselves!) so as to avoid corruption of your original raw data files. It is also a good practice to keep a log of when and where each session of your experiment was conducted, how many subjects participated, how much these subjects were paid each or on average, and other important characteristics of the data collected (e.g., subjects' demographic data).

5.1 What is an Independent Observation?

A **unit of observation** is an object for which data is collected. For example, the amount that a subject bids in an auction. One of the most difficult issues that experimentalists face is determining what data unit constitutes an *independent* unit of observation. Is the choice made by each subject in your experiment an independent observation? If your experiment is an individual choice experiment, this may be the case, but if there are strategic or market interactions among the subjects in your experiment, then individual subject choices may no longer be independent of one another.

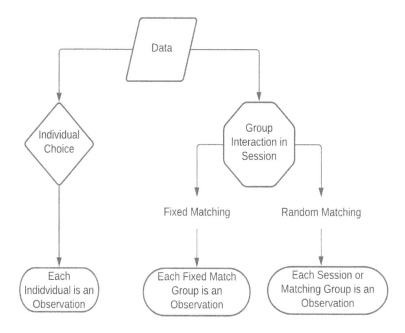

Figure 5.1: Decision tree for what constitutes an independent observation.

In such cases, one could take the group or the market decision as an observation, but if decisions are made repeatedly, after the first repeated instance, individual, group, or market observations may no longer be considered independent observations as well; they may not be independent of the history of prior outcomes. As **independence of observations** is an important assumption underlying most statistical analyses, the consideration of what constitutes an independent observation requires some thought.

Figure 5.1 provides a decision tree for assessing the experimental data unit that might be considered an independent observation in your data analysis. If you have individual choice data, then, unsurprisingly, you should be able to treat each individual as a separate observation. However, if you have data pertaining to the decisions made by groups of subjects, then you should carefully consider whether groups remained in the same fixed match with one another for all rounds of your study or whether there was random re-matching to form groups in every round. If the former case, then each group in which individuals remained in the same fixed match may be the most appropriate unit of observation. If the latter, then the largest unit in which individuals were chosen to form randomly matched groups, typically an experimental *session*, may be the most appropriate unit of observation. A hybrid case is to divide a session of N subjects into two or more **matching groups** of size $n < N$ and then only randomly form groups within the confines of those matching groups of size n. In this way, each matching group serves as an independent observation, as there are no spillovers/contamination across matching groups.

If one has repeated data measures for each unit of observation, say, over a number of "periods," then one might wish to use group average values per period as the time series unit measure.

5.2 Preliminary Data Analysis

A first step in analyzing your data should be to compute means, standard deviations, medians, and minimum and maximum values for each of your outcome variables by treatment condition in your experiment. Typically, one of the first tables in the results section of an experimental paper reports on such statistics by treatment in order to provide the reader with an overview of the more detailed data analysis that is to follow.

Another important first step is to *visualize* your data by making **scatter plots**, **histograms**, and **cumulative distribution functions** of your data observations broken down by treatment and observation unit (individual, group, or session). **Box plots** of outcome variables by treatment provide a concise means by which to summarize the minimum, maximum, the sample median, and the first and third quartiles of your experimental data and are conveniently pre-programmed in many statistical packages. Such a plot can reveal whether your data is symmetrical around the median, how tightly your data is grouped, and whether and how your data is skewed. Some box plot programs also identify data **outliers**, which are individual data points that stand out from the rest of the dataset due to their unusual values. As a rule, experimental social scientists do not discard outlier values generated by human subjects but do highlight them and attempt to address their presence in statistical analyses of the data.[1]

The first-best analysis of your experimental data is visual. Organizing your mean outcome variable(s) by treatment, can you clearly see whether your various treatments had the hypothesized effect or not? Joe Berkson, a

---

[1]Outlier values can be caused by human error, such as when a subject intends to bid 100 but instead types "1,000". To avoid generation of such data, experimenters often place restrictions on the choices that subjects can make and explain such restrictions in the instructions given to subjects.

researcher at the Mayo Clinic, calls this approach the "Inter Ocular Trauma" (IOT) test. It involves plotting your data by treatment and then observing whether the treatment effects hit you "between the eyes." If your data passes the IOT, then you may not even need to conduct a more sophisticated data analysis; a well-constructed figure may suffice.

A data visualization is useful not only for understanding the likely impact of treatment effects but also for the appropriate choice of the econometric approach that you will use to analyze your data. For instance, **parametric methods** such as linear or logit regression make assumptions about the parameters of the distribution from which the sample is drawn, e.g., a normal or logistic distribution. **Non-parametric** approaches do not require such distributional assumptions and are therefore more flexible as to when they can be applied. On the other hand, tests using parametric methods (e.g., t-tests) typically have more statistical power than do nonparametric tests. Thus, using a parametric test, you may be more likely to detect a significant effect when one truly exists than if you use a non-parametric test.

A good reference/cookbook on non-parametric tests as applied to experimental data is Siegel and Castellan Jr. (1988), *Nonparametric Statistics for the Behavioral Sciences*, 2nd Ed. New York: McGraw Hill. A good reference on parametric regression analysis for experimental data including finite mixture models and the method of maximum simulated likelihood is Moffatt (2016), *Experimetrics: Econometrics for Experimental Economics*, London: Macmillan. In the remainder of this chapter, I will sketch out some simple non-parametric and parametric approaches to the analysis of experimental data; but, for a more detailed treatment of the subject matter, the reader is referred to these two books or others on the subject matter.

5.3   Non-parametric Methods

Unless a visual inspection of your data suggests that parametric assumptions are valid and/or you have a very large number of observations, parametric methods may not be appropriate. In this case, you will want to consider non-parametric methods. The appropriateness of parametric methods may also depend on your view of the unit of an observation: individuals, groups, or sessions. Some experimentalists will use parametric methods applied to all of the data generated in their experiment and then try to correct for the lack of statistical independence using panel data methods, e.g., that cluster standard errors at the unit of observation, whether that is at the individual, group, or session level, in order to take account of interactions. Other experimentalists will take a more conservative approach by treating each experimental session as an independent observation. In the latter approach, it may be the case (due to budget constraints) that one has too few observations to satisfy distributional assumptions and so nonparametric methods would be the more appropriate choice.

For example, suppose you want to test whether data from two different treatments (independent samples) come from different distributions with different means. A *t*-test assumes that the difference between two samples is normally distributed while the nonparametric Wilcoxon–Mann–Whitney test makes no such distributional assumption. In small samples, as is typical for costly experimental data, the normality assumption may not hold. This is precisely where the appeal of non-parametric tests lies.

In the following sections, I discuss some common non-parametric tests. Most of these are pre-programmed in statistical packages like Stata and R, but I also provide some additional pointers as to how these tests work.

5.3.1 Wilcoxon–Mann–Whitney test

This test relies on ordinal/ordered data from two independent samples, e.g., n_A session means from treatment A, and n_B session means from treatment B. It is perhaps the most popular non-parametric test used by experimental social science researchers. As already noted, it is asymptotically equivalent to a *t*-test as the sample size becomes large.

To illustrate how the test works, let us consider a specific example. Suppose there are two treatments, A and B, with observations $n_A = n_B = 5$ per treatment. The treatment A mean scores are 11, 8, 12, 14, and 13. The treatment B mean scores are 5, 9, 6, 4, and 7. Note that the samples sizes need not be the same, but it must be the case that min $[n_A, n_B] \geq 3$.

The hypotheses may be specified as follows. Null: A and B come from the same population, $\Pr[A > B] = \frac{1}{2} = \Pr[A < B]$. Alternative (two-tail): A and B come from different distributions.

If one has a directional hypothesis, then one may specify the alternative hypothesis, e.g., as A is stochastically larger than B $\Pr[A > B] \neq 1/2$. (One can also study the opposite case.)

Many statistical packages are programmed to implement this type of test, but it is instructive to manually work out the test results for our simple example data if we want to better comprehend what is actually going on. To do so, we first rank the data from lowest to highest and then assign ranks to the entire sample. As there are 10 total observations in this example, there are 10 ranks to be assigned: rank 1=lowest to 10=highest. The ranking is shown in Table 5.1. Note that ranks can be sensitive to the rounding of the data. In the event of ties, one assigns the same rank to all tied elements. The next step is to sum up the ranks for each treatment. Denoting the sum

Table 5.1: Ranking of data in the example.

Rank: Low-High	1	2	3	4	5	6	7	8	9	10
Mean	3	5	6	7	8	9	11	12	13	14
Treatment	B	B	B	B	A	B	A	A	A	A

of ranks for treatment i by RS_i, we have $RS_A = 5 + 7 + 8 + 9 + 10 = 39$ and $RS_B = 1 + 2 + 3 + 4 + 6 = 16$. Note further that the sum of the first N integers, $1 + 2 + 3 + \cdots + N = N(N + 1)/2$.

Thus, if we have $n_A + n_B = N = 10$, total observations, the sum of the first N integers is $10(10 + 1)/2 = 55 = RS_A + RS_B$. If the null hypothesis of no difference is true, then the sums of the ranks should be roughly equal for each treatment, or, in this case, around $55/2 = 27.5$ each. Note that in our example case where $n_A = n_B = 5$, the maximum $RS_i = 40$ and the minimum $RS_i = 15$.

Suppose the alternative, H_1, is that treatment A is different from treatment B (a two-sided test). Then we first compute the Mann–Whitney U statistic for each treatment i, which is given by $U_i = RS_i - n_i(n_i+1)/2$. The U-test statistic subtracts the minimum possible rank sum for each group i, $n_i(n_i + 1)/2$, from the rank sum for each treatment i, RS_i.[2]

For treatment A, we have that $U_A = 39 - 15 = 24$ and for treatment B we have that $U_B = 16 - 15 = 1$. The U-test statistic to choose is always the lower of the two statistics, i.e., $U = \min(U_A, U_B)$ in this case $U = U_B = 1$. When the null hypothesis is true, this test statistic has a known distribution (available, e.g., in Siegel and Castellan Jr. (1988) or programmed into many computer statistical packages). In our example, the probability (p-value) of observing a U-test statistic of 1 with $n_A = n_B = 5$ is 0.016. Generally, a statistical significance level of 5% is the standard in experimental economics

---

[2]In another variant of U_i, RS_i is *subtracted* from the maximum possible rank sum for group i, $n_i \cdot n_j - n_i(n_i + 1)/2$, i.e., $U_i = n_i \cdot n_j - n_i(n_i + 1)/2 - RS_i$.

research. If that is the chosen significance level, then in this example we would reject the null of no difference between the treatments.

As mentioned, the Wilcoxon–Mann–Whitney test is pre-programmed in many statistical packages. In Stata, for instance, one would use the following command: ranksum data, by(treatment)

5.3.2 Robust rank-order test

The Wilcoxon–Mann–Whitney test assumes that variables from treatments A and B are sampled from the same continuous distributions—that is, while the form of the distribution is not specified, it is assumed that they have the same variance. The null is that the means are the same and the alternative is that they are different. We can relax the assumption that the variances are the same (i.e. the underlying distributions are different) and still test whether there are differences in the means using the robust rank-order test (which involves a less restrictive set of assumptions).

This non-parametric test also requires you to rank the data from both treatments, but the robust rank-order test statistic involves a measure of the *placement* of each element of the A data sample relative to the B data as well as the reverse (the placement of each element of the B data sample relative to the A data). These measures are used to construct indices of the variability of the two datasets since we no longer assume the data in treatments A and B come from the same distribution. The variability indexes are used to adjust differences in the mean placements. Not surprisingly, the robust rank-order test is much less sensitive to changes in distributional assumptions than is the Wilcoxon–Mann–Whitney test. For further details on this test, see Feltovich (2003). This test is less commonly used but still programmed in many software packages. For instance, in Stata, one would use the following command: pfrank data, by(treatment) Applying the robust rank-order test statistic to the example from the previous section would mean we would have to reject the null hypothesis of no difference as the robust rank-order test statistic, 7.188, has a (two-sided) p-value of 0.0000.

5.3.3 Kruskal–Wallis test

This test asks the following question: Do $k > 2$ independent samples (ordinal/ ordered data) come from the same or different populations? In essence, this rank-based test extends the scope of the Wilcoxon–Mann–Whitney test to three or more samples. Thus, it is the analogue to the F-test used in the analysis of variance but without the assumption that all populations under comparison are normally distributed. It is this that makes it a non-parametric test.

In applying this test, the null hypothesis is that all k samples have the same distribution functions. An alternative hypothesis is that at least two of the samples have different distribution functions. In Stata, the Kruskal–Wallis test is performed using the following command: `kwallis data, by(treatment)`.

5.3.4   Fisher's exact test

This test, formulated by Fisher (1935), addresses whether there are non-random associations between *two* categorical variables. To apply this test, one needs two independent samples of categorical data that result from two different classifications, e.g., treatment 1 and treatment 2 and outcome 1 and outcome 2.

This test reveals the significance of the association (contingency) between the *two* kinds of classifications and is therefore an excellent test for the benchmark 2×2 experimental design. This test is the non-parametric analogue of Pearson's chi-squared test. Specifically, suppose we have two treatment variables and two outcome variables

	Outcome 1	Outcome 2
Treatment 1	a	b
Treatment 2	c	d

The null, H_0, is that the number of observations, a, b, c, or d in the 2×2 contingency table above, are evenly distributed across all four cells. Rejecting the null is evidence of an association between one or both of the contingencies.

As an example, consider a study conducted by Duffy and Fisher (2005) (discussed later in Chapter 10) in which they reported the categorical data in Table 5.2. The two contingencies are (1) whether a double auction or call market mechanism is used to determine market prices and (2) whether or not random price coordinating announcements (sunspots) are followed by market participants or not followed. The units are sessions: there were 9 sessions of the double auction market and 6 of the call market. Imposing the null hypothesis that sunspot announcements are randomly followed or not across both types of market, Fisher's exact test has a p-value of

Table 5.2: 2 × 2 Contingency table from Duffy and Fisher (2005).

Market	Sunspot Announcement	
Mechanism	Followed	Not Followed
Double Auction	4	5
Call Market	6	0

Source: Duffy and Fisher (2005).

0.044. Thus, the null hypothesis of no difference can be rejected at the 5% significance level. In this instance, the call market institution greatly mattered for whether the sunspot announcements were followed.

5.3.5 Chi-squared test

This non-parametric test also requires two independent samples. The null hypotheses is that there is no difference in the frequencies with which 2 or more discrete, mutually exclusive categories are observed between the two samples.

The Chi-squared test is a generalization of Fisher's exact test to more than two discrete categories. To successfully implement this test, the expected frequencies in each discrete category should not be too small.

5.3.6 Kolmogorov–Smirnov test

The Kolmogorov–Smirnov (KS) test is a non-parametric test used to determine whether there are differences in the *distributions* of some choice variable relative to some theoretical prediction (one-sample test) or between treatments (a two independent sample test). Figure 5.2 illustrates the two situations. The KS test is a non-parametric test that uses differences between cumulative distribution functions (CDFs). These CDFs themselves are valuable tools for representing individual choice data and illustrating disparities in distributions across treatments. Notably, the KS test operates by comparing the distinctions between the two distributions across the entire feasible range, as illustrated by the arrows in Figure 5.2

The one sample null hypothesis: the CDF for a choice variable is no different from some hypothesized/theoretical CDF (e.g., a best response function), is illustrated in the left panel of Figure 5.2

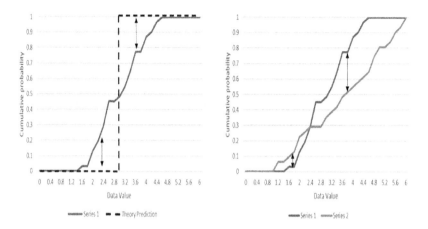

Figure 5.2: Left panel, CDF compared to a theoretical prediction (of 30): use the KS one-sample test; Right panel, CDF of data from two treatments: test for differences using a KS two-sample test of differences between distributions.

The two independent sample null hypothesis: the cumulative distribution functions (CDFs) for a given choice variable is no different between treatments or samples, is illustrated in the right panel of Figure 5.2.

For an example illustration of the KS test to experimental data, consider the study by Charness and Gneezy (2000), which involved a 2×2 experimental design. One treatment variable was whether subjects participated in a dictator or an ultimatum bargaining game (discussed later in Chapter 8). The other treatment was whether the name of the recipient (the other player in the bargaining match) was known to the player making the bargaining proposal (Names) or was not known (No Names). Further details are shown in Figure 5.3 below.

In this example, there are four independent samples of data, which are used to create four CDFs. Application of a two-sided KS test reveals that there is a significant difference in the cumulative distributions of proposer allocations (the outcome variable on the horizontal axis) in the dictator game ($p < .02$) but not in the ultimatum game ($p = .60$). While the test makes this result clear, the differences (or lack of differences) between the two pairs of CDFs are also quite evident in this case.

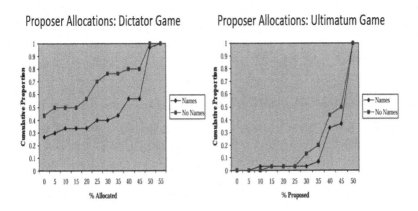

Figure 5.3: CDFs of proposer amounts offered to recipients.
Source: Charness and Gneezy (2000), used with permission of the authors.

5.3.7 Sign test

The sign test is used to assess a hypothesis regarding the *direction* of differences, e.g., +, − or 0 (no change) between *matched pairs* of data. Such data typically come from *within-subject* designs, where subjects are exposed to some treatment intervention; the data pair typically takes the form of a before-and-after set of data for each subject or group. However, it can also be used to assess trends in series of ordinal measurements.

As an example, suppose subjects are first asked how likely it is that they will vote for some political issue or candidate. Then, they are confronted with some new information, e.g., some poll results about the issue or candidate. Finally, they are asked to revisit the question of their likelihood of voting for the same issue or candidate. The sign test can be used when precise quantitative data are not available or might be difficult to gather, e.g., when the direction of change is the only information collected. The null hypothesis is that the median difference is 0, or that there are approximately equal numbers of +'s and −'s.

Following up with voting example, suppose you have 20 matched pair (before and after) observations. Sixteen observations show before-after differences in the negative direction and 4 in the positive direction. The null hypothesis of an equal occurrences of signs has a known distribution: it is a binomial distribution with a success probability equal to $1/2$. Using the example scenario of 16 negative and 4 positive changes, the null hypotheses of no difference has a p-value of .012, meaning that, at the 5% level of significance, you would reject the null of no difference from the treatment intervention.

5.3.8   Wilcoxon signed-rank test

Frank Wilcoxon (1945) proposed this test in the same paper in which he proposed the Wilcoxon–Mann–Whitney Test. Like the Wilcoxon–Mann–Whitney test, this distribution-free test is based on ranks. However, it goes beyond considering just the order of differences in matched pairs within a single sample; it incorporates the magnitude of these differences as well. This nuanced approach makes it more powerful than the signs test. However, it does require information on the *magnitudes* of differences. The test is particularly effective for within-subject designs where you have *matched pairs* of observations from two treatments, say A and B for each observation or subject i. In many applications, this test is used in place of the one sample t-test when the normality assumption is questionable, or when dealing with small samples, or both.

The test proceeds as follows: Using n pairs of matched data, the first step is to take differences, $d_i = A_i - B_i$, for $i = 1, \ldots n$. The null hypothesis is that the median $d_i = 0$, and the alternative hypothesis is that the median $d_i \neq 0$. One begins by sorting the differences according to size in absolute value terms and then assigning ranks to the d_i's without regard to the sign, with the lowest difference being assigned rank 1. Ties are awarded the average of the ranks that would have been assigned absent ties. Once all the differences are ranked, the sign of the difference ($-$ or $+$) is attached to the rank. Finally, one sums up the ranks of the positive differences, yielding the measure T^+, and sums up the negative ranks, yielding the measure T^-. If there is no difference between the matched pairs, then the positive and negative sums of the ranks should be approximately the same and equal to $1/2$ times the sum of the first n integer ranks, or $n(n+1)/4$.

As an example, consider matched pairs data reporting subject i's willingness to pay (WTP) and the same subject i's willingness to accept (WTA) in monetary terms for an object, say, a coffee mug, as elicited by using, say, a Becker–DeGroot–Marschak mechanism (discussed earlier in Chapter 3). The example matched pairs data are shown in Table 5.3.

In this example, $T^- = 12$ and $T^+ = 66$ and $n = 12$. If there were no differences, we would expect the sum of the ranks to be roughly the same,

Table 5.3: Wilcoxon signed-rank test, example data.

WTP	WTA	d_i	Rank
5.73	6.47	0.74	4
6.00	5.00	−1.00	−10.5
5.10	5.98	0.88	8
5.19	5.92	0.73	3
5.10	6.10	1.00	10.5
5.86	6.84	0.98	9
4.90	6.00	1.10	12
5.48	6.25	0.77	6
6.00	5.50	−0.50	−1.5
5.50	6.25	0.75	5
5.74	6.59	0.85	7
5.00	5.50	0.50	1.5

or approximately $12(12 + 1)/4 = 39$, in this example. Using the sum of the ranks and the expected sum, one can obtain a p-value for the null. In this case, the p-value is 0.034, so we would be inclined to reject the null at the standard significance level of 0.05. In this example, it appears that the WTA is greater than the WTP—that is, there is a WTA-WTP gap, which is a common finding in the experimental literature using such elicitations.

Like other non-parametric tests, the Wilcoxon signed-rank test is pre-programmed for use in many statistical packages. In Stata, for instance, one can use the following command: `signrank wta = wtp`.

The Wilcoxon signed-rank test can also be used on a single (non-matched pairs) sample. For instance, suppose you have data on a variable x_i from i subjects or groups. Suppose further that your theory predicts that x should be a certain fixed value, v (e.g., an equilibrium bid prediction). The Wilcoxon signed-rank test can be adapted to test the null hypothesis that $x = v$. The same principle used in the matched pairs design applies here. Differences from v are calculated and ranked before being assigned a sign depending on whether the deviations are above or below the target value, v. In this case, the appropriate Stata command would be: `signrank x = v`.

If the sum of the ranks above and below v are roughly the same, then one cannot reject the null hypothesis; otherwise, the null may be rejected.

A word of caution regarding *corner solutions* is necessary. Suppose your prediction for v lies at the boundary of the permissible choice set. For instance, the theory predicts that everyone "free-rides" and contributes 0 to a public good (discussed later in Chapter 7), but 0 is the minimum contribution amount that anyone can make. In such a case, you cannot use a sign-rank test to assess whether your contribution data are equal to 0 because the data cannot feasibly lie below 0, which violates the premise that negative and positive differences could be equally likely.

5.4   Parametric Approaches

There are a wide variety of parametric approaches that depend on whether one is using continuous, censored, or discrete outcome variables as the dependent variable in data analysis. Like non-parametric tests, parametric tests assume that your data comprise independent observations. Unlike non-parametric methods, parametric methods typically assume that your data are (approximately) normally distributed and exhibit a similar amount of variance within each group being compared.

5.4.1   *t*-Tests

A *t*-test is a parametric statistical test that can be used to detect differences between a target value or between treatment groups. Just as with non-parametric tests based on ranks, t-tests can be applied to one sample, two samples, and to matched pairs of observations. The main difference is the assumption that the variables of interest are normally distributed.

Suppose, for example, that one has one sample of data on some choice variable, y_i for $i = 1, 2, \ldots, n$ subjects, and one is interested in whether the mean of some data, $\bar{y}$, is equal to some theoretically predicted value, μ, for instance, the equilibrium bid amount in an auction or contest.

The t-test statistic for a single sample is

$$t = \frac{\bar{y} - \mu}{SE_{\bar{y}}},$$

where μ is a predicted value and $SE_{\bar{y}}$ is the standard error of the data y approximated by $\sqrt{s_y^2/n}$, where s_y^2 is the sample variance of y. This test statistic is used to determine whether the coefficient estimate is significantly different from μ or not, i.e., the null hypothesis is that $\bar{y} = \mu$ and the alternative is that $\bar{y} \neq \mu$. The non-parametric analogue is the one-sample Wilcoxon signed ranks test.

The t-statistic follows a recognized distribution known as the Student's t distribution. Suppose that you have a sample of n observations. In the case of a one-sample test, the degrees of freedom are $n - 1$. In combination with a significance level, α, representing the probability of making a Type I error (rejecting the null hypothesis when it's true)—common values are 0.05 or 0.01—critical values for the t-statistic can be determined. If the computed t-statistic falls within these critical values, the null hypothesis is not rejected; otherwise, it is rejected. Statistical packages will readily compute this t statistic for you. For instance, in Stata, one would use the following command: `ttest` $y == \mu$.

For two independent samples, the question is whether the means of the two samples are the same or not. For instance, suppose you have n_1 observations for treatment 1 and the mean is $\bar{y}_1$, and you have n_2 observations for treatment 2 and the mean is $\bar{y}_2$. Assuming that both groups are sampled from normal distributions, one can apply a t-test to the difference in these means using the statistic:

$$t = \frac{\bar{y}_1 - \bar{y}_2}{SE_{y_1 - y_2}},$$

where $SE_{\bar{y}_1 - \bar{y}_2} = \sqrt{\frac{s_1^2}{n_1} + \frac{s_2^2}{n_2}}$, and s_i^2 is the sample variance of data from treatment i.

The non-parametric analogue is the Wilcoxon–Mann–Whitney test. The null hypothesis is that the $\bar{y}_1 = \bar{y}_2$, while the alternative is that $\bar{y}_1 \neq \bar{y}_2$.

If you have a *directional* hypothesis, e.g., as predicted by some theory, then you can use a *one*-sided test, e.g., the alternative is that $\bar{y}_1 \geq \bar{y}_2$ or $\bar{y}_1 \leq \bar{y}_2$. However, otherwise, you should consider using the *two*-sided test (which is more conservative). Given a significance level α and the number of degrees of freedom for a two sample test, $n_1 + n_2 - 2$, you can determine whether the t-statistic lies within the critical region or not. Again, this test is pre-programmed for use in many statistical packages.

The same type of t-test can be applied to *matched pairs* of data in the same manner as in the two independent sample case. This would be the parametric analogue to the Wilcoxon signed-rank test for matched pairs.

5.4.2   Linear regression analysis

A simple and standard approach to determine whether treatment conditions have an effect on some outcome variable, $y_{i,t}$, is to pool one's data together and to conduct a **linear regression analysis** of treatment effects on that outcome variable. Here, i refers to the unit of observation, while t refers to the period in which it was obtained (in the event of repeated data collection). Linear regression is a statistical method used to modeling the relationship between a dependent variable and one or more independent variables (treatment indicators or data features). Its primary goal is to establish a linear relationship that allows the researcher to make predictions or understand the influence of the independent variables on the dependent variable.

A simple linear regression specification for a $k \times 1$ experimental design might be written as follows:

$$y_{i,t} = \beta_0 + \beta_1 T_1 + \beta_2 T_2 + \cdots + \beta_k T_k + \gamma X_{i,t} + \epsilon_{i,t}. \qquad (5.1)$$

In this regression model, T_k is a binary treatment dummy variable that is equal to 1 if treatment k was in effect and 0 otherwise, while $\epsilon_{i,t}$ is the error term. $X_{i,t}$ is a vector of *covariate* terms, which are variables or factors that may influence the relationship between the independent and dependent variables being studied in a regression analysis. Covariates might include data on subjects' age, gender, cognitive abilities, risk attitudes, or other factors that are unlikely to be affected by any treatment interventions. Covariates or control variables do not have to be included in the regression analysis, especially if subjects are randomly assigned to different treatments, but they may enable a more precise estimate of treatment effects. When in doubt, consider specifications both with and without such covariates.

If equation (5.1) is estimated using ordinary least squares regression, then the coefficient β_0 on the constant term measures the average value of the outcome variable, y, for the baseline or control treatment, T_0, which is why a dummy variable for that treatment has been omitted. The coefficient estimate, β_0, measures the average effect of the baseline treatment on the outcome variable y.

The coefficients on the other dummy variables, T_1, T_2, etc. measure the amount by which those treatments change the average value of the outcome variable y, relative to the control treatment 0. Relative to β_0, β_k gives the *additional change* resulting from each treatment condition, k. In the case of linear regression, the impact of moving from the conditions of the control treatment 0 to those of treatment 1 would be captured by the difference in the coefficient estimates $\beta_1 - \beta_0$. To detect whether this difference is statistically different from zero, one would apply a parametric t-test.

More generally, as suggested above, you may be interested in knowing if there are significant treatment differences *between* the means of two different treatment groups. For instance, whether treatment 1 has a different mean for the outcome variable y than for the control treatment 0. For this we can apply a t-test to the difference in estimated β coefficients using the test statistic:

$$t = \frac{\hat{\beta}_1 - \hat{\beta}_0}{SE_{\hat{\beta}_1 - \hat{\beta}_0}}.$$

If there was just one treatment variable—for instance, whether all subjects know some information about their opponent(s) (T_1) or no subject has this information (T_0)—then the difference $\hat{\beta}_1 - \hat{\beta}_0$ will capture the *average treatment effect* of such information on the outcome variable y. Note that the validity of such tests requires that subjects were randomly assigned to the two treatments; that is, treatment assignment does not depend on other environmental factors.

Beyond gauging the extent of this effect, one may also wish to determine whether this difference is significantly different from zero. The t-test statistic above can be used to assess whether or not it is appropriate to reject this null hypothesis, given the sample size and chosen significance level. Again, statistical packages can compute such t-statistics for you quite easily. For instance, in Stata, the command `ttest y, by(treatment)` will give t-test results for *all* treatment conditions $1, 2, \ldots, k$ as identified by the variable labeled treatment.

5.4.3   Interaction effects

In addition to determining whether there are treatment differences, one may also be interested in understanding whether there are **treatment interaction effects**.[3]

For instance, suppose that one has a 2×2 experimental design, as in Figure 4.1. The treatment dummy variable T_i $i = 1, 2$, can either be "on or

---

[3]Researchers in the behavioral and psychological sciences often use analysis of variance (ANOVA) techniques for this purpose, while experimental social science researchers typically use linear regressions with dummy variables. The latter focuses on the estimation of coefficients that can be useful for prediction purposes. The ANOVA approach focuses instead on evaluating how treatment conditions contribute to explaining the variability observed in the outcome variable, emphasizing explanation rather than prediction.

off" depending on whether or not the treatment conditions V_{1i} or V_{2i} are set equal to their baseline values, say V_{11} and V_{21}, or not. In this case, one could study the interaction of treatment conditions 1 and 2 by including the multiplicative dummy variable $T_1 \times T_2$ in the regression specification as follows:

$$y_{i,t} = \beta_0 + \beta_1 T_1 + \beta_2 T_2 + \beta_3 (T_1 \times T_2) + \gamma X_{i,t} + \epsilon_{i,t}. \qquad (5.2)$$

In this specification, the coefficient on β_3 provides an estimate of the average interaction effect of the two treatment conditions together, relative to control settings where both treatment conditions are set to baseline values (as estimated by the β_0 coefficient).

Researchers are sometimes interested in exploring the interaction effect of treatment conditions with the personal characteristics of subjects (e.g., the subjects' age, gender, or educational attainment). For instance, suppose one is interested in gender differences in first-mover proposals made in dictator games (where the second mover has no response) as compared with ultimatum bargaining games where the second mover can reject or accept a proposal (these games are discussed later in Chapter 8). While gender may not have been a treatment variable, assuming gender is coded as a binary variable with female=1 and male=0, one can study the interaction of gender with treatment conditions in this 2×1 experimental design as follows:

$$y_{i,t} = \beta_0 + \beta_1 T_1 + \beta_2 \text{female} + \beta_3 (T_1 \times \text{female}) + \gamma X_{i,t} + \epsilon_{i,t}. \qquad (5.3)$$

In this example, the baseline treatment 0 is the dictator game, while treatment 1 is the ultimatum bargaining game. Thus, the coefficient estimates, β_0 and β_1, indicate the average proposal amounts made by the baseline male gender in the dictator game and in the ultimatum bargaining game, respectively. Moreover, the coefficient estimate on the female dummy variable β_2 tells us by how much we need to adjust β_0 to account for the average female proposal in the dictator game, while β_3 tells us by how much we need to adjust β_1 to account for the average female proposal in the ultimatum bargaining game.

5.4.4 Limited dependent variables and data censoring

In many experimental studies, the data collected are *binary* (e.g., enter or stay out) or restricted in some sense (e.g., only non-negative values). In such cases, the researcher will typically want to use some **nonlinear estimation methods** that account for the limited range or censoring of the dependent variable. Examples include **probit**, **logit**, and **Tobit** regression analyses.

One common issue noted earlier is that of censored data at the lower or upper bounds of the admissible choice set. For instance, in public good games subjects are constrained to give some amount to the public good between 0 and their endowment. In the standard public good game (discussed in Chapter 7), the marginal per capita return on the public good is less than 1. This makes it rational for participants to contribute 0 to the public good (that is, to free-ride), leading to a notable frequency of observations at this lower boundary. However, because contributions cannot fall below zero or exceed the endowment, ω, conventional statistical methods cannot be employed to test the null hypothesis that players contribute 0 to the public good. This is due to there being a constraint imposed on the experimental data, preventing it from crossing 0 or surpassing the endowment value. One way to deal with this *data censoring* is to employ a Tobit regression analysis, which accounts for such censoring:

$$y_{i,t}^* \ = \ X_{i,t}\beta + \epsilon_{i,t},$$

$$y_{i,t} \ = \ \begin{cases} 0 & \text{if } y_{i,t}^* \leq 0 \\ y_{i,t}^* & \text{if } 0 < y_{i,t}^* < \omega \\ \omega & \text{if } y_{i,t}^* \geq \omega. \end{cases}$$

Here, $y_{i,t}$ denotes the observed data while $y_{i,t}^*$ denotes the desired or aspirational amount for the outcome variable, which can fall into one of three categories: (1) negative, lying below the lower bound of 0; (2) within the admissible bounds $(0, \omega)$; or (3) in excess of the upper bound of the subject's endowment, ω. This is known as the 2-limit Tobit model, which estimates the coefficients β by maximum likelihood estimation and is programmed in many statistical packages. The Tobit approach adjusts for the fact that data are only observed in the region $(0, \omega)$; if one were to use OLS on such censored data, then the slope coefficients could be biased relative to the Tobit model, which adjusts for the data censoring.

5.4.5 Clustering of standard errors

In experimental work, it is common to report standard errors that account for the clustering of units for which the unobserved components may be correlated. If the observations within a **cluster** are similar, then the errors within that cluster may be more correlated than those of the entire sample, meaning it is important to adjust the standard errors accordingly. Most statistical packages will cluster standard errors for you if you specify the unit on which clustering is to occur. The unit choice will depend on the experimental design, but it is typically related to what the experimenter regards as an independent observation. For instance, if one is conducting an individual choice experiment where the same subject makes decisions repeatedly and in isolation from others, then one may choose to cluster standard errors at the participant level. If one is conducting experiments involving strategic interactions by subjects participating in *groups*, then it may make more sense to cluster standard errors at the group level. If these groups are repeatedly randomly formed within each experimental session, then clustering may be more appropriate at the experimental *session* level. If the experimental design implies that the clustering of observations can be done in more than one way, say at the group or at the session level, then the researcher might adopt an empirical approach and choose to cluster on the unit for which the observations are more related to one another. For a good discussion of the clustering of standard errors and when and how to apply such clustering see Kim (2022).

5.4.6   Correcting for multiple hypothesis testing

Generally, an experiment tests one or more hypotheses. However, using the *same* data to test **multiple hypotheses** can be problematic in that it increases the likelihood of committing a type I error of mistakenly rejecting a true null hypothesis. Specifically, suppose that one wishes to test whether, given some experimental data set, $k = 1, 2, \ldots, m$ different null hypotheses, $H_1, H_2, \ldots, H_m$, all simultaneously hold, where all m hypotheses are assumed to be independent of one another. The type I error probability for each hypothesis is α, meaning that the probability of rejecting each null hypothesis is $1 - \alpha$. Supposing that all independent null hypotheses are true, it follows that the probability of rejecting at least one of them is $1 - (1 - \alpha)^m$, which goes to 1 in the limit as m becomes large. To address this multiple hypothesis testing problem, it is advisable to minimize the number of hypotheses, m, that are tested using the *same* dataset. Alternatively, one can apply one of various corrections for multiple hypothesis testing. For example, the simple and widely used Bonferroni procedure rejects H_k at the α significance level only if one would also reject H_k at the α/m significance level. For example, if you have a single dataset that you use to test 4 hypotheses and you choose a significance level α of 0.05, then you would use an adjusted α of $0.05/4 = 0.0125$ in tests of each hypothesis. This chapter has provided an introduction to the variety of methods that experimental researchers use to analyze the data collected from their experiments. The list of methods discussed here is very basic and certainly not exhaustive. It should be noted that the nature of the data analysis most appropriate for examining data from a particular experiment will likely depend on specific elements of the researcher's experimental design. Still, armed with the knowledge of the basic techniques presented in this chapter, the researcher should be well equipped to begin to make sense of the data they have collected and to determine whether the experimental results provide support for the hypotheses under investigation.

Chapter 6

Game Theory Experiments

Game theory is the study of strategic interactions between two or more players with common, mixed, or opposed interests. Good introductions to the subject matter and solution concepts can be found in Myerson (1997) and Maschler *et al.* (2020). Game theoretic predictions have been the subject of many experimental social science studies to date, perhaps because game theory is most relevant to the small population sizes that are used in most experiments. In this chapter, we will discuss experiments involving simple games; more complex games build upon the design elements of these simple game.

Game theory experiments tend to focus on the predictions of Nash equilibrium or Bayesian Nash equilibrium. A Nash equilibrium is a solution concept in which each player, knowing the strategies of others, chooses a strategy to maximize their payoff, and no player has an incentive to unilaterally change their strategy. Bayesian Nash equilibrium extends the Nash equilibrium idea to situations with incomplete information, incorporating players' probabilistic assessments of the actions played by others. In a Bayesian Nash equilibrium players make decisions based on their private beliefs and their strategies are optimal given those beliefs.

Treatment variables in game theory experiment often involve parametric changes that allow the experimenter to assess the *comparative statics* implications of the theory. This approach is adopted because the empirical validation of exact Nash equilibrium "point" predictions is often challenging, given the limited volume of observations typically gathered by experimental researchers. For Bayesian Nash equilibrium predictions, experimenters often elicit subjects' beliefs in addition to their actions so that they may understand the extent to which subject are playing a best response to their beliefs.

To properly implement game theoretic models in the laboratory, there are a number of important conceptual issues that experimenters should be aware of when designing tests of game-theoretic models.

1. Inform subjects of the payoffs earned by themselves and by all opponents. In a mutual best response or Nash equilibrium, players play best responses to the strategies of their opponents. To construct such best responses, it is necessary that players know the payoffs or payoff functions that their opponents face in addition to knowing their own payoffs or payoff function.

2. Provide any and all other information necessary for subjects to compute solutions to the game. For instance, if the Bayesian Nash equilibrium requires knowledge of the distribution of player types, then be sure to carefully explain this distribution function.

3. In an effort to induce "common knowledge" of the rules of the game, read the experimental instructions aloud. This can be done in person or via a pre-recorded video. Game theoretic predictions rely on *common knowledge* assumptions—essentially, that each player knows the rules of the game, knows that all others know the rules of the game, and that all others know that all others know the rules of the game, and so on, ad infinitum. By reading the instructions aloud, one makes it clear that all subjects are issued with the *same* instructions, which may better approximate the common knowledge assumption. As for common knowledge of the rationality of other players, one can demand that all subjects complete comprehension test questions prior to completing the main experimental task and publicly announce that no subject will be allowed to enter into the experimental task until they have successfully completed the comprehension quiz.

4. Maintain restrictions on identity, communication, matching, etc. Game theory typically presumes that agents interact strategically via their available sets of actions and not through other means, including knowledge of the personal characteristics of their opponents or communication. Of course, these other means of interaction may be an object of experimental interest. For instance, pre-play communication (or "cheap talk") as well as gender differences in strategic

behavior have been extensively studied. If this is one's interest, then it is often desirable to consider these other means of interaction as a separate treatment condition so as to prevent confounding factors from influencing game-theoretic predictions.

6.1 Dominant Strategy, Prisoner's Dilemma Games

The Prisoner's Dilemma (PD) is the 2-player, 2-action (2 × 2) game most often used to illustrate the notion of a dominant strategy (i.e., the strategy a player should play regardless of the strategies chosen by other players). In this game, the dilemma stems from the fact that if both players choose their other, non-dominant strategy, they would collectively earn more than in the dominant strategy Nash equilibrium.

This trade-off between social efficiency and individual dominance characterizes many socioeconomic issues. Hence, it is not surprising that the PD game was one of the first to be studied experimentally at the Rand Corporation in Santa Monica, CA in 1950 by Dresher and Flood and reported on by Flood (1952). Only later, in 1951, was the PD game given its storyline involving two prisoners by mathematician Albert W. Tucker.

The game that Flood and Dresher studied experimentally is shown in Table 6.1. Note that this is an *asymmetric* PD game in that one player

Table 6.1: Flood and Dresher's PD game.

		Column Player	
		C1	C2
Row	R1	−1, 2	0.5, 1
Player	R2	0, 0.5	1, −1

Source: Flood (1952)

can earn higher payoffs, but the dominant strategy Nash Equilibrium, where Row plays the dominant strategy R2 and Column plays the dominant strategy C1, is inefficient relative to the R1-C2 efficient outcome.

This game was played 100 times by two participants for money; the payoffs in Table 6.1 are given in cents, with the first number in each cell representing the Row Player's payoff and the second number the Column player's payoff. In the 100 trials, the Row player chose his dominant strategy R2 only 32 times and earned $0.40, while the Column player chose his dominant strategy of C1 22 times and earned $0.65. The Nash Equilibrium (R2, C1) was played just 14% of the time, while the efficient outcome was played 60% of the time. Flood and Dresher concluded that "It seems unlikely that the Nash equilibrium point is in any realistic sense the correct solution of this game."

When told about these experimental results, John Nash, the mathematician and Nobel laureate in Economics who developed the Nash equilibrium solution concept, wrote to Flood:

> "The flaw in this experiment as a test of equilibrium point theory is that the experiment really amounts to having the players play one large multimove game. One cannot just as well think of the thing as a sequence of independent games as one can in zero-sum cases. There is much too much interaction, which is obvious in the results of the experiment . . . Since 100 trials are so long . . . it's fairly clear that one should expect an approximation to behavior which is most appropriate for indeterminate end games with a little flurry of aggressiveness at the end and perhaps a few sallies, to test the opponent's mettle during the game."

Indeed, Nash was pointing out that in repeated games with fixed matches the set of Nash equilibria can be much larger than in the static, one-shot version of the game.

Subsequent research on the PD game has sought to allow both repetition of the game, enabling players to gain experience, yet employ random, anonymous matchings in each repetition so as to frustrate collusive cooperative behavior. While there have been many PD game experiments, a particularly pertinent example is the study conducted by Cooper *et al.* (1996). These experimenters used a random, no repeat matching protocol (discussed earlier in Section 3.10) wherein each game is truly "one-shot." The 40 subjects were divided into two equal-sized groups: "red" and "blue." Each member of the red group played each member of the blue group *exactly once* (20 rounds total). One parameterization of the PD game used by Cooper *et al.* (1996) is shown in Table 6.2.

Table 6.2: Prisoner's dilemma game payoff table used in Cooper *et al.* (1996).

		Column Player	
		C1	C2
Row	R1	350, 350	1000, 0
Player	R2	0, 1000	800, 800

Note that in this version of the PD game, the dominant strategy for the Row player is R1 and for the column player it is C1.

The frequencies with which the four cells of the game matrix were played over all 20 rounds are shown in Table 6.3. Thus, with care taken to make

Table 6.3: Prisoner's dilemma game results.

		Column Player		
		C1	C2	Sum
Row	R1	62.0%	16.0%	78.0%
Player	R2	15.5%	6.5%	22.0%
	Sum	77.5%	22.5%	

Source: Data from Cooper *et al.* (1996).

the game more like a one-shot game but while allowing for repeated play, we see that there is much greater coordination on the Nash equilibrium (R1,C1), which accounts for 62% of all outcomes. Furthermore, subjects play their dominant strategy approximately 78% of the time. This is a good example of a typical experimental game theory outcome; indeed, while there is not unanimous support for the Nash equilibrium prediction, the evidence suggests that the dominant strategy Nash equilibrium outcome is the most likely choice that pairs of players will make when playing this game.

6.2 Mixed Strategies: Matching Pennies

A mixed-strategy equilibrium (MSE) is a Nash equilibrium where players mix across the available pure strategies with certain probabilities. For example, in Rock, Paper, Scissors (RPS), the MSE is to play the pure strategies Rock, Paper, Scissors with probabilities $\{\frac{1}{3}, \frac{1}{3}, \frac{1}{3}\}$.

MSE have been studied in the laboratory usually in settings (such as RPS) where the MSE is unique and the game is zero or constant sum. In such cases, the equilibrium strategy involves minimizing one's possible losses and maximizing one's possible gains (the so-called minimax strategy). As humans are bad at randomizing, experimenters studying MSE have sometimes provided subjects with a randomization device.

Consider, as an example, the experimental study of Ochs (1995), who studied versions of the "matching pennies" (or hide-and seek) game which are the simplest 2-player games with a unique MSE. Ochs used versions of

Table 6.4: Matching pennies game payoff table used in Ochs (1995).

		Player 2 A	B
Player 1	A	X, 0	0, 1
	B	0, 1	1, 0

the payoff matrix shown in Table 6.4 In this game, the treatment variable is the payoff value for $X > 0$. Notice that the Row Player 1, who is the "seeker," wants to choose the same action (A or B) as the Column Player 2, the "hider," but that Player 2 is best served if she chooses the opposite action to that chosen by Player 1. Ochs conducted three between-subjects experimental treatments using this game where the value of the variable X was set to either 1, 9, or 4.

The unique mixed strategy Nash equilibrium of this game calls for Player 1 to choose action A with probability 0.5 in all three treatments (all 3 values for X) but for Player 2 to play A with probability $1/(1 + X)$, or with probabilities 0.5, 0.1, or 0.2, depending on whether $X = 1$, 9, or 4, respectively.

The somewhat counterintuitive prediction being tested here is that changes in Player 1's payoff X only affect Player 2's behavior; intuitively, in a MSE, one needs to keep one's opponent guessing. If the payoff to Player 1 (the seeker) from choosing action A, i.e., X increases, then Player 2 (the hider) needs to best respond by playing A less frequently. In Ochs's experiment, participants were assigned distinct roles as either Player 1 or Player 2. This setup was intentionally chosen to facilitate an assessment of their ability to grasp and apply a MSE. The design employed a strategy method and a randomization device. Subjects were asked to formulate strategies for 10 rounds at a time by specifying how many A balls they wanted to place in a 10-vector cell. They were given three options:

1. All 10 balls A.

2. All 10 balls B.

3. Specify the number of A balls in the cell and A will be chosen probabilistically based on that number.

The experiment involved conducting 10 rounds simultaneously, wherein participants were presented with their individual vector of "balls," the vector

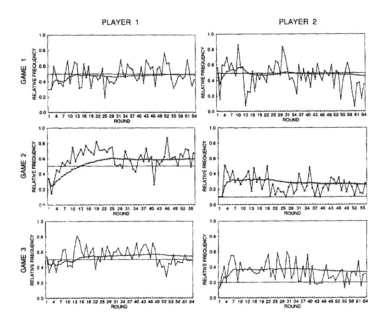

Figure 6.1: ▲ Relative frequency of A choices. ■ Long-run average frequency of A choice and—mixed strategy Nash equilibrium prediction. Game 1: X=1, Game 2: X=9, and Game 3: X=4.
Source: Ochs (1995), copyrighted material reproduced with the permission of Elsevier.

of their opponent, and their corresponding payoffs for this set of 10 rounds. The process was then repeated several times. The experimental results for the three treatments are shown in Figure 6.1, which reports the relative frequency of play of A choices by Players 1 and 2 (left and right columns) versus the three treatments (rows): Game 1: $X = 1$, Game 2: $X = 9$, and Game 3: $X = 4$. It can be seen in the baseline, symmetric treatment, where $X = 1$, that both Player 1 and Player 2's strategies are consistent with the unique mixed strategy Nash equilibrium, i.e., both are playing A around 50% of the time. However, as that equilibrium simply involves players uniformly mixing between their two actions, it does not provide the strongest test of the theory. Indeed, as X is changed, so that payoffs become *asymmetric*, it becomes clear that Player 2 does not fully adjust their behavior to this change and their frequency of play of action A remains too high relative to the lowered mixed strategy Nash equilibrium prediction. Having said this, there does appear to be some very slow adjustment to the mixed strategy NE prediction (indicated by the horizontal line in the figures) over time, as indicated by the long run average frequency of A choices. Still, the evidence suggests that players have difficulty playing according to the MSE even when it is the unique equilibrium.

6.3 Coordination Games: Stag Hunt, Battle of the Sexes

A coordination game is one for which there exist *multiple* Nash equilibria. The *coordination problem* is as follows: Which of these equilibria will strategic, interacting agents choose to coordinate upon? Such coordination problems are well suited to experimental study; after all, theory alone cannot tell us which equilibrium will be selected, and so empirical evidence is useful in resolving such coordination problems.

Consider the game payoff table shown in Table 6.5. Assume for now that

Table 6.5: A general 2×2 coordination game.

		Column Player	
		X	Y
Row	X	A, a	D, c
Player	Y	C, d	B, b

the game is symmetric, so that $A = a$, $B = b$, $C = c$, and $D = d$. Assume further that $a > c$ and $b > d$. In that case there exist two pure strategy Nash equilibria to this two player game, namely (X, X) and (Y, Y), where the first element is the choice of the row player and the second element is the choice of the column player. There is also a mixed strategy Nash equilibrium where both players play X with probability $p = (b - d)/(a + b - c - d)$.

One question that experimenters have explored using different versions of this coordination game is whether payoff efficiency is used as an equilibrium selection criterion. If we further assume that $a > b$, then equilibrium (X, X) is referred to as the "payoff dominant" or Pareto efficient equilibrium, while equilibrium (Y, Y) is considered inefficient. If it is further the case that $a + d < c + b$, then the equilibrium (Y, Y) is termed "risk dominant" in the terminology of Harsanyi and Selten (1988). This means that if one assigns the prior belief that one's opponent is equally likely to play X or Y, then one's expected payoff from playing X, equal to $(a + d)/2$, is less than one's expected payoff from playing Y, equal to $(c + b)/2$. Therefore, risk-neutral expected payoff maximizers would choose to play Y.

The experimental evidence is mixed regarding whether subjects use risk or payoff dominance as an equilibrium selection criterion in simple 2 player, 2 action games (see, e.g., Cooper *et al.* (1990) Straub (1995), Rankin *et al.* (2000), Battalio *et al.* (2001), Dal Bó *et al.* (2021) and Kendall (2022)).

Consider, for example, an experiment conducted by Battalio *et al.* (2001), who explore the role of the "optimization premium," i.e., the steepness of the best response function for equilibrium selection. They consider three versions of the "Stag Hunt" coordination game as shown in Figure 6.2. In all the parameterizations of this game that they study, (X, X) is payoff-

	X	Y
X	45,45	0,35
Y	35,0	40,40

Game 2R

	X	Y
X	45,45	0,40
Y	40,0	20,20

Game R

	X	Y
X	45,45	0,42
Y	42,0	12,12

Game 0.6R

CONTINGENCY TABLE I

TREATMENT BY PERIOD 1 SUBJECT CHOICE

	X	Y	Total
0.6R	41 (0.64)	23 (0.36)	64 (1.00)
R	45 (0.70)	19 (0.30)	64 (1.00)
2R	34 (0.53)	30 (0.47)	64 (1.00)
Total	120 (0.63)	72 (0.37)	192 (1.00)

CONTINGENCY TABLE II

TREATMENT BY PERIOD 75 SUBJECT CHOICE

	X	Y	Total
0.6R	28 (0.44)	36 (0.56)	64 (1.00)
R	16 (0.25)	48 (0.75)	64 (1.00)
2R	3 (0.05)	61 (0.95)	64 (1.00)
Total	47 (0.24)	145 (0.76)	192 (1.00)

Figure 6.2: Three stag hunt games. The monetary incentive (optimization premium) to select a best response to an opponent's strategy is twice as large in game 2R and six-tenths as large in game 0.6R relative to the baseline game R.
Source: Battalio *et al.* (2001), copyrighted material reproduced with the permission of John Wiley and Sons.

dominant while (Y, Y) is risk-dominant. The baseline "Game R" has $a = 45$, $b = 20$, $c = 40$, and $d = 0$. The mixed strategy NE is to play X with probability $p = (b - d)/(a + b - c - d) = 20/25 = 0.80$ in this game. In the other two treatments, they hold the mixed strategy NE constant and change the parameters of the game so as to increase, in game 2R, or lessen, in game 0.6R, the attractiveness of the risk-dominant equilibrium (Y, Y).

The results, which are also shown in Figure 6.2, indicate that in the first period of play of all three games, subjects have an overall (Total) 63%-to-37% preference for strategy X over strategy Y. However, as subjects gain experience, i.e., by period 75, the risk-dominant strategy Y becomes the majority choice of all subjects in all 3 games, most of all in game 2R and least of all in game 0.6R. This experiment neatly illustrates how both payoff differences and learning (experience) matter for experimental outcomes. The results are also clearly mixed as to whether concerns regarding payoff dominance or risk dominance matter most, though the evidence from this study points more toward risk dominance as the equilibrium selection criterion favored by experienced experimental subjects.

Table 6.6: Battle of the Sexes Game used in Duffy *et al.* (2017).

		Column Player X	Y
Row	X	9, 3	0, 0
Player	Y	0, 0	3, 9

The Battle of the Sexes game is another coordination game that has been studied by experimentalists (see, e.g., Cooper *et al.* (1989), Cooper *et al.* (1993), or Duffy *et al.* (2017)). It differs from the Stag Hunt game in that the two pure strategy Nash equilibria are not Pareto rankable. For example, consider the study of this game by Duffy *et al.* (2017) who used the payoff matrix shown in Table 6.6. Note that this game involves some asymmetric payoffs. Specifically, in this example we have $A = 9$, $a = 3$ and $B = 3$, $b = 9$, while all other parameters are 0. The two pure strategy Nash equilibria remain (X, X) and (Y, Y), but both are equally efficient, suggesting that efficiency concerns alone cannot easily resolve this coordination problem. In addition to the two pure strategy Nash equilibria, there is a mixed strategy NE where Row Player (Column Player) plays X with probability 3/4 (1/4). Duffy *et al.* (2017) report on a number of experimental treatments but, in one treatment dimension, they compare whether subjects are randomly matched to play the game in each repetition (the "stranger" design) with whether subjects remain in fixed matches (the "partners" design) over 60 periods of play, thus enabling the use of history-dependent strategies. In the random matching treatment, play in the majority of sessions was consistent with the mixed strategy Nash equilibrium prediction in the sense that the most frequently observed outcome was (X, Y) followed by (X, X) and (Y, Y), while the least frequent outcome was (Y, X). By contrast, under fixed matchings, many pairs of subjects learned to coordinate on an "alternation" strategy, wherein they switch with some periodicity between playing

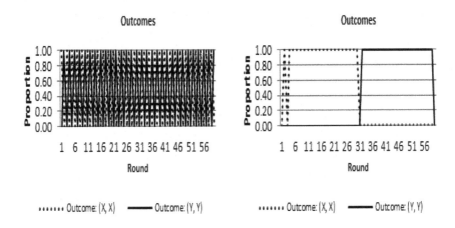

Figure 6.3: Example pairs of players playing the Battle of the Sexes under fixed matches.
Source: Duffy *et al.* (2017), copyrighted material reprinted with the permission of Springer Nature.

the (X, X) and the (Y, Y) strategies. The logic behind this outcome is that the average payoff from the alternation strategy is greater than the average payoff from the mixed strategy since the latter involves the play of some of the zero payoff outcomes of the game. Figure 6.3 shows the behavior for two examples of such alternating pairs of players. In the left panel, a pair learns to alternate between playing two pure strategy Nash equilibria in every other period, while in the right panel, a pair largely divided up the 60 periods of play coordinating on (X, X) for much of the first 30 periods followed by (Y, Y) for the remaining 30 periods. These experimental results illustrate how the matching protocol that is used can have a crucial impact on the experimental outcomes that are observed. Fixed matching facilitates tacit collusion on efficiency-enhancing alternation outcomes that is not possible under random matching.

6.4 Backward Induction: Centipede and Trust Games

Thus far, we have considered simple 2-player simultaneous-move games. It is also of interest, though, to consider 2-player sequential-move

games. Two well-studied versions of such games are the "Centipede" game
and its final round truncation known as the "Trust game."

Let us first consider the Centipede game, so named because the extensive
form of the game resembles a centipede. Two players move sequentially,
alternately facing a choice between "taking" or "passing." The amount at
stake, "the pie" they are to divide, increases at every new decision stage
reached. The game ends when one player chooses to "take" or when the
last stage is reached.

An illustration of a 6-round version of the game, in its extensive form
as studied by McKelvey and Palfrey (1992), is provided in Figure 6.4.

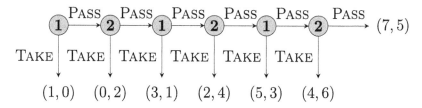

Figure 6.4: A 6-round Centipede game.
Source: McKelvey and Palfrey (1992).

The players, labeled 1 and 2, alternate turns; when it is a player's turn,
they must decide whether to take or pass, with take terminating the game.
Assuming common knowledge of rationality, the application of backward
induction leads to the unique prediction that Player 1 will choose "take"
at the first opportunity, meaning that the payoff to the two players will be
(1,0).

McKelvey and Palfrey (1992) conducted an experimental study of the
Centipede game using university subjects and the 6-round version shown
in 6.4. In addition, they also considered a 4-round version of the Centipede
game. They found that regardless of the length of the game, players do
not play "take" at the first opportunity but instead—and in violation of
the backward induction prediction—they pass until a few stages from the
end of the game. Repeated experience with play of the same 2-player game
helps, but does not entirely eliminate the failure of backward induction
play. This outcome from play of the Centipede game has been replicated by
many other researchers. One notable exception to the failure of backward
induction was documented in a lab-in-the-field experiment conducted by
Palacios-Huerta and Volij (2009), who used a subject pool that included
grandmaster chess players, who one might expect to be quite adept at

backward induction. Indeed, when such players were matched to play the game, nearly 100% of the games ended at the first decision node.

One well-studied variant of the Centipede Game is known as the "Trust" Game (also referred to as the "Investment" Game). This game was originally proposed by Berg *et al.* (1995) and can be viewed as the final, two round truncation of the Centipede game. In this Trust game, there are two players, 1 and 2, both of whom are endowed with some amount X.

Trust is captured by the willingness of the investor to invest a positive amount $I \leq X$ with the trustee in the first stage, knowing that any amount transferred will be exogenously increased (by the experimenter) to the level $3 \times I$. Reciprocity is the willingness of the trustee to return some or all of this tripled investment amount $0 \leq R \leq 3 \times I$ in the second stage, keeping $3 \times I - R$ for him/herself. The extensive form of the trust game is shown in Figure 6.5. In the one-shot version of the trust game, the subgame perfect

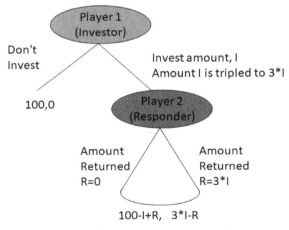

Figure 6.5: The trust (or investment) game.

Nash equilibrium, which is found by applying backward induction, has the second mover player 2 (Responder) returning $R = 0$ so that the first mover player 1 (Investor) rationally best responds by investing nothing, $I = 0$ (i.e., no trust).

As noted, this game was first studied by Berg *et al.* (1995), who gave all subjects an endowment, $X = \$10$, and established the convention of tripling of any amount invested or sent by the first mover. They ran the experiment with inexperienced student subjects and the results from one session of their "No History" treatment are shown in Figure 6.6. This figure

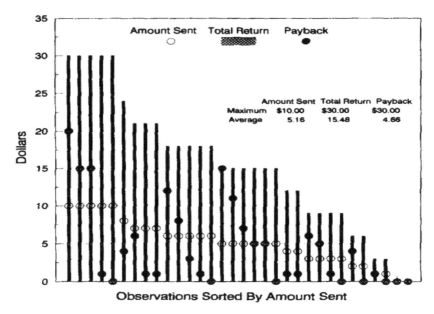

Figure 6.6: Trust game results.
Source: Berg *et al.* (1995), copyrighted material reproduced with the permission of Elsevier.

shows the amount sent (or invested) by player 1 as open circles and the data are sorted by this amount. The height of each bar corresponds to three times the investment value, denoted as $3 \times I$. Finally, the solid black circle is the amount returned, R, by player 2 to player 1. Several intriguing insights arise from this experiment, findings that have been consistently replicated by other researchers on numerous occasions. First, in violation of the subgame perfect/backward induction prediction, there is a surprising amount of blind trust. Indeed, the average amount sent by player 1 is $5.16 of the $10 endowment (51.6%) and 5 out of 32 subjects sent their entire $10 endowment. Only 2 out of 32 subjects played according to the subgame perfect Nash equilibrium and sent 0. Finally, the return on investments by player 1 is poor; the average amount returned by player 2 to player 1 was just $4.66. More generally, the average amount invested, I, is around 1/2 of X. The average amount returned is approximately 1/3 of the total return or $3 \times I$. Thus, the average return to the investor (player 1) is roughly 0; on average, they typically get their investment of I back. Conditional on a positive investment, $I > 0$, responders (player 2) get around 2/3 of I.

Finitely repeated versions of the trust game have also been studied, such as by Cochard *et al.* (2004), who report that investors invest more and trustees return a higher percentage in the finitely repeated trust game with fixed matches (7 rounds) as compared with the one-shot version. This behavior can be rationalized using a sequential equilibrium notion with different types of responders, e.g., those who return more than 1/3 and those who do not. In particular, they find evidence of two main types— those returning 2/3 (fair-minded types) comprise 62% and those returning 0 (selfish) comprise 10%; the remainder cannot be easily categorized into either of these two types.

6.5   Contests and Over-dissipation

Contests are games where the participants' effort choices or investments affect their probability of winning a fixed prize. The first contest experiments were conducted by Millner and Pratt (1989, 1991), who tested Tullock (1980)-type contests where n active players compete for a resource of common value $V > 0$. Each player i chooses an effort or investment amount $x_i \geq 0$. Given an individual's investment x_i and a vector of opponents' investments $x_{-i} = (x_j)_{j \neq i}$, player i's chance of winning the resource or contest is given by

$$p_i(x_i, x_{-i}) = \begin{cases} \frac{x_i^r}{\sum_j x_j^r}, & \text{if } \sum_j x_j \neq 0, \\ \frac{1}{n}, & \text{otherwise,} \end{cases}$$

where the Tullock constant $r \in (0, \infty)$ determines the sensitivity of winning probabilities to levels of individual investments; this game becomes an all-pay auction (discussed later in Chapter 9) as $r \to \infty$. The expected payoff to player i: $E\pi_i = p_i V - x_i$. The unique symmetric Nash-equilibrium investment is: $x_i = x = \frac{r(n-1)}{n^2} V$.

Millner and Pratt studied the case where $n = 2$, $V = \$8$, subjects had a \$12 budget, and r was, in one treatment, set equal to 1 and, in the other treatment, set equal to 3. Thus, in the NE x=$\frac{r}{4}$8 or \$2 when $r = 1$ and x=\$6 when $r = 3$. Contest experiments often focus on the *dissipation rate*, which is the amount of total expenditures by all participants relative to the value of the prize, i.e., $\sum_i x_i / V$. Thus, the mean *dissipation* rate should be 50% when $r = 1$, and 150% when $r = 3$.

Millner and Pratt's results are shown in Figure 6.7, which reports mean expenditures and the rate of over-dissipation in the last five rounds (trials) of their experiment by the r exponent value. When $r = 1$, the mean

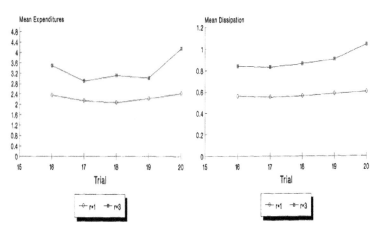

Figure 6.7: Results from Millner and Pratt's contest experiment, $r = 1$ versus $r = 3$. Mean expenditures (left panel) and mean dissipation rates (right panel) from trials 16–20.
Source: Millner and Pratt (1989), copyrighted material reproduced with the permission of Springer Nature.

expenditure of $2.24 and the mean dissipation rate of 56% of the lottery prize are both significantly greater than the NE of $2 and 50%. When $r = 3$, both the mean expenditure of $3.34 and the mean dissipation rate of 84% are significantly less than the NE of $6 and 150%.

Most experimental contest studies find support for the comparative statics predictions of contest theory but not the point predictions. See Dechenaux *et al.* (2015) for a comprehensive survey. Indeed, a common finding in lottery contests and all-pay auctions is that there is *significant overbidding* relative to the Nash equilibrium predictions. Furthermore, for $n \geq 4$, a general finding is *over-dissipation*, which refers to aggregate spending in excess of V. Relatedly, there is evidence for so-called "joy of winning" preferences, where players appear to gain utility from simply competing, regardless of the cost of doing so. For instance, in Sheremeta (2010), after the main contest experimental task, players can invest effort in another contest, in which the prize $V = 0$. Many subjects choose to bid positive amounts in such a contest! A further observation is that there is significant *dispersion* in the behavior of individual subjects, suggesting that the symmetric NE might not be an appropriate characterization of strategic behavior. Finally, impulsivity and cognitive abilities, as reflected in CRT scores, matter greatly in explaining departures from NE predictions Sheremeta (2018).

6.6 Level-k Reasoning: The Beauty Contest Game

The avoidance of dominated strategies is fundamental to game theory, e.g., cooperation in a one-shot PD game, passing in the centipede game. An understanding of whether subjects obey dominance is best examined in settings where dominance can be applied iteratively, as this can reveal the extent of subjects' ability to apply the iterated elimination logic. Thus far we have primarily considered 2-player games, but it is also possible to study n-player dominance solvable games. One example we already considered (in Chapter 1) was the market entry game. Another example, though, is the beauty contest game, which spawned the development of *level-k* reasoning.

The beauty contest game is named after a famous metaphor of John M. Keynes regarding how financial market investors form expectations about the average opinion.[1] When Nagel (1995) experimented with this game, N = 15–18 subjects were asked to guess a number, x_i, in the interval [0,100]. Subjects were instructed that the winner of this game was the person(s) whose guess x_i was closest in absolute value to

$$p \times \overline{x},$$

where $\overline{x} = \frac{1}{n}\sum_{i=1}^{n} x_i$, i.e., the mean of all guesses. The winner earned a fixed prize amount, while all others earned 0. More recent variants of this game eschew the tournament payoff structure in favor of a distance payoff function where each player i's payoff $\pi_i = f(x_i - p\overline{x})$.

Typically, p is some value different from 1, e.g., Nagel (1995) considered three treatment values: $p = 1/2$, $2/3$, and $4/3$. If $p < 1$, then iterated elimination of dominated strategies leads to the choice of 0 as the unique equilibrium outcome. By contrast, if $p > 1$, then both 0 and the upper bound of the guessing interval, 100, are equilibrium outcomes. An experimental design where $p \neq 1$ allows for the detection of the number of *levels* of iterated reasoning that subjects employ before stopping. In Nagel's experiment, the same group of subjects played the beauty contest game under a constant p-value four times. After each repetition, they received feedback on the winning number and then made new guesses. Some results from

---

[1]Keynes likened professional investment decisions to newspaper beauty contests of the era in which participants had to choose the prettiest picture from an array of faces. As Keynes put it: "It is not a case of choosing those [faces/investments] that, to the best of one's judgment, are really the prettiest, nor even those that average opinion genuinely thinks the prettiest. We have reached the third degree where we devote our intelligences to anticipating what average opinion expects the average opinion to be. And there are some, I believe, who practice the fourth, fifth and higher degrees" (Keynes, 1936, 136).

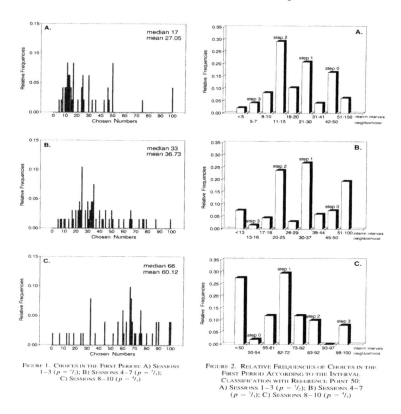

FIGURE 1. CHOICES IN THE FIRST PERIOD: A) SESSIONS
1–3 ($p = \frac{1}{2}$); B) SESSIONS 4–7 ($p = \frac{2}{3}$);
C) SESSIONS 8–10 ($p = \frac{4}{3}$)

FIGURE 2. RELATIVE FREQUENCIES OF CHOICES IN THE
FIRST PERIOD ACCORDING TO THE INTERVAL
CLASSIFICATION WITH REFERENCE POINT 50:
A) SESSIONS 1–3 ($p = \frac{1}{2}$); B) SESSIONS 4–7
($p = \frac{2}{3}$); C) SESSIONS 8–10 ($p = \frac{4}{3}$)

Figure 6.8: Beauty contest game results.
Source: Nagel (1995). Copyright: American Economic Association; reproduced with the permission of *American Economic Review*.

this experiment are presented in Figure 6.8. The left panels show for each treatment A: $p = 1/2$, $B : p = 2/3$, and $C : p = 4/3$, the distributions of guesses in the first round of play. The right panels characterize subjects by level-k type.

The level-k approach to reasoning proceeds as follows. Imagine there is some level-0 belief—say, a winning guess is 50—which corresponds to the midpoint of the guessing interval.[2] A level-0 type makes this guess. A level-1 type reasons further that if everyone guesses 50, then the average

---

[2]The level-0 choice is not pinned down by theory; in principle it can be any value. A more reasonable approach might be to start with the assumption that the highest the mean guess could possibly be is 100 (given the rules of the game) and to then assign this value to level 0.

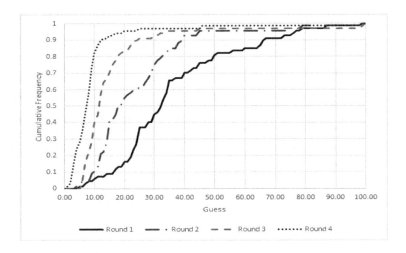

Figure 6.9: Cumulative frequency of guesses in Nagel's 2/3 the average game over Rounds 1–4.
Source: Nagel (1995), data used with permission of the author.

will be 50 and his best response is therefore $p \times 50$. Similarly, a level-2 type reasons that if every level-1 type guesses $p \times 50$, then her best response is $p \times p \times 50$ or $p^2 \times 50$, and so on ...

The right panel of Figure 6.8 bins together guesses around the neighborhood of these step-levels of reasoning. For example, if $p = 2/3$, then a level-1 guess would be around $2/3 \times 50$ or 33.33 corresponding to guesses in the bin 30-37, labeled "Step 1." In the same $p = 2/3$ the average game, a level-2 guess would $(2/3)^2 50$ or 22.22, corresponding to guesses in the bin 20-25, labeled Step 2. As this figure reveals, most subjects employ just 1–2 steps of iterated best response reasoning.

Repetition of the game over four rounds does move guesses in the direction of the equilibrium predictions. For instance, Figure 6.9 shows the cumulative distribution functions (CDFs) of guesses in Nagel's $p = 2/3$ the average game over the four rounds played. Note that the CDFs, however, are not degenerate at the equilibrium prediction of 0 even after four rounds. Rather, strategic uncertainty reflecting a lack of common knowledge of rationality continues to play a role.

The level-k behavioral model was first proposed by Nagel (1995), Stahl II and Wilson (1994), Stahl and Wilson (1995) with further extensions by Ho *et al.* (1998), Costa-Gomes *et al.* (2001), and Camerer *et al.* (2004).

A subject's level of reasoning in this game has been used as a measure of their degree of strategic sophistication.

A number of variants of the beauty contest game have been studied in the literature. For instance, Duffy and Nagel (1997) change the order statistic from mean to median and play the game for a longer period of time (10 rounds). Still, they find that players submit choices greater than 0. The fastest convergence to equilibrium obtains using the median, an unbiased measure of central tendency. Costa-Gomes and Crawford (2006) and Grosskopf and Nagel (2008) study the *two* player BCG. This game is isomorphic to the game: Choose a number, and the person who chooses the smallest number wins. Nevertheless, an overwhelming majority continue to choose dominated strategies. Other researchers, e.g., Güth *et al.* (2002), Sutan and Willinger (2009), and Anufriev *et al.* (2022), have studied cases where the equilibrium is interior to the guessing interval and more complex to determine (e.g., where the guessing target is $100 - 2/3\bar{x}$; in that case, the Nash equilibrium is 60. In all of these extensions, systematic departures from the Nash equilibrium predictions continue to be found. Finally, Gill and Prowse (2016) show that more cognitively able subjects choose numbers that are closer to equilibrium predictions, earn more, and converge more frequently to equilibrium play than do less cognitively able subjects.

6.7   Summary

The major solution concept of game theory is the Nash or Bayesian Nash equilibrium. A major finding across many different game theory experiments is that there is mixed evidence for Nash equilibrium play. While the Nash equilibrium concept is often quite valuable in anticipating how differences in treatment conditions will influence the adjustment of subjects' behavior, such as in various contest experiments or in the beauty contest experiment, subjects may fail to play according to the precise "point" predictions of Nash equilibrium and so behavioral modifications to this solution concept may be needed.

We have already considered one behavioral approach, the level-k analysis, for understanding departures from Nash equilibrium. Another approach, however, involves considering the fact that agents are boundedly rational and are learning over time—or, in other words, that their motivation is not merely to maximize their own payoffs but rather to take into account *other-regarding* social concerns. These possibilities will be covered later in

Chapter 8. Finally, we note that an important generalization of Nash equilibrium is that subjects are playing *noisy* best responses that take account of the fact that other players are not perfectly best-responding to the payoff incentives of the game. A noisy best response *equilibrium*, where players best respond to the noisy best responses of all others, has been formalized in the notion of a "quantal response" equilibrium (QRE) by McKelvey and Palfrey (1995, 1998). The QRE approach has been found to be particularly useful for rationalizing aggregate experimental findings from a broad variety of game theory experiments. For an introduction to the notion of QRE and applications, the interested reader is referred to a complete monograph on this topic (Goeree *et al.* (2016)).

Chapter 7

Public Economics Experiments

Public economics studies the way in which government policies shape and influence economic activity. More generally, public economics is often viewed as the study of collective action decisions (Olson (1965)), with a particular focus on economic efficiency and equity. In this chapter, we cover three main types of public economic experiments: voluntary contributions to public goods, tax compliance, and voting behavior. All three areas have received wide attention in the experimental economics literature and here we present the basic experimental designs used in this literature.

7.1 Public Good Experiments

One of the first areas of economics in which experimental methods were applied was the voluntary provision of public goods. For comprehensive surveys of public good experiments, the reader is referred to Ledyard (1995) or Vesterlund (2016).

Public goods have two defining characteristics (Pigou (1932)), which are as follows:

1. Nonrival—goods that can be consumed by one person without detracting from the consumption opportunities available to others.

2. Nonexcludable—goods that, once provided, are available to all.

Examples of goods that satisfy these properties include roads, parks, public radio and television, streetlights, flood control, clean air and water initiatives, police, firefighters, and national defense.

The main problem with the private, voluntary provision of public goods, as first identified by Samuelson (1954), is that of *free-riding*, i.e., those who benefit from voluntarily provided public goods have a strong incentive to avoid paying for those public goods and therefore free-ride on the generosity of others. Hence, many public goods (e.g., streetlights, police, firefighters, and national defense) are financed via taxation.

Much of the experimental literature on public goods focuses on *voluntarily* provided or funded public goods, such as donations to charities, environmental clean-up efforts, or the construction and maintenance of informational websites. Here, a central focus is on free-riding problems and the ways in which such problems might be mitigated.

One of the first studies of the public good problem and the prevalence of free-riding behavior was by two sociologists Marwell and Ames (1979, 1980, 1981). In one study, they assigned 256 high school students to 64 4-player groups, where each group consisted of 2 males and 2 females and subjects could earn payments based on their choices. More specifically, each subject was given an endowment of tokens which s/he could invest either in a private or a public good. The private good yielded a payoff of 1 cent per token allocated while the payoff for the tokens allocated to the public account varied according to whether a known threshold "public good provision point" was met or not. Beyond the provision point, tokens allocated to the public good returned far more money per token invested than did those allocated to the private good. They studied two group sizes of 4 or 80 subjects. They allocated 900 tokens to each 4-player group and 18,000 to larger groups (225 tokens per group member). Their main finding was that the mean investment in the group exchange was 127.5 tokens per subject, or 56.67% of available resources, which exceeded the provision point. The most efficient outcome would have been full contribution by all to the public good (as that would maximize the joint payoffs of all participants.) Marwell and Ames studied many other variants of their experimental design and repeatedly produced similar findings. This led them to conclude that "subjects are not rational free riders ... but do not approach optimality in their investments."

These findings piqued the interest of economists who understood from the early work of Vernon Smith and his associates that it sometimes takes time for subjects to learn the economic incentives of a model environment. This suggests that the one-shot nature of the experiments conducted by

Marwell and Ames might not be so representative of the extent or absence of free-riding behavior. The changes implemented to Marwell and Ames' original experimental design by economists Isaac *et al.* (1984); Isaac and Walker (1988); Isaac *et al.* (1994) resulted in what is today known as the linear voluntary contribution mechanism (VCM) or the "public goods game."

The game can be described as follows. In each of $t = 1, 2, \ldots, T$ periods, N players repeatedly decide how many tokens, x, from their per-period endowment, ω, of "tokens" they want to contribute toward a public good. Tokens not allocated to the public good ($\omega - x$) remain in the player's private account. Player i's objective is to maximize, by choice of their public good contribution amount $x_i \in [0, \ \omega]$, their payoff in this N-player game:

$$\pi_i(x_i) = \omega - x_i + \beta G \text{ where } G = \sum_{j=1}^{N} x_j, \tag{7.1}$$

where β is the known, constant *marginal per capita return* on total contributions to the public good, G. Unlike Marwell and Ames, there is no provision point for the public good in the standard public good game, though there are versions of the game with such provision points (known as threshold public good games). Typically, it is assumed that $N^{-1} < \beta < 1$. In that case:

- In both the one-shot and in the finitely repeated games, the unique dominant strategy Nash equilibrium is the same; since $\partial \pi_i(x_i)/\partial x_i = \beta - 1 < 0$, it is to choose $x_i = 0$ for all i.

- This zero-contribution (full free-riding) equilibrium is Pareto-dominated by the full contribution outcome, $x_i = \omega$, for all i, which is *not* an equilibrium but would maximize group welfare (that is, it comprises the *social optimum*).

Isaac *et al.* (1984) were the first to use the linear voluntary contribution mechanism to characterize payoffs in a finitely repeated public goods game (this is now standard). Their baseline 2×2 experimental design varied the group size $N = 4$ or 10, and the MPCR, β between 0.30 and 0.75. Specifically, their four main treatments were parameterized as follows: $(N, \beta, N\beta) = \{(4, 0.3, 1.2), (4, 0.75, 3), (10, 0.3, 3), (10, 0.75, 7.5)\}$. Notice that, using this design, comparisons between treatments 1–2 and 3–4 enable the detection of MPCR effects. Moreover, comparisons of treatments 1–3 and 2–4 enable detection of group size effects for fixed β. Finally, a comparison of treatments 2–3 enables an assessment of the group size effect holding fixed the group benefit amount at $N\beta = 3$. As a further treatment variable, they also considered the behavior of "experienced" subjects, i.e., those who previously participated in at least one other public good game, but not involving the same composition of other participants. As the behavior of these experienced subjects is not so different—they do contribute a little less on average—we focus here on the behavior of the inexperienced subjects, which has been the subject of much subsequent research.

Also of note is the fact that this experiment was one of the first to be computerized. Subjects were in a fixed match, partners design: the same 4 or 10 players played $T = 10$ periods of the public good game. Each was given the same number of tokens and instructed that they had to choose how many tokens they would place in a public account and how many they would place in a private account, with no carryover between periods. Following each period of play, subjects received feedback on their own contribution to the total contributions to the public good G and their payoff for the period π_i.

Table 7.1 reports on the mean percentage of the token endowment that subjects contributed to the public good in each of the four main treatments of the Isaac *et al.* study.

Table 7.1: Mean percentage of tokens contributed to the public good in the experiment of Isaac *et al.* (1984).

Group	Marginal Per Capita Return	
Size	$\beta = 0.3$	$\beta = 0.75$
$N = 4$	26.4 %	65.1 %
$N = 10$	32.9 %	65.1 %

Figure 7.1 shows contributions to the public good as a percentage of subjects' token endowments over time, i.e., over each of the 10 periods of the experiment.

Notice that holding N fixed, mean contributions increase with β for both values of N. For $\beta = 0.3$, an increase in N from 4 to 10 leads to a statistically significant increase in contributions. This is not true for $\beta = 0.75$, though. Note further that contributions decrease with an increase in N when $N\beta$ is held fixed as in the comparison between the $N = 4$ and $\beta = 0.75$ treatment and the $N = 10$ and $\beta = 0.3$ treatment. The latter finding suggests that a larger group size tends to depress contributions to the public good, all else being held equal. A final important finding, as revealed in Figure 7.1, is that contributions decrease over time, especially

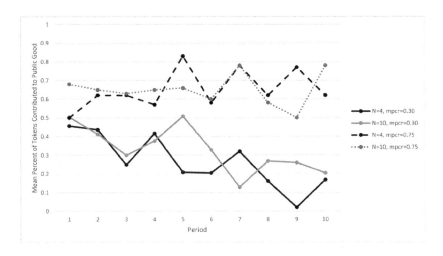

Figure 7.1: Mean percent of tokens contributed to the public good in each of the 10 periods of the 4 treatments of Isaac *et al.* (1984).
Source: Figure constructed using data reported in Isaac *et al.* (1984).

with a lower β. In other words, subjects initially over-contribute to the public good, relative to the no-contribution Nash equilibrium prediction, but they learn to free-ride over time—which indicates the value of studying the public good game repeatedly. In many subsequent repetitions of the public good game, a pattern emerges of over-contribution to the public good and a gradual decline in public good contributions as subjects learn to free-ride. This trend of behavior suggests that this finding is very robust.

7.2   Variations on a Theme

A wide variety of variations on this basic public good game have been studied. Many of these involve mechanisms to manipulate the extent of free-riding or contributions to the public good in order to better understand subject behavior.

The corner solution critique of the public good game is that the predicted Nash equilibrium of the standard game is at the zero lower bound (where all contribute zero to the public good). A problem with this design is that errors can only go in one direction (that of over-contribution), which means the absence of complete free-riding might be attributable to this

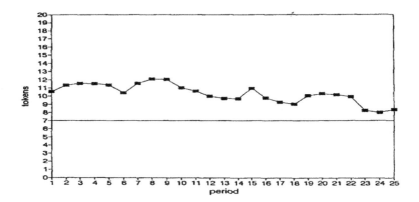

Figure 7.2: Token contributions over time in a public good game with a non-corner solution; $\omega = 20$, equilibrium contribution $= 7$.
Source: Keser (1996), copyrighted material reproduced with the permission of Elsevier.

design feature. One solution is to use regression methods that adjust for *censoring* in the dependent variable, e.g., Tobit regressions as in Chaudhuri *et al.* (2006). Another remedy explored by Saijo and Nakamura (1995) and Keser (1996) is to make the Nash equilibrium *interior* to the choice space. For example, Keser replaces the payoff function of the standard game with a quadratic version:

$$\pi_i(x_i) = a(\omega - x_i) + b(\omega - x_i)^2 + cG.$$

In this case, $x_i^* = \omega + \frac{c-a}{2b}$; Keser chose $\omega = 20$, $a = 41$, $b = 1$, and $c = 15$, so that $x^* = 7$, meaning that the Nash equilibrium is not zero and is 35% of the endowment of 20. In her experiment, she continues to find over-contribution to the public good, as shown in Figure 7.2. Still, the point of this exercise is that it is possible to avoid corner solutions by revising the payoff objective.

In a further effort to understand the source of over-contributions in the public good game, experimentalists have considered whether interactions with the *same* group of players over time might play a role. The standard "partners" design has $N = 4$ players in a fixed match playing the public goods game for a number of rounds. An alternative "strangers" design randomly forms groups of N players in each repetition. The aim of the strangers design is to make the game more closely resemble a one-shot game and avoid any dynamic game effects. The cost of such a design is that one needs a multiple of N players to randomly form groups of N subjects in each repetition, which means that the unit of independent observation is no longer a single group of N subjects but rather the *matching set* of subjects from which groups of N subjects are randomly formed. The evidence regarding whether partner or stranger matching has an influence on contributions is mixed. See Andreoni and Croson (2008) for details.

An issue related to the manner in which subjects are matched is that, in the standard design, contributions are repeatedly made by the *same* group of subjects without entry (birth) or exit (death) of subjects participating in the experiment. Duffy and Lafky (2016) explored the role of subject

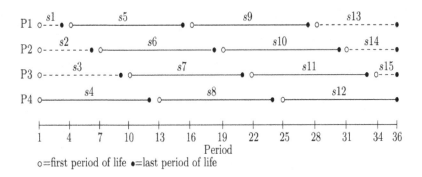

Figure 7.3: Overlapping generations matching design showing the lifetimes of subject numbers s1–s15 in the four positions, P1–P4 of the experiment of Duffy and Lafky (2016). Subjects with partial lifetimes of 3, 6, or 9 periods are depicted using dashed lines; full 12-period-lived subjects are depicted using solid lines.
Source: Duffy and Lafky (2016), copyrighted material reproduced with the permission of Springer Nature.

turnover by using an overlapping generations matching protocol, which is illustrated in Figure 7.3. In this design there are four active positions P1–P4 in any period of the game and 15 total subjects s1–s15 per observation. Only subjects who are active make contributions to the public good. Every three periods, one of the four active subjects "dies" (leaves the experiment) and a new subject enters the experiment to take their place, i.e., is "born." No subject lives for more than 12 periods in total, and some at the beginning or toward the end live as few as 3 periods. Each subject's lifetime is known and finite. In this design, the group size is always $N = 4$, but

Table 7.2: Mean percentage of endowment contributed to the public good over 10 rounds in the three treatments, Regular, RegRank, and Rank.

	Round										
Condition	1	2	3	4	5	6	7	8	9	10	All
Regular	56.0	59.8	55.2	49.6	48.1	41.0	36.0	35.1	33.4	26.5	44.07
RegRank	45.8	45.4	32.6	25.0	23.1	17.8	11.3	9.5	8.3	9.0	22.79
Rank	32.7	20.3	17.7	9.9	9.2	6.9	8.1	8.3	7.1	5.4	12.55
RegRank–Rank	13.2	25.1	15.0	15.1	13.9	11.0	3.2	1.3	1.2	3.6	10.24
As % of Regular	23.5	42.0	27.1	30.4	28.9	26.7	8.9	3.6	3.6	13.5	20.82

Source: Andreoni (1995). Copyright: American Economic Association; reproduced with the permission of *American Economic Review*.

there is heterogeneity among subjects in terms of *experience levels*. Duffy and Lafky demonstrate that this design, characterized by overlapping generations, effectively curbs the decline in contributions to the public good over time. This contrasts with the standard design, where all participants commence and conclude their participation in the experiment concurrently.

Andreoni (1995) explores whether subjects making contributions in the linear VCM game are "kind" (altruistic) or simply confused. His design involves a stranger matching protocol with variations in the information that subjects receive as well as the manner in which subjects are paid. The baseline "Regular" treatment is the standard repeated public good game under a stranger matching protocol played for 10 rounds. In a second "Rank" treatment, subjects' monetary payoff is not the standard payoff (7.1) but is instead based on their ranking among the other subjects in their group, with top rank (the player earning the highest standard payoff (7.1) being awarded to the subject who earned the most. Finally, a RegRank treatment provides subjects with their relative rank information but pays them in the standard manner (7.1). The aim of the second treatment is to reinforce the notion that free-riding behavior is the dominant strategy; top rank (and the highest payoff) is achieved by contributing nothing, so paying base on rank reinforces non-cooperative behavior and should reduce/eliminate any confusion that subjects have about what they should be doing. On the other hand, if subjects are altruists—that is, if they are inclined to cooperate—they should not behave differently in the rank treatment relative to the regular treatment. The third RegRank treatment considers whether information on rank alone would reduce confusion. The results of this experiment are shown in Table 7.2

In the Regular treatment, we observe the standard pattern of over-contribution and its decay. In the Rank treatment, there is significant reduction in contributions in every round relative to the Regular treatment. Contribution percentages in the RegRank treatment lie in between these two extremes. Andreoni concludes from this experiment that contributions to the public good in the standard VCM are partly due to confusion but are also part attributable to genuine kindness as well. This is reflected in the fact there are a certain percentage of subjects who refuse to contribute zero even in the rank treatment where non-contribution is reinforced.

Having established that kindness plays some role, this raises the question of what *kind* of kindness is at work. Warm glow is *impure* altruism: one gives to the public good because it makes one feel better about *oneself* and not necessarily because one cares about others. Altruism, by contrast, is true (or *pure*) concern for the welfare of others. Is the over-contribution phenomenon in public good games caused by the desire to feel a warm glow or by genuine altruism? This question is addressed by Palfrey and Prisbrey (1996, 1997). In their experiments, subjects in a given public good game all face the same marginal per capita return from investment in the public good, β, but they have different payoffs for r_i, the private good, which are drawn randomly from a commonly know distribution. With knowledge of both β and r_i, player i's payoff objective is as follows:

$$\pi_i = r_i(\omega - x_i) + \beta G,$$

where G is once again total contributions to the public good. Variations in β across treatments affect the social cost of giving; if subjects are pure altruists, then contributions should increase directly with increases in β. By contrast, variations in $r_i - \beta$ affect the *private cost* of giving. Palfrey and Prisbrey posit that a subject's warm-glow behavior follows this rule: Contribute if $r_i - \beta < g + \epsilon$ and don't contribute if $r_i - \beta > g + \epsilon$. Here g is a measure of a subject's "warm-glow threshold" and ϵ is unaccounted-for noise. By varying $r_i - \beta$, g can be estimated. They find that variations in β have almost no effect on giving, suggesting that pure altruism plays little role. By contrast, variations in $r_i - \beta$ do matter for giving amounts and the impure altruism threshold g is estimated to be significantly greater than zero.

An alternative to the notion that subjects are impure altruists is that some subjects are *conditional cooperators*—that is, they contribute to the public good if others contribute and they do not contribute otherwise. Fischbacher *et al.* (2001) propose a strategy method to address whether such conditional behavior is operative in the VCM. They study what has become the standard parameterization of the public good game payoff function (with $\omega = 20$, $\beta = .4$, and $N = 4$):

$$\pi_i = 20 - x_i + 0.4G$$

and use a strategy method for a one-shot play of the game. Subjects were given $\omega = 20$ tokens and were asked to make two kinds of contribution decisions:

1. **Unconditional:** How many of your 20 tokens do you wish to contribute to the public good?

2. **Conditional:** For each of 21 possible average amounts contributed by the other three members of your group (integers $0, 1, \ldots, 20$), how many of your 20 tokens do you wish to contribute to the public good?

To incentivize truthful revelation, subjects were told that, after making both decisions, three of the four group members would have their *unconditional* contribution implemented while the fourth would have their *conditional* contribution decision played out for them according to the average contributions of the other three subjects. Since it was not known which subject would have their contribution schedule played out, all subjects' schedules were effectively incentivized and thus valid for data analysis. The results from 44 subjects (11 groups of 4) are depicted in Figure 7.4. Of the 44 subjects, 50% (or 22) provided schedules of contributions that largely increased with the average contributions made by the other three players. Only 30% of subjects submitted schedules indicating that they would contribute 0 for all the mean contribution levels of others, which is the subgame perfect Nash equilibrium prediction. Finally, 14% of subjects—those labeled "hump-shaped" in the figure—were conditionally cooperative up to a point, equaling 50% of their endowment of 10 tokens and beyond that point reducing their tokens as the group average increased. This evidence suggests that there is a great heterogeneity of behaviors among subjects playing the public goods game—a heterogeneity result that has been replicated in many other studies. For instance, Kocher *et al.* (2008) recruit participants from three different locations—North Carolina, U.S.A.; Innsbruck, Austria; and Tokyo, Japan—and apply the Fischbacher *et al.* (2001) approach. A majority of the participants act as conditional cooperators: U.S. (81%), Austria (44%), and Japan (42%). Similarly, Herrmann and Thöni (2009) recruit 160 participants at four separate universities spread across Russia, two in rural areas and two in small cities. They find that, overall, 56% of participants behave as conditional cooperators. Note that

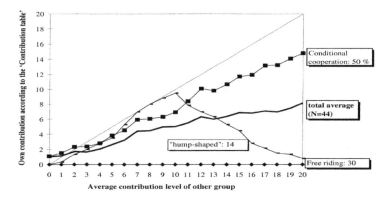

Figure 7.4: Average own contribution level for each average contribution level of the other group members (diagonal line = perfect conditional cooperation). Classification of the 44 subjects reveals that $22/44$ (50%) are conditional cooperators; $13/44$ (30%) are free-riders; $6/44$ (14%) are "hump-shaped."
Source: Fischbacher *et al.* (2001), copyrighted material reproduced with the permission of Elsevier.

a mix of some conditional cooperative types together with some free-riders can readily account for the pattern of over-contribution and its decay over time in finitely repeated public good games, as shown by Ambrus and Pathak (2011).

7.3 Mechanisms to Increase Public Good Contributions

In addition to trying to understand the cause of declining contributions over time, researchers have also attempted to consider various mechanisms that might increase or sustain contributions to the public good while maintaining the voluntary nature of the VCM. In this pursuit, several mechanisms have received wide attention and study.

One mechanism is to suppose that there is a certain threshold, $T > 0$, for voluntary contributions that has to be reached in order for the public good to be provided. Specifically, suppose that

$$\pi_i(x_i) = \begin{cases} \omega - x_i & \text{if } \sum_{i=1}^n x_i < T, \\ \omega - x_i + \beta T & \text{otherwise.} \end{cases}$$

In addition to the free-riding, zero contribution Nash equilibrium, this *threshold* public good game has another Nash equilibrium in which the group contributes just enough to meet the threshold, T, yielding the fixed reward payout, βT, with $1 > \beta \geq 1/n$. To contribute less involves not achieving the threshold, hence sacrificing the reward. To contribute more involves sacrificing part of the endowment without affecting the reward. In either case, the player's payoff falls. However, there are many such threshold equilibria because there are many ways in which contributions can add up to the threshold amount. The symmetric equilibrium where each player i contributes $x_i = T/n$ is a plausible candidate for the focal equilibrium outcome, but in the absence of communication, coordination on such an equilibrium outcome can be difficult. Indeed, Croson and Marks (2000) report mixed success rates for public good provision in such threshold public good games. A general finding is that while some groups achieve the threshold, others do not. Further refinements to the threshold public good game involve refunding contributions if the public good threshold is not reached or rebating contributions in excess of the threshold level. Both of these modifications tend to increase public good contributions in threshold public good games relative to their absence.

A second mechanism is punishment of free-riders by other members of the group. Fehr and Gächter (2000a,b, 2002) study a two-stage version of the public good game:

1. **Stage 1:** 4 subjects play the linear VCM, with $\beta = 0.40$, $\omega = 20$ tokens.

2. **Stage 2:** Contributions of individual members are revealed and any member of the 4-player group may choose to reduce the earnings of any other member of his own group at some lesser cost to himself.

Working backwards in the one-shot (or finitely repeated game), the sub-game perfect equilibrium is that agents should never punish in stage 2 as doing so only reduces their payoff; hence, through backward induction, punishment should *not* be a factor in decisions in stage 1, meaning we should expect *no contributions* in stage 1 as usual. By contrast, the experimental finding is that punishment *is* chosen and that it increases contributions to the public good relative to settings without punishment. This is illustrated in Figure 7.5, which presents the results from *within-subject* studies that consider repeated play of the public good game either with or without punishment opportunities (and both orders of play). Without punishment,

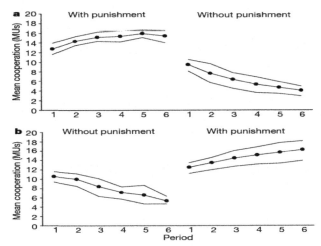

Figure 7.5: Time trend of mean cooperation together with the 95% confidence interval. In panel a, over the first six periods, subjects have the opportunity to punish other group members. Afterwards, the punishment opportunity is removed. In panel b, over the first six periods, punishment of other group members is ruled out. Thereafter, punishment becomes possible.

Source: Fehr and Gächter (2002), copyrighted material reproduced with the permission of Springer Nature.

there is a downward trend in contributions to the public good, but with punishment this trend is reversed.

A third mechanism for sustaining contributions to public goods is *ostracism*, or endogenous group formation, as studied by Cinyabuguma *et al.* (2005), Page *et al.* (2005), and Ahn *et al.* (2008). As an example, consider the "regrouping treatment" applied by Page *et al.* (2005), which uses the payoff function $\pi_i(x_i) = 10 - x_i + .4G$. At the end of each *third* period (periods 3, 6, 9, 12, 15, and 18), there is a regrouping decision made by the four groups of 4 subjects each. Each subject is shown a list—without other identifying information and in a random order—of each of the other 15 subjects' average contribution to their group accounts over the experiment up to that point. Subjects are then given the opportunity to express a preference among possible future partners by ranking them 1–15 at some cost. Groups are then reformed according to these rank preferences. This mechanism also leads to increases in group contributions as the threat of exclusion or ostracism works to limit free-riding and increase contributions to the public good. Page *et al.* show that a combination of punishment and endogenous group formation is the best in terms of the amount of public good that is provided.

A final mechanism that has been the focus of much study is the use of prizes awarded by lottery to incentivize public good contributions. As Morgan (2000) shows, treating public good contributions as purchases of tickets toward winning a lottery prize can overcome the free-rider problem in the voluntary contribution mechanism. Specifically, suppose a charity offers a fixed prize of R to those making voluntary contributions to a public good. The probability of winning this prize is increasing in individual i's contribution (think of raffle tickets costing $1 each). In this case, the public good payoff function changes to the following:

$$\pi_i(x_i) = \omega - x_i + \frac{x_i}{G}R + \beta(G - R) \text{ where } G = \sum_{j=1}^{N} x_j.$$

The lottery introduces a *negative* externality—each ticket purchased decreases the chance that a given ticket wins. This partially counteracts the positive externality of public good provision, thus bringing the marginal benefit of contributing closer to the social benefit.

This mechanism was tested experimentally by Morgan and Sefton (2000). Their two main treatments were the standard VCM game (no lottery) versus a lottery treatment (LOT), which adds the lottery. In their design, $\omega = 10$ tokens, $\beta = 0.75$, and $N = 2$. In treatment LOT, each point contributed was a lottery ticket to win a prize of 8 points. In this case, the equilibrium prediction is that both players should contribute $x_i = 8$ tokens. To make the no lottery VCM treatment comparable, 8 points were added to the group account in the VCM treatment. Nevertheless, since $\beta < 1$, the equilibrium prediction in the VCM treatment remains $x_i = 0$ for all i. The mean contribution levels in these two treatments are show in Figure 7.6.

As is clear from this figure, contributions to the public good are significantly larger with the lottery prize than without it; in the absence of the prize, we see decay in contributions with repetition, but with the lottery, we see that contributions are increasing toward the interior equilibrium prediction of 8 tokens per player. Subsequently, many papers have explored reward mechanisms to induce voluntary contributions (see, e.g., Schram and Onderstal (2009), Corazzini *et al.* (2010), Duffy and Matros (2021), and Carpenter *et al.* (2022)).

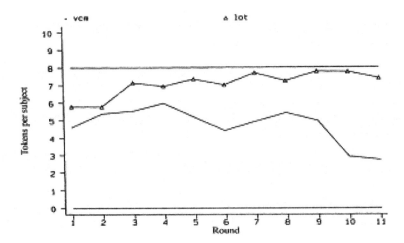

Figure 7.6: Mean contributions to the public good over 12 rounds. VCM game without a lottery (VCM) compared to VCM game *with* a lottery (LOT).
Source: Morgan and Sefton (2000), copyrighted material reproduced with the permission of Oxford University Press.

7.4   Tax Compliance

Public goods are typically financed through taxes and not through voluntary private contributions. Still, just because many public goods are provided through tax revenues does not mean that free-riding is no longer a concern. Indeed, *tax compliance*, namely the accurate reporting of income and payment of the appropriate amount of tax owed, can be viewed as the analogue of voluntary contributions under compulsory (tax) systems. Tax compliance has also been studied experimentally and there is now a large, mature literature on the subject matter (see, e.g. Alm and Malézieux (2021)).

Here, the framework most frequently used is the standard "economics-of-crime" model of tax compliance proposed by Allingham and Sandmo (1972). In this model, an individual has income I and must decide how much of it to declare, D, or not. The tax rate is t, the detection probability/audit rate (by the government) is p, and the fine on income undeclared for tax purposes if detected is f. The individual's income if not caught is $I_N = I - tD$, while her income if caught is $I_C = I - tD - f[t(I - D)]$. In this setting, individuals maximize by choice of D, their expected utility $EU(I) = (1 - p)I_N + pI_C$.

Suppose that $U(I) = \frac{I_i^{1-\sigma}}{1-\sigma}, i = C, N$. For reasonable values, e.g., $\sigma = 1$, $t = 0.4$, $f = 2$, $p = 0.02$ the optimal $D^* = 0$!

The first experimental test of this framework was conducted by Friedland *et al.* (1978). They gave subjects a gross income amount in each period that increased over time and asked them how much taxable income to declare, D. The experimental treatments varied model parameters: the tax rates t, fines f, and the audit probability p. The audit probability was always chosen to be the inverse of the fine magnitude f so that the expected value of gains from tax evasion were always zero. They found that income was under-reported by 50% when the tax rate was $t = 0.25$ and by 80% when the tax rate was $t = 0.50$. A main takeaway from this study is that the fraction of income declared for tax purposes was highly elastic with respect to the tax rate!

A further study by Alm *et al.* (1992) explores non-expected utility explanations for why people might pay taxes. They look at (1) whether subjects overweight audit probabilities and (2) whether they respond to (or recognize) the value of the public goods funded by tax revenues (as in a VCM). In their experiment, a period begins with each of 8 subjects receiving an income level randomly drawn from the set $\{0.25, 0.50, \ldots, 2.00\}$. Second, subjects report taxable income and pay taxes. Here, the tax rate is $t = 0.40$. Third, an audit occurs with some probability p. If an audit occurs and there is unreported income, then a fine multiple $f = 15$ is applied to the amount of the unreported income. Finally, all taxes and penalties are summed and included in a group tax fund. This group fund is multiplied by a factor and the total is distributed back to subjects as in the public good component of the VCM game. The experiment involved six treatment conditions—three values for the audit probability, $p = 0$, 0.02, and 0.10—and three group multiplier amounts—0, 2, and 6—corresponding to marginal per capita returns (mpcrs) on the public good (tax revenue redistribution) of 0, 0.25, and 0.75.

The risk-neutral, expected utility maximizing prediction is to disclose $D = 0$ if $p < 0.05$ but to fully comply with $D = I$, when $p = 0.10$. The mean compliance rates as a function of p are shown in the left panel of Figure 7.7. The compliance rates are responsive to changes in p but are not equal to the extreme predictions of 0 or full compliance (1.0).

Holding $p = 0.02$ constant, the risk-neutral expected utility maximizing prediction is $D = 0$ when the public account multiplier m is 0 or 2, but full compliance, $D = I$, when $m = 6$. Varying the multiplier on the public

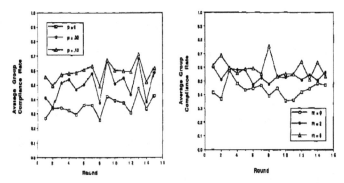

Figure 7.7: Mean tax compliance rates across six experimental treatments of Alm *et al.* (1992).
Source: Alm *et al.* (1992), copyrighted material reproduced with the permission of Elsevier.

good component of the payoff also has little effect on compliance rates, as shown in the right panel of Figure 7.7.

With regard to tax compliance, a natural question arises as to the external validity of experimental evidence using student subjects as in Alm *et al.* (1992). For instance, student subjects may not have much experience with the tax system and may not pay much or anything in taxes. To address this external validity question, Alm *et al.* (2015) ask the following questions: (1) whether behavior observed in the lab is likely to be similar to behavior observed in a *naturally* occurring environment; and (2) whether *non-student* subjects in tax compliance laboratory experiments behave differently than student subjects in identical laboratory experiments. For (1), Alm *et al.* (2015) consider the audited tax returns of 1,101 U.S. taxpayers whose sole source of income in tax year 2001 was a Schedule C proprietorship *and* who were found to have positive taxable income. These taxpayers are those who are most likely to be audited as their income is mostly self-reported, which is also true in the experimental studies. Alm *et al.* (2015) report that the mean reported compliance rate in their experimental sample is 0.286 when the audit rate is zero and 0.368 when the audit rate is 0.05. Using the 2001 tax year audit rate of 1.72% for Schedule C filers, they interpolate a reporting compliance rate of **0.314** for the experimental sample for this audit rate and they compare it with the compliance rates in actual audited returns. As they note, "this rate is essentially identical to the unweighted mean reporting compliance rate for [U.S. individual tax-filers] of **0.313** using the audited taxpayer sample."

To address question (2), they brought both student and non-student taxpayers to a laboratory tax compliance study similar to the one already described and, in doing so, they found no difference in compliance rates between student and non-student subjects. This is an excellent example of cross-validation of experimental results with non-experimental data as well as with non-student subjects, and makes a strong case for the external validity of the experimental findings from tax compliance experiments.

7.5   Voting

Researchers in the political economy and political science fields have conducted experiments in many different contexts. Many of these experiments use game-theory-based models in combination with some voting rule to determine outcomes. Here we discuss a standard framework for implementing voting experiments. In line with this chapter's focus on public good provision, one can think of the costly decision to turn out and cast a vote as providing a kind of public good, while abstention from voting (if allowed) can be thought of as a form of free-riding. In short, one can think of voting decisions as another type of collective action problem.

We begin by noting the famous paradox of voting (or not voting). Suppose the cost to individual i of voting is c_i. The benefit to i of voting, conditional on i's candidate/alternative winning, is B_i, and assume it is 0 otherwise. The probability that i's vote is *pivotal* is p_i. Player i's vote is pivotal if i's vote tips the outcome of the election in favor of the candidate or alternative preferred by player i, while a non-vote (abstention) results in i's candidate or preferred alternative losing. Rational choice theory says that voter i will choose to vote only if $p_i B_i \geq c_i$ and i will abstain otherwise. Downs (1957) was the first to point out that the probability a single voter casts a pivotal vote in large elections is very small. In such settings, if there is any cost to voting, it may be rational to abstain. Note that the rational choice framework ignores any "civic duty" or social norm motivations for voting.

More generally, the electorate size may not be so large that the probability of being pivotal is near zero. Pivotal-voter models (e.g., Ledyard (1984) and Palfrey and Rosenthal (1983, 1985), endogenize the probability, p, that a voter's vote is pivotal to the voting outcome. They do this by modeling voting as a *participation game* that is easily tested experimentally.

To be more specific, suppose there are two teams, 1 and 2, of size M and N, respectively. An action $s_i \in \{0,1\}$ for any team member is to participate, that is vote, 1, or not, 0. A mixed strategy is a probability of voting, denoted by p_i for a member of team 1 and q_i for team 2. The costs of voting to player i are c_i, which could be fixed or could be a random draw from a known distribution.

The payoff function for the team participation game is typically that the team with the larger participation, $\sum_i s_i$ (or votes), wins a prize of value 1, while the other team loses and earns 0, i.e., the winner takes all. Ties result in a payoff of $1/2$ to each team. For M, $N \geq 2$, for any $c_i \in (0,1)$, there exist mixed strategy equilibria, with pure strategy equilibria being rare. Generally, if $M > N$, $p_i < q_i$, which is known as the "underdog" effect.

The predictions of the pivotal voter model using participation games have been studied experimentally by Schram and Sonnemans (1996), Levine and Palfrey (2007), Duffy and Tavits (2008), and Faravelli *et al.* (2020), among others. Consider the experiment of Levine and Palfrey (2007), who study the participation game under strategic uncertainty; specifically, the individual costs of voting are stochastic and are drawn from a known distribution. There are two teams, A and B, with different numbers of members N_A and N_B. Members of both teams simultaneously decide whether or not to vote (participate). Subjects on the winning team earn 105 points while those on the losing team earn 5 points. Prior to voting, each subject gets a random draw $c_i \in [0,55]$, which is their opportunity cost (in points) of voting. This amount is received as a bonus for not voting. The equilibrium assumption is that voters correctly perceive the probability of being pivotal on average and rationally decide whether to vote or to abstain. The equilibria involve *cut-off strategies*: voters whose cost of voting lies below some critical level choose to vote, while all others abstain. For any given set of parameters, there is a unique Bayesian Nash equilibrium that is characterized by such a cut-off strategy.

One of Levine and Palfrey's treatment variables was the size of the electorate, i.e., the size of the two combined teams $N = N_A + N_B$. They studied cases where the electorate consisted of $N = 3$, 9, 27, and 51 subjects. The other treatment variable was whether the two teams were of almost equal size—the "toss-up" condition—or whether two-thirds of voters belonged to the same team (or party) and the remaining one-third to the other team—the "landslide condition". Thus, they implement a 4×2 experimental design which they use to test three main hypotheses:

1. **Size Effect:** Holding the distribution of preferences constant, a larger total electorate size leads to lower turnout (participation).

2. **Competition Effect:** Holding the size of the electorate constant, turnout is higher in toss-up ("close") elections than in "landslide" elections.

3. **Underdog Effect:** Voters whose preferences are in the minority participate more than voters whose preferences are in the majority. Note that the three voter case has a reverse underdog effect.

Table 7.3 reports on equilibrium and actual participation rates across all treatments of the Levine and Palfrey study.

Table 7.3: Treatment conditions and mean turnout rates: Equilibrium (Eq.) versus actual for teams A and B.

Treatment Vars.			Participation Rates, Groups A, B.			
N	N_A	N_B	Eq_A	Actual A	Eq_B	Actual B
3	1	2	0.537	0.539	0.640	0.573
9	3	6	0.413	0.436	0.374	0.398
9	4	5	0.460	0.479	0.452	0.451
27	9	18	0.270	0.377	0.228	0.282
27	13	14	0.302	0.385	0.297	0.356
51	17	34	0.206	0.333	0.171	0.266
51	25	26	0.238	0.390	0.235	0.362

Source: Levine and Palfrey (2007), copyrighted material reproduced with the permission of Cambridge University Press.

While the data do not precisely conform with the equilibrium *point* predictions (as is typical in experimental studies), there is strong support for the *comparative statics* predictions of the theory as formulated in the three hypotheses. First, as the size of the electorate, N, increases, voter participation rates among members of both teams decreases. Second, participation rates are higher in close elections than in landslides. For example, compare the close case (where $N = 27$ and there are $N_A = 13$ and $N_B = 14$ team members) with the landslide case (where $N = 27$ and there are $N_A = 9$ and $N_B = 18$ team members); here, participation rates (both actual and equilibrium predicted rates (Eq)) are higher in the former than in the latter. Finally, there is evidence for an underdog effect: participation rates by members of the disadvantaged group A are greater than the participation rates of members of the advantaged group, B (with the exception of $N = 3$).

This team participation game design has been implemented on an even grander scale in an on-line experiment by Faravelli *et al.* (2020) involving 1,200 participants recruited using Amazon's Mechanical Turk. The experiment adopted a 2×2 between-subjects design where the treatment variables were, once again, the size of the electorate (either small ($N = 30$) or large ($N = 300$)) and whether team membership made for close or lopsided outcomes. In this study, voting also required costly *real effort*, namely the completion of online slider tasks. Some researchers believe that involving participants in real tasks that require genuine effort provides a better means by which to capture the motivation and exertion of real-world situations than simply endowing subjects with earnings or subtracting costs from their point earnings. Another feature of this study is that the group, A or B, that had the most players complete the real effort slider task were the group that won the election, with all members of the winning team sharing a common prize of $5 regardless of whether they had paid the cost (completed the task) or not. In this experimental setting, the treatment effects are weaker than the theory predicts; for instance, there is always over-participation in the costly task relative to theoretical predictions. These findings suggest that details of the experimental design (e.g., the implementation of the voting cost), and perhaps the use of online subject pools, can matter for the accordance of experimental findings with the theory.

Finally, in regard to pivotality, the rational choice theory of voter turnout relies heavily on the notion that voters carefully weigh whether their vote will be pivotal to the outcome of voting or not. To address whether such concerns are truly operative, Duffy and Tavits (2008) elicit subjects' beliefs regarding the pivotalilty of their vote prior to deciding whether or not to vote.

Specifically, they study a two-team participation game with 10 subjects per team (20 total). In their experiment, subjects have to decide whether or not to buy a token (i.e., vote) at a cost of c, which was the same for everyone. The team with the highest number of tokens was the winner. In this setup, the winning team earned $1 per round, the losing team earned $0, and $c = \$0.18$; thus, a player should vote if $\$1p > \$0.18$ or if $p > 0.18$, and abstain otherwise.

In one treatment, prior to voting, subjects were asked to state the probability that their decision to buy a token (vote) would be pivotal to the outcome or not. The meaning of a pivotal token purchase was carefully explained to subjects, who were also tested on their understanding of pivotality. Accuracy in beliefs was incentivized using a quadratic (proper) scoring rule, of the type discussed earlier in Section 3.7, for which subjects received a small additional payment. In the baseline control treatment, subjects were not asked to decide whether their voting decision would be pivotal; they simply made token purchase (voting) decisions without the belief elicitation stage.

Duffy and Tavits (2008) report that eliciting beliefs about pivotality or not does not have any effect on voter turnout, which was the same across the two treatments. That is, the elicitation of beliefs was unobtrusive to the main outcome variable, voter turnout. In the case where subjects' beliefs about pivotality *were* elicited, subjects were more likely to record a greater subjective belief in their own pivotality, consistent with rational choice theory. However, subjects initially greatly *overestimated* the probability that their votes would be pivotal. Despite this, given that the experiment was repeated for 20 rounds, as subjects gained experience and learned their true pivotality following each repetition, they did learn to reduce their belief in their own pivotality over time, as shown in Figure 7.8. Still, the over-estimation of belief in one's pivotality may explain the over-participation

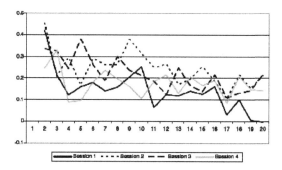

Figure 7.8: Difference between the elicited subjective probability of being pivotal (decisive) and the actual probability of being pivotal from four experimental sessions of Duffy and Tavits (2008) with 20 subjects each. *Source*: Duffy and Tavits (2008), copyrighted material reproduced with the permission of John Wiley and Sons.

that we often see in collective action games such as voting or contributions to public goods.

7.6   Summary

Public goods are resources or services that are non-excludable and non-rivalrous, meaning they are available to all individuals and that one person's use of the good does not diminish its availability to others. Experiments have been conducted to study how people behave when asked to make voluntary contributions to public goods. The most common framework uses the linear voluntary contribution mechanism (VCM) where groups of participants are given an endowment and must decide how much to contribute to a public good that benefits everyone and how much to keep for themselves. The total contributions are then multiplied by some factor and evenly distributed among all participants. This setup creates a tension between individual self-interest and collective benefit. The experimental findings reveal that while some individuals contribute generously, others contribute less or not at all, leading to a decay in contributions over time. Various measures have been explored to arrest this decay, including partner rather than stranger matching, punishment of free-riders, ostracism, and prizes for giving.

Voting is closely linked to the concept of public goods and collective decision-making. Through voting, citizens collectively make decisions that impact not only public goods and services but also the overall direction of governance. In voting, individuals face a trade-off between expressing their preferences for a policy/candidate and the cost of voting. Rational choice theory suggests that an individual's incentive to vote depends on their perception of the impact their vote will have on the outcome. The paradox of voting is that the probability that any single vote changes the outcome of an election is exceedingly small, which might discourage participation. Still, the pivotal voter model of voting predicts robust amounts of participation and has been put to the test, with the experimental findings providing some support for this rational choice approach to understanding voting.

Tax compliance refers to individuals and businesses adhering to tax laws and fulfilling their tax obligations. This is another example of collective action and cooperation for the greater good of society. Tax revenue funds public goods and services like infrastructure, education, and healthcare. However, tax compliance is not always guaranteed, as individuals might wish to evade or avoid taxes in order to maximize their own wealth. Experimental evidence suggests that individuals do comply with reporting requirements but not as sharply as is implied by rational choice theories of tax compliance.

In summary, these topics are all interconnected in their exploration of how individuals make decisions in collective situations. The voluntary provision of public goods experiments shed light on cooperation in situations where self-interest conflicts with the common good. Voting illustrates the challenges and motivations behind participation in collective decision-making, while tax compliance reflects the complex interplay between individuals' self-interest, societal obligations, and government policies aimed at ensuring public goods provision.

Chapter 8

Social Preferences

Social comparisons are a fact of life. Most of us care about our standing relative to others in any number of dimensions, such as income, beauty, social class, power, and influence. However, many (though not all) economic models abstract from such other-regarding concerns. One of the key findings of behavioral and experimental social science research to date is that such other-regarding concerns can be important factors in decision-making and that taking such concerns into account can help us to rationalize departures from theoretical predictions made under the standard assumption of self-interested, *money-maximizing* preferences.

To be more precise, suppose the payoff to player i from some action is π_i. The idea of social preferences is that subjects may not just get utility from their own payoff, but rather their payoff may depend on the payoffs earned by others. Specifically,

$$u_i = u_i(\pi_i, f(\pi_i, \pi_{-i})),$$

where u_i is i's utility function and $f(\pi_i, \pi_{-i})$ is some function of i's payoff in relation to the payoffs of all other agents $(-i)$ with whom i interacts or makes comparisons. For instance, if there are n other agents, f might be $\frac{\pi_i}{\sum_{j=1}^{n} \pi_j}$. If there is just one other agent, j, whose payoff is relevant to i, then f might be $\pi_i - \pi_j$. Social preferences or other-regarding concerns can influence utility in a positive or negative manner; that is, $\partial u_i / \partial f$ can be positive or negative. By way of contrast, the standard money-maximizing preferences do not include the f term, i.e., $u_i = u_i(\pi_i)$. While many theories posit money-maximizing preferences, subjects often bring other-regarding concerns with them to experimental studies, meaning that

143

one should always be mindful of how such preferences affect experimental outcomes.

If social preferences are not a part of a theory or hypothesis that is being tested—for instance, the theory presumes money-maximizing preferences or self-regarding preferences—then it might be best to try and minimize other-regarding concerns by, for example, making players anonymous to one another, having large numbers of players, or providing information only about a subject's own payoff. However, in game theory experiments, as our first example illustrates, the number of players is often small and it is not generally possible to restrict payoff information to a subject's own payoff. This is because the outcome of play is fully revealing about both players' payoffs.

8.1   Ultimatum Game Bargaining

Social preferences or other-regarding concerns have been well known to arise in settings with few players, such as in bargaining when two players negotiate as to how they will split the gains from trade. Perhaps the most famous example of social preferences comes from the ultimatum bargaining game, first studied experimentally by Güth *et al.* (1982) and subsequently by many others.

In this game, two players A and B have to decide how to divide up a cake of size C representing the total gains from trade. Player A moves first, proposing the fraction $x \in (0,1)$ of the cake to be given to player B and keeping fraction $1 - x$ of the cake for herself. Player B then chooses whether to accept or reject player A's allocation. Acceptance means that player A earns $(1 - x)C$ and player B earns xC, while rejection means that both players earn 0. The game, in its extensive form, is depicted in Figure 8.1. If this game is played once or a finite number of times, the logic of backward induction reveals that the subgame perfect Nash equilibrium (SPNE) is for player A to keep all of C for herself (i.e., choose $x = 0$) and player B will agree to this allocation since his payoff is made no better or worse by rejecting or accepting. To make the Nash equilibrium strict, player A can offer B $x = \varepsilon$, where $\varepsilon > 0$ is the *smallest monetary increment possible*, e.g., 1 cent, in which case player B will strictly prefer to accept this allocation over rejection and a payoff of 0.

In the design proposed by Güth *et al.* (1982), the cake size, C, ranged between 4 and 10. Inexperienced subjects were randomly and anonymously

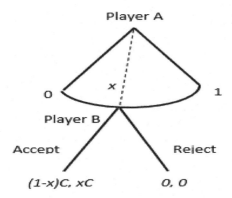

Figure 8.1: The ultimatum game in extensive form. Player A determines the fraction x of the cake C to give to Player B, who then decides whether to accept the allocation $(1 - x)C$, xC or to reject the proposal, in which case both players earn 0.

matched and faced different C-values. The mean Player A proposal was $x = 0.37$ and the mode was $x = 0.50$. While the smallest admissible fraction was $\varepsilon = 0.01$, all offers by Player As were above this level. Subjects were then recalled 1 week later (now "experienced") and asked to play the game again. This caused the mean to drop only slightly to $x = 0.32$, but equal split options became less frequent. Güth et al.'s findings indicated systematic deviation from the SPNE prediction and provided evidence against game theoretic reasoning. However, as we will see, the findings can be reconciled by considering social preferences.

Before we consider the social preference explanation, we should first note that many variants of the ultimatum game (UG) have been studied with the aim of restoring the theoretical prediction or better understanding what motivates subjects. For instance, Binmore et $al.$ (1985) studied the two-round UG where the responder can accept at the end of round 1 or make a counterproposal. If the counterproposal is chosen, the value of the cake is reduced to δC. They use $\delta = 0.25$, $\varepsilon = 0.01$, and $C = £1$. Here, the equilibrium prediction is that player A offers B $x = \delta$ in round 1 and player B accepts as he will fare no better by waiting until round 2. They find that subject behavior accords with this prediction. Harrison and McCabe (1996), meanwhile, had players make decisions both as proposers and responders. The responders state their minimum acceptable offer, or

MAO in a strategy method design. After that, players' roles were randomly determined in each round and their role-dependent decisions were played out. By the 15th period, proposers were offering a mean of $x = 0.14$ to responders. Another modification includes increasing the cake size, e.g., to \$100, or in a field study, to 3 times monthly expenditures. Larger cake sizes can affect the amount given but it remains the case that x is substantially greater than 0 and that responders reject positive offers (see, e.g., Andersen *et al.* (2011) and Slonim and Roth (1998). Many authors have also used the UG to examine gender and cultural differences. Regarding gender, Solnick (2001) reports mixed results: men and women make similar proposals, but if gender is known, male recipients receive higher offers, particularly from female proposers. Moreover, across countries, there are cultural differences in how subjects play the game, as documented by Henrich (2004). For instance, Machiguenga farmers in Peru offer much less, $x = 0.26$, on average and seldom reject, while Lamalera whalers in Indonesia offer the most, $x = 0.58$, on average.

The result that the subgame perfect Nash equilibrium is not played in UG games is relatively robust. According to a meta study of 75 UG experiments conducted by Oosterbeek *et al.* (2004), the mean offer is 40.4% and the rejection rate is 16.67%.

8.2   Dictator Games

One reaction to the UG results is that subjects have *fairness concerns*; in other words, they do not accept that Player A can gain all or nearly all of the cake for themselves. Building on this, Forsythe *et al.* (1994) introduced the "dictator game" variant of the UG where the proposer decides on an allocation and the receiver has *no opportunity* to reject the allocation. The dictator game variant enables a clean test of the fairness hypothesis: If fairness explains the UG results, there should be no difference in the distribution of giving between ultimatum and dictator games. In addition, as a secondary hypothesis, they asked whether paying subjects had an influence on outcomes. Thus, they implemented a 2×2 design: Dictator or Ultimatum Game, Pay or Don't Pay. The results are shown in Figure 8.2.

The main finding is that, in the paid sessions, there *is* a significant difference in the distributions of allocations between the dictator and the UG. Dictators, on average, offer $x = 0.22$, while in the UG, the average is more than double that at $x = 0.46$. Furthermore, there is a greater

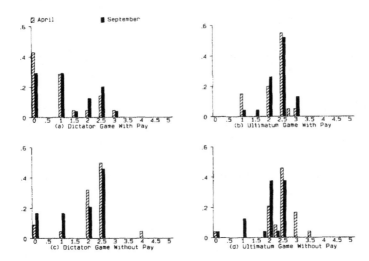

Figure 8.2: Histograms of proposals made in the ultimatum game (left) and dictator game (right) with pay (top row) and without pay (bottom row). April and September refer to two different sessions.
Source: Forsythe *et al.* (1994), copyrighted material reproduced with the permission of Elsevier.

concentration of allocations in the dictator game at the subgame perfect equilibrium of 0. There are also significant differences between the pay and no-pay dictator game treatments, but not between the pay and no-pay UG. When there is no other player involved and payoffs are hypothetical, as in the no-pay dictator game, subjects in the proposer role (i.e., the Player A role) claim that they would be more generous, yet in the actual paid setting, they are significantly less generous. This finding demonstrates the importance of paying subjects, as hypothetical scenarios may not properly incentivize the truthful disclosure of action choices.

The dictator game has been studied by many researchers. A common finding is that mean contributions are significantly different from zero. For instance, Engel (2011) reports on a meta study of 128 dictator Games and finds that the mean percentage given is 28%.

Numerous variants of the dictator game have been explored in the literature. For one example, Bardsley (2008) and List (2007) study dictator games where both the dictator and recipient are initially given money ($5), after which the dictator has the option to either give some of her endowment to the recipient or to take money ($5) that has been given to the recipient. This change in the action set reduces the willingness of dictators to give positive offers to the recipient. For example, in the study by List (2007), the baseline action space for the dictator is to give an amount in the set Baseline $= \{0, 0.5, \ldots, 5\}$. In a first treatment, this set is changed to Take1 $= \{-1, 0, 0.5, 1, \ldots, 5\}$ and, in a further treatment, the set is changed to Take5 $= \{-5, -4.5, \ldots, 0, 0.5, 1, \ldots, 5\}$. These changes to the *framing* of the action set have a significant effect on the rate of positive offers and mean offers. While in the Baseline treatment, positive offers are 71% and the mean offer is \$1.33, in Take 1 the rate of positive offers falls to 35% with a mean of \$0.33. Meanwhile, in Take 5 the rate of positive offers is just 10% and the mean offer is $-\$2.48$—that is, dictators on average take approximately half of the recipient's endowment. This experiment shows that results can be sensitive to frames (action choice sets), which is important to keep in mind when making claims, for instance, that giving in the standard dictator game reveals that the mean subject is altruistic.

In another variant, the dictator has to *earn* their endowment through some menial task that requires real effort as opposed to receiving "manna from heaven" from the experimenter. It is thought that requiring dictators to earn their endowment creates a stronger feeling of ownership or property rights, and, indeed, we do observe that dictators with earned endowments reduce their giving relative to those with unearned endowments (Hoffman *et al.* (1994); Fahr and Irlenbusch (2000); Oxoby and Spraggon (2008); Jakiela (2011); Danková and Servátka (2015)).

In a third and final variant, the recipient is a *charity*. Dictator allocations to charities tend to be higher than those to student recipients for two reasons: (1) the dictators typically have the option to choose which charity their donation goes to and they do not get such a choice with a matched student recipient (Fehrler and Kosfeld (2014); (2) as a result, subjects may also receive some residual benefit from the public good provided by the charity. Supporting this, a meta-study by Umer *et al.* (2022) confirms that unearned endowments and charitable recipients increase dictator allocations.

8.3 Market Games

A second reaction to the UG results is that social or other-regarding concerns are less likely to arise in settings where individual subjects have little power, as in larger market games. Market economies involving many traders buying and selling goods often result in competitive equilibrium allocations that can involve highly unequal distributions of the gains from trade (see, e.g., Crockett *et al.* (2011)). Moreover, as Dufwenberg *et al.* (2011) show, if preferences did depend on the distribution of final allocations in a non-separable way, then the First Welfare theorem of Economics (that every competitive equilibrium is Pareto optimal) may not generally hold! Indeed, it appears that the domain of social or other-regarding preferences may be limited to settings with only a small number of players.

An example illustrating these different domains is provided by the four-country experiment of Roth *et al.* (1991). This experiment—conducted in Jerusalem, Ljubljana, Pittsburgh, and Tokyo—was among the first to use similar instructions and subject pools across four different countries, allowing for cross-cultural comparisons. In each location, the UG was played with the monetary equivalent of $10 pies or $30 pies. In addition to the standard UG, there was also a "market game" variant where there were 10 players in each match, with 9 of the 10 playing the first-mover proposer role, which we can think of as representing buyers in a market. The remaining player in each match was the second-mover responder or, in the market game sense, a seller. All proposers had the same valuation for the single (virtual) good offered by this seller, namely $10 or $30 depending on the treatment. The game starts with all proposers making bid proposals of $0–$10 or $0–$30 for the good offered by the single seller. In this market game, due to competition among proposers (buyers), the subgame perfect Nash equilibrium involves all 9 proposers offering $10 or $30 to the seller (depending on the treatment). Consequently, the prediction is that the seller appropriates all of the surplus. By contrast, in the UG, a single proposer proposes a portion of their allocation of $10 or $30 (depending on the treatment) to allocate to the matched responder, who either agrees or disagrees to the amount being offered. Both the market game and UG treatments were repeated for 10 rounds. The results for rounds 1 and 10 involving either $10 or $30 pies are shown in Figure 8.3.

The figure very clearly shows that by the 10th round of the UG with either $10 or $30 pies, most proposals made to responders are at the 500 level, representing a 50% or equal division of the pie. By contrast, by the 10th round of the market game variant, under either $10 or $30 pies, most proposals made to responders are at the 1000 level, representing 100% of the pie. While this finding may not be particularly surprising, since there is considerably more competition among proposers in the market game, it nevertheless illustrates the fragile nature of social preferences, here in the form of fairness concerns, to the number of participants in a match. It also shows that extreme (i.e., corner solution) game-theoretic equilibrium

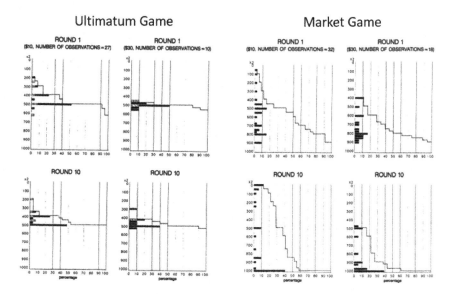

Figure 8.3: UG, left four panels, and Market Game, right four panels: distribution of amounts allocated by proposers to responders in round 1 (top) versus round 10 (bottom). First columns of each treatment are $10 pies and second columns are $30 pies.
Source: Roth *et al.* (1991). Copyright: American Economic Association; reproduced with the permission of *American Economic Review*.

predictions are *not* the issue. Can non-monetary considerations (e.g., fairness considerations) explain these differences across the two treatments? We address this question in the next section.

8.4   Inequity Aversion

Suppose you have income level x. Suppose you are told the income level of a "comparison person" is y. The case where $y > x$ is regarded as one of *disadvantageous* inequality. Surveys show that this type of inequality is strongly disliked by many; they would give up some income if, by doing so, the inequality was further reduced. By contrast, the case where $y < x$ represents *advantageous* inequality. Surveys show that this is also disliked by some but not as strongly disliked as disadvantageous inequality. For instance, most of us choose not to discuss how much income we make with our colleagues or peers, which is likely a result of inequity aversion.[1]

Fehr and Schmidt (1999) and Bolton and Ockenfels (2000) were the first to propose that experimental subjects might exhibit inequity aversion, i.e, that they might have preferences over the *distribution* of payoffs earned in an experiment. Note that in many experiments, this distributional information can be suppressed, but, most notably in game theory, experiments such as the UG and market games, where one player's gain is another's loss, distributional information on payoffs will be known to all.

To be precise, suppose that there are n players, $i = 1, 2, \ldots n$, each having earned a non-negative monetary payoff of x_i. In the Fehr and Schmidt (1999) specification, player i's utility function is imagined to be the following:

$$U_i(x_i) = x_i - \frac{\alpha_i}{n-1} \sum_{j \neq i} \max[x_j - x_i,\ 0] - \frac{\beta_i}{n-1} \sum_{j \neq i} \max[x_i - x_j,\ 0].$$

Here, it is assumed that $0 < \beta_i < 1$ and $\alpha_i > \beta_i$. The α parameter captures "envy" or disadvantageous inequality, which is thought to be more harmful in utility terms than is advantageous inequality, or "guilt," which is measured by the β parameter (hence the assumption that $\alpha_i > \beta_i$). In the $n = 2$ player version, the above specification simplifies to:

$$U_i(x_i) = x_i - \alpha_i \max[x_j - x_i,\ 0] - \beta_i \max[x_i - x_j,\ 0],\ i \neq j.$$

Note that standard "neoclassical" or "money-maximizing" preferences have $\alpha_i = \beta_i = 0$; thus, inequity aversion (either disadvantageous or advantageous) reduces utility relative to this benchmark level. Bolton and Ockenfels (2000) differ from Fehr and Schmidt (1999) in allowing for a more general, nonlinear social preference specification:

$$U_i(x_i) = V(x_i, \sigma_i)$$

where

$$\sigma_i = \begin{cases} \frac{x_i}{\sum_{j=1}^{n} x_j} & \text{if } \sum_{j=1}^{n} x_j > 0, \\ \frac{1}{n} & \text{if } \sum_{j=1}^{n} x_j = 0. \end{cases}$$

represents the other-regarding component. While both approaches are useful, we will focus here on rationalizing the UG and market game results using the linear approach adopted by Fehr and Schmidt (1999) (FS).

---

[1]Inequality in comparisons between/among "third party" individuals is typically ignored: self-centered inequity aversion is the norm.

Consider first behavior in the UG under FS preferences. Assume the cake (also known as the "pie") is of size 1. Let $(1-s, s)$ denote the proposer's allocation, with s being the fraction/amount allocated to the responder. Let us first consider the responder's (r's) behavior. If $s > 0.5$, then $U_r(s) = s - \beta_r(2s - 1) > 0$, which implies that the responder should always accept. If $s < 0.5$, then $U_r(s) = s - \alpha_r(1 - 2s)$. Solving for the critical $s'(\alpha_r)$ s.t. $s - \alpha_r(1 - 2s) = 0$, we obtain the responder's best response, which is to accept if $s > s'(\alpha_r) = \frac{\alpha_r}{1+2\alpha_r}$ and reject otherwise. Notice that: $0 < s'(\alpha_r) < 0.5$.

Consider next the Proposer's behavior. Given the responder's behavior, the proposer never offers $s > 0.5$ because this is always accepted and the proposer can do better by offering $s \leq 0.5$. If the proposer were perfectly informed of the responder's preferences, then the proposer would offer $s = s'(\alpha_r)$. If the proposer knows the CDF of αs, $F[\alpha_r]$ and its support $[\underline{\alpha}, \overline{\alpha}]$, then the proposer's optimal offer is $s \in (s'(\underline{\alpha}), s'(\overline{\alpha}))$. This equilibrium strategy under FS preferences is consistent with many of the stylized facts from numerous ultimatum games, e.g. most offers never exceed 0.5 and low offers are almost always rejected.

By comparison, consider how the equilibrium under FS preferences changes in the market game setting. First, let $\overline{s} = \max[s_1, s_2, \ldots, s_{n-1}]$ of the $n - 1$ proposer offers (recall n was 10 in the Roth *et al.* 1991 market game). Beginning again with the second-mover responder's decision, it is clear that the responder will always accept $\overline{s}$ since this is the maximum proposal and $U_r(\overline{s}) = \overline{s} - \frac{1}{n-1}\beta_r(2\overline{s} - 1) - \frac{n-2}{n-1}\beta_r(\overline{s} - 0) \geq 0 \Leftrightarrow (n - 1)\overline{s} \geq \beta_r(n\overline{s} - 1)$ which always holds since $\beta_r, \overline{s} \leq 1$.

As for the proposers, an equilibrium where $\overline{s} < 1$ does not exist, regardless of α, β. As there is only one winning proposer, there will be lots of inequality. This inequality can be mitigated only if the proposer increases her own monetary payoff which she does by increasing her own proposed offer. A proposer who loses gets

$$U_p(1 - s_i) = \frac{-\alpha_i}{n - 1}\overline{s} - \frac{\alpha_i}{n - 1}(1 - \overline{s}) = \frac{-\alpha_i}{n - 1}.$$

A proposer who wins gets

$$U_p(1 - s_i) = 1 - s_i - \frac{\alpha_i}{n - 1}(2s_i - 1) - \frac{n - 2}{n - 1}\beta_i(1 - s_i) \geq \frac{-\alpha_i}{n - 1},$$

$\forall s_i \leq 1$. It follows that in the market game, no single individual can enforce an equitable outcome. Since there will be inequality anyway, the only way to reduce this inequality is for each proposer to increase his own payoff. The only way for a proposer to increase his own payoff is to bid more aggressively, i.e., to propose to give more to the responder. By contrast, in the two-player UG bargaining game, the responder can enforce an equitable outcome by destroying wealth (rejecting proposals), and for sufficiently inequality-averse subjects, this is in fact a best response.

The discussion above concerns sequential move games, but now let us turn our attention to one-shot simultaneous move games, such as the Prisoners' Dilemma or the public goods game. Consider, as an illustration, the two-player Prisoner's Dilemma game,

Player 2

		C	D
Player 1	C	*a,a*	*c,b*
	D	*b,c*	*d,d*

where C = confess, D = don't confess and $b > a > d > c$.

To consider the role of FS preferences, we first transform payoffs using those preferences so that the payoffs to the game can be written as

	C	D
C	a, a	$c - \alpha_1(b - c), b - \beta_2(b - c)$
D	$b - \beta_1(b - c), c - \alpha_2(b - c)$	d, d

In the one-shot Prisoner's Dilemma game, where players have social preferences ($\alpha_i > \beta_i \geq 0$), Duffy and Muñoz-García (2015) show that the following strategy profiles can be supported as Nash equilibria of the game:

1. (D,D), if $\beta_i \leq \frac{b-a}{b-c}$ for any player; and

2. (C,C), (D,D), and a mixed strategy Nash equilibrium where every player i randomizes according to probability $\bar{q}(\alpha_j, \beta_j) = \frac{d-c+\alpha_j(b-c)}{a+d-c-b+(\alpha_j+\beta_j)(b-c)}$ if $\beta_i > \frac{b-a}{b-c}$ for both players.

In other words, FS preferences can turn the one-shot PD game into a coordination game if players' disadvantageous inequality parameter β_i is sufficiently high. These possibilities are illustrated in Figure 8.4.

Finally, let us return to the dictator game variant of the UG, which is itself a kind of one-shot simultaneous move game. Here, FS preferences have more difficulty rationalizing the observed behavior. Again, let the proposer or dictator's allocation be $(1 - s, s)$. The dictator's utility if $s < 0.5$ is $1 - s - \beta_d(1 - 2s)$. So, if $\beta_d < 1/2$, the dictator gives $s = 0$, while if $\beta_d > 1/2$, the dictator gives $s = 0.5$. However, why should $\beta_d > 1/2$? In this case the dictator prefers to give a dollar to someone with a lower

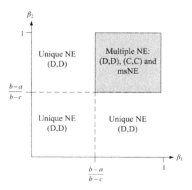

Figure 8.4:   Prisoner's dilemma equilibria under Fehr and Schmidt preferences.
Source: Duffy and Muñoz-García (2015), copyrighted material reproduced with the permission of Springer Nature.

income than himself than to keep a dollar in his own pocket. Fehr and Schmidt propose a nonlinear (concave) specification to resolve this issue so that $s \in [0, .5]$, in accordance with the data.

The social preference specifications of Fehr and Schmidt (1999) and Bolton and Ockenfels (2000) have been criticized for focusing too strongly on payoff differences. Aside from minimizing inequities, another goal of subjects may be to maximize group payoffs (an efficiency preference) or to maximize the minimum group payoff (a maximin preference). As an illustration, consider the one-shot, dictator allocation choice experiment designed by Engelmann and Strobel (2004). In this three-player dictator game, the only player who makes an active choice is "Person 2." This subject must choose from among three possible allocations—A, B, and C—where the amounts going to Persons 1, 2, and 3 are as indicated in Table 8.1.

Notice that in treatment F, allocation A is aligned with the three objectives of minimizing inequities (Fehr & Schmidt preferences), maximizing efficiency (the sum of the three payoffs), and maximizing the minimum group member's payoff (Maximin). Indeed, 83.3% of subjects choose allocation A in treatment F. However, in treatment E, the efficient allocation remains choice A while the choice to minimize inequity and maximize the minimum payoff becomes choice C. In this case, subjects most frequently choose option A, though there is also weight on option C. Finally, in treatment R, the maximin choice, option C is the most frequently chosen

Table 8.1: Dictator allocation experiments. Person 2 makes a dictator
allocation choice that is paid out to all three persons.

	Treatment F			Treatment E			Treatment R		
	A	B	C	A	B	C	A	B	C
Person 1	8.2	8.8	9.4	9.4	8.4	7.4	11	8	5
Person 2	5.6	5.6	5.6	6.4	6.4	6.4	12	12	12
Person 3	4.6	3.6	2.6	2.6	3.2	3.8	2	3	4
Total	18.4	18	17.6	18.4	18	17.6	25	23	21
Inequity	X						X	X	
Efficiency	X			X			X		
Maximin	X						X		X
% Choosing	83.8	10.3	5.9	39.7	23.5	36.7	26.7	20	53.3

Source: Engelmann and Strobel (2004). Copyright: American
Economic Association; reproduced with the permission of *American Economic Review*.

allocation. The point of this simple experimental exercise is to demonstrate
that inequity concerns alone may not be the most important driver of agent
decisions. Instead, agents may be heterogeneous in their social concerns.

For another example, consider the study of Xiao and Houser (2005), in
which the price sensitivity of other-regarding concerns is examined. Specifically, they report on a UG with $20 pies. In addition to the standard control
treatment, they add a further emotional expression "EE" treatment where
they allow responders to send free written messages to Proposers in addition to deciding whether to accept or reject the Proposer's offers. When
the only punishment mechanism available to responders is the relatively
costly option of rejecting an offer, as in the control treatment, then responders use that punishment mechanism. However, evidently, other-regarding
behavior can be price sensitive! Given the less costly option of punishing
selfish Proposers with verbal abuse in text messages sent by Responders
to Proposers, many Responders facing 80/20 splits in particular chose that
route rather than giving up any positive allocations made to them by the
proposer. Specifically, the opportunity to vent led to a significant reduction in rejection rates for 80/20 splits, though not for other allocations.
Still, one implication is that outcome-based models like that of Fehr and
Schmidt (1999), which only consider pecuniary outcomes, are likely to miss

important aspects of subjects' behavior when players have a wider array of responses to perceived inequities.

8.5 Reciprocity/Intentions-Based Models

Indeed, a second type of social preference model is based on *reciprocity and intentions*. Here, the application is typically to sequential-move settings as these allow for the role of intentions and reciprocity. To illustrate this idea, consider the experimental design of Falk *et al.* (2003), who study the role of intentions for behavior using simple, binary-choice ultimatum games. In a binary-choice game, the proposer has just two allocation options while the responder, as before, can choose to accept or reject the proposal. In their study, the cake is of size 10 and the first-mover (proposer) choice always includes an allocation of (8,2), i.e., 8 to the proposer and 2 to the responder. The other proposer allocation choices are treatment conditions and are either (5,5), (2,8), (8,2), or (10,0). The results of these four different treatments are summarized in Table 8.2.

Table 8.2: Proposal and acceptance frequencies in the binary UG experiment of Falk *et al.* (2003).

Binary Choices	% Choosing (8,2) Offer	% Rejecting (8,2) Offer
(8,2) vs. (5,5)	31%	44%
(8,2) vs. (2,8)	73%	27%
(8,2) vs. (8,2)	–	18%
(8,2) vs. (10,0)	100%	9%

Source: Table constructed from data reported in: Falk *et al.* (2003), copyrighted material reproduced with the permission of John Wiley and Sons.

As this table reveals, rejection rates of (8,2) proposals are higher if the *other* allocation the proposer could have made was more "fair", e.g., (5,5), versus the case where it was less fair, e.g., (10,0). This suggests that responders take into account the intentions of proposers to act fairly, given the proposers' available actions, and then, accordingly, the responders reciprocate kindness with kindness.

Indeed, intentions-based reciprocity models assume that the desire to raise or lower others' payoffs depends on how fairly those others have behaved toward a player, i.e., what their intentions were (see, e.g., Charness and Rabin (2002) for further evidence). Responders are kind to those who were kind to them and not kind to those who have "misbe-haved." Consider, for example, two players A and B with payoffs x_A and x_B. Charness and Rabin (2002) specify the utility of a responder, the second-mover player B, as follows:

$$U_B(x_A, x_B) = (\rho r + \sigma s + \theta q)x_A + (1 - \rho r - \sigma s - \theta q)x_B$$

where $r = 1$ if $x_B > x_A$, 0 otherwise; $s = 1$ if $x_B < x_A$, 0 otherwise. $q = -1$ if A has "misbehaved" and $q = 0$ otherwise. Here, ρ and σ capture distributional concerns, while θ captures reciprocity concerns. Thus, this model nests FS and BO and social welfare models. Generally, a choice of $\theta \neq 0$ improves the model's fit to the data.

Finally, we note that pure reciprocity models rely on psychological game theory (see, e.g., Rabin (1993), Dufwenberg and Kirchsteiger (2004)) where players have to form *beliefs* about other players' intentions and what constitutes misbehavior. However, this can be context-dependent, e.g., a 10% restaurant tip in the U.S. would be considered harsh, but in Europe it would be considered generous. These models are relatively complicated and often generate multiple equilibria even in the simplest games (e.g., in the UG).

8.6   Image Concerns/Social Norms

Another explanation for pro-social behavior concerns self-image concerns. Subjects may feel compelled to act in a pro-social manner in certain situations—even though they prefer the own-payoff-maximizing outcome—because they do not want to *appear* selfish, either to themselves or to others. To address this possibility, Dana *et al.* (2007) study a binary dictator game, where the dictator must choose either option A, an unequal (6,1) allocation between the dictator and another player, or option B, an equal (5,5) allocation. In the Baseline treatment, the dictator is aware of both the allocation to himself and to the other player. In a Hidden Information treatment, regardless of the dictator's A or B choice, the other player gets 1 or 5, with probability 0.5. In such a treatment, the dictator could ex-post choose to know only the payoff consequences of an A or B choice for himself and not the other, or look at what the other player got as well. A third treatment, called Two Dictators, has two players playing dictator roles, enabling them to both make decisions regarding allocations. Both dicta-tors have to choose A in order to implement the unequal allocation (6,6,1), where the other (non-dictator) player gets the payoff of 1. If at least one of the two dictators chooses B, the allocation is always (5,5,5). A fourth and final treatment is called "Plausible Deniability." This is similar to the baseline treatment except that the dictator has only 10 seconds to make a decision, and, during that time, there is some chance that the computer program randomly chooses A or B before the dictator makes his decision. Notably, recipients are unaware if the decision was made by the dictator or the computer. The results of these various treatments are shown in Table 8.3.

Table 8.3: Results from Dana *et al.* (2007). An A choice is the allocation (6,1) or (6,6,1) in the two-dictator game. The B choice is an allocation of (5,5) or (5,5,5).

Treatment	% Dictators Choosing A	% Look at Payoffs
Baseline	5/19 (26%)	–
Hidden Information	23/32 (72%)	18/32 (56%)
Two Dictator	13/20 (65%)	–
Plausible Deniability*	12/22 (55%)	–

Note: *If choice made by dictator and not the computer.
Source: Dana *et al.* (2007), copyrighted material reproduced with the permission of Springer Nature.

Relative to the full information baseline, providing various types of "moral wiggle room" leads to more self-regarding behavior. That is, dictators engage in a greater number of unequal "A" choices. These results suggest that image concerns play some role in the incidence of pro-social behavior.

A related experiment by Andreoni and Bernheim (2009) argues that the spike at 50–50 giving in dictator games is likely due to subjects following a social norm of appearing fair rather than simply maximizing some type of social preference function. Andreoni and Bernheim supplement the fairness hypothesis of Fehr and Schmidt with an additional assumption that people like to be *perceived as fair by others*. To illustrate this, suppose there are two players—a dictator, D, and a recipient R—who split a pie normalized to have unit value. Suppose that with probability $1 - p$, D chooses to give the responder $x \in [0,1]$ and, with probability p, Nature chooses to give the responder an amount x_0. What is the purpose of this design? While both p and x_0 are common knowledge, the responder does not know if D or Nature made the decision. The dictator's preferences are assumed to be given by

$$U(x,m,t) = F(1 - x, m) + tG(x - x^F)$$

where F, G are payoff functions, and m is the dictator's "image" payoff (assuming there is an audience, A, including the R and possibly the experimenter), t is D's taste for fairness $t \in [0, \bar{t}]$, and $x^F = 1/2$, the 50–50 norm.

The social image, m, is assumed to depend on A's perception of D's fairness. With $p > 0$ and x_0 close to zero, the distribution of voluntary choices has mass not only at $1/2$ (if t is sufficiently large), but also at x_0; the potential for nature to choose x_0 regardless of the dictator's type reduces the stigma associated with voluntarily choosing x_0.

Andreoni and Bernheim (2009) ask the following question: Does increasing p increase the mass of dictators who choose any given x_0 (close to zero) and reduce the mass of dictators who split the payoff equally? The answer is yes. The design involves \$20 pies and discrete choices of how much D can give to R: $x = 0, 1, \ldots, 20$. The experiment varies $p \in \{0, 0.25, 0.5, 0.75\}$ and $x_0 \in \{0, 1\}$. The results are shown in Figure 8.5. As this figure reveals, the

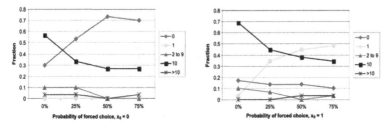

Figure 8.5: Fractions of various amounts of \$20 endowment allocated by dictator to responders as a function of p. The left panel shows results for the case where $x_0 = 0$ and the right panel for the case where $x_0 = 1$.
Source: Andreoni and Bernheim (2009), copyrighted material reproduced with the permission of John Wiley and Sons.

fraction of those giving 10 (half the \$20 endowment) declines as p increases from 0% to 75%, while the fraction of those giving 0 steadily increases over the same range for p. As in Dana *et al.* (2007), this evidence suggests that social image concerns play a role in maintaining the social norm of 50–50 giving in dictator games.

8.7 Social Identity

Distributional or reciprocity models rely on individuals attributing weight to the payoffs of others but spend little time explaining where these weights come from. Casual empiricism suggests that individuals do not treat others equally. For instance, if a good friend asks you for $20, you might well give them the money without even asking why they need it. Yet, if a random person on the street asks for the same amount of money, your response is not likely to be so positive.

The economics literature on social identity, starting with Akerlof and Kranton (2000), examines a plausible source of differing weights on the payoffs of others: people identify as members of various categories, and utility is determined in part by how much a person's actions conform to the norms for those categories. Chen and Li (2009) experimentally tested this notion. They started by creating a group identity in the lab using the famous minimal group paradigm protocol of Tajfel (1974). To do this, subjects are asked to express a preference for the art of Wassily Kandinsky or Paul Klee after being shown a number of pictures of both artists' work (see, for an example pair, Figure 8.6).

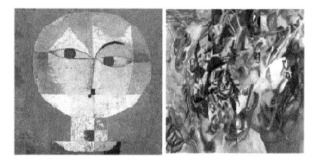

Figure 8.6: Klee or Kandinsky? Construction of a minimal group paradigm.

Based on their reported painting preferences, subjects are then divided into two groups: the Klee group and the Kandinsky group. Group identity was then further primed in some sessions by having the groups perform an additional artist identification task and/or engage in a series of decisions allocating money between two other subjects. All subjects then played a series of two-person sequential move games including dictator games as well as games where the second player makes a decision, making it possible to separate the effect of group identity on preferences from the effect on beliefs. Control sessions had no groups (and hence no group identity) and advanced directly to the final stage of playing two-person sequential move games.

The main outcome was that participants exhibit charity (envy) when their match receives a lower (higher) payoff than they do. Their charity (envy) toward an ingroup match is significantly greater (less) than that toward an outgroup match.

Players may not only have distributional concerns. Another type of social identity relates to preferences for an individual's *relative position* or *status* in a community. Indeed, if people have a strong preference for social status, it would not be surprising if a high-ranking individual in a poor country could be happier than a low-ranking individual in a rich country even if they have the same real income.

Evidence for relative social concerns abound. As Glazer and Konrad (1996) observe, charities frequently publish the names of contributors providing various threshold amounts of giving in clearly defined, rank-ordered categories with labels such as "contributor", "benefactor", and so on (in lieu of reporting the actual amounts given). Indeed, charities seem to exploit such tastes for relative social position.

An experimental test of this idea was undertaken by Duffy and Kornienko (2010). They studied 5-round dictator game *contests*. In each round, five dictators are ranked in one treatment in terms of their giving to others (Competitive Altruism). In a second treatment they are ranked according to the amount they kept for themselves (Competitive Selfishness). Finally, in a control treatment (Control) they are spuriously ranked. At the end of each round, the ranking is made known to all 5 members of the group, but subjects are only identified by their ID letter: A,B,C,D, or E (e.g., subject E was ranked first, followed by subject B, and so on).

Table 8.4: Giving by rank order in the dictator contest experiment of Duffy and Kornienko (2010). Observations are 200 for total giving, 20 for round 1 giving and 180 for rounds 2–10 giving.

Giving Amounts by Dictator to Recipient	Selfish Treatment	Altruistic Treatment	Control Treatment
Total giving, Mean (St. Dev):	$0.74 (1.49)	$2.59 (2.60)	$1.37 (1.99)
Round 1 giving, Mean (St. Dev):	$1.77 (1.99)	$3.00 (2.64)	$1.25 (1.97)
Rounds 2–10 giving, Mean (St. Dev):	$0.62 (1.39)	$2.54 (2.60)	$1.38 (1.99)

Source: Duffy and Kornienko (2010), copyrighted material reproduced with the permission of Elsevier.

As Table 8.4 makes clear, the mean amount that dictators gave to Recipients was greatest in the Altruistic treatment and was least in the Selfish treatment. Mean amounts in the Control treatment were intermediate to the two ranking treatments. These findings suggest that social rank or position is another important element of social preferences.

8.8 Social Preferences in the Field

The impact of social preferences is well documented in the laboratory, but how prevalent is it in the field? Falk *et al.* (2013) designed two studies to address this question. In their first study, they ask "Do pro-social students select into laboratory experiments?" For this purpose, they consider 16,666 undergraduates who registered for experiments at the University of Zurich between 1998 and 2004. In total, 1,783 students participated in at least one lab study, amounting to a lab participation rate of around 11% of the student population. Conditional on participating at least once, the students participate in 2.5 experiments on average.

To test whether experimental participants are more pro-social, they exploited a naturally occurring decision that each student at Zurich must make each semester: Upon enrolling for classes, every student has to decide whether or not to contribute a predetermined amount to two social funds that provide charitable services (financial support for foreign students (CHF 5) and free loans for needy students (CHF 7), where CHF 1 = $1.03 (May 2013)). Students could therefore give CHF 0, 5, 7, or 12 (both funds together). The level of possible donations is similar to the stake sizes typically used in lab settings. They found that giving amounts were statistically indistinguishable between subjects who participated in laboratory studies versus those who did not.

In a second study, they asked whether students were more pro-social than non-student subjects. To do this, they conducted trust game experiments with two groups of participants: University of Zurich students and non-student participants recruited from the city of Zurich using the same recruitment methods. Subjects from both pools received an endowment of CHF 20. The first mover then decided how much of his endowment to transfer to the matched second mover. The transfer could be any amount in steps of 2 CHF—that is, $0, 2, 4, \ldots$, or 20 CHF. The chosen transfer was then tripled by the experimenter and passed to the second mover. Contingent upon the first mover's transfer, the second mover decided on a back transfer. This back transfer could be any integer amount between 0 and 80 CHF. A total of 1,296 subjects participated in the experiment (295 from the student pool and 1,001 from the general population). Ultimately, it was found that first-mover transfers are *not* significantly different between students and non-students: 13.17 CHF for non-students versus 13.47 CHF for students. Furthermore, second-mover returns are actually *lower* for students than for non-students. However, the slope between first-mover

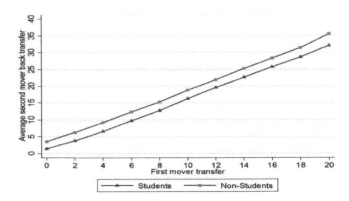

Figure 8.7: Back transfer amount by the second mover as a function of the transfer amount by the first mover, students versus non-students. *Source*: Falk *et al.* (2013), copyrighted material reproduced with the permission of Oxford University Press.

transfer amounts and second-mover returns is very similar, indicating similar reciprocation patterns, as illustrated in Figure 8.7.

In an field study looking for evidence of reciprocity, DellaVigna *et al.* (2022) considered how workers respond to changes in the piece rate for a rote task. The authors recruited 446 workers from Craigslist for a six-hour clerical job, where subjects prepared mailers for multiple charities and a grocery store. In one study the treatments were different piece rates offered for 20-minute envelope stuffing batches: $7 fixed pay, no piece rate; $3.5 fixed pay, 10¢ piece rate; and no fixed pay and a 20¢ piece rate. Here the results suggest significant increases in output from increases in the piece rates, which the authors consider evidence of a form of reciprocity.

8.9   Summary

As we have seen, social preferences can play an important role in the decisions of subjects in experiments. These can take many different forms, including concerns about payoff inequities, intentions, efficiency and a player's social image. Fairness and other social preference concerns are typically absent from economic models of behavior, which tend to assume that all agents have money-maximizing preferences. If your aim is to test such models, then you should be aware of the possibility that social preferences may alter your conclusions. Indeed, while it may sometimes be possible to limit information on the payoffs earned by others, such restrictions cannot always be imposed. For instance, in game theory experiments, strategic reasoning requires knowledge of the payoff opportunities available to opponents.

One approach to dealing with the issue of social preferences is to study behavior in "one-shot" games where players make decisions with payoff consequences for themselves and others on just a single occasion. The advantage of such one-shot experiments is that there is no feedback on distributional payoff information, which helps to circumvent the role of social or other-regarding concerns. This approach offers clarity, as there is no need for re-matching subjects; rather, each game, played only once, can be treated as an independent observation. Still, as we saw earlier in the work of Fischbacher *et al.* (2001), other regarding concerns such as conditional cooperation can arise even in the one-shot case.

A potential problem with one-shot play of games is that subjects might not fully understand the environment and, as a result, they may make mistakes that could be incorrectly construed as exotic preferences. Plott (1996), for instance, advances a "discovered preference" hypothesis that responses in experiments reflect a type of internal search process in which subjects use outcome experiences and trial and error to "discover" what they really want. Only with experience would their preferences become understood and reflected in their behavior.

An alternative approach to dealing with other regarding concerns is to pair subjects with robot players who play according to certain known strategies or are programmed to play like human subjects. In principle, telling subjects that they are playing against robot players should eliminate other-regarding concerns for these robot players. However, the results here are not as clear as one might hope. For instance, Houser and Kurzban (2002) conducted public good game experiments in which three of the four players were known to be computer robot players while the fourth player was a human subject. The robot players were programmed to behave as if they were human subject players. Relative to the more standard 4-human subject treatment, Houser and Kurzban (2002) found that the sole human subject in the robot treatment gave less to the public good on average, yet perfect free-riding by the human subject in each group of the robot treatment was still not observed! They attribute this outcome to confusion on the part of subjects.

Another question regarding social preferences is whether to use a direct-choice or a strategy method to gather data. The evidence to date suggests that strategy methods may lead to different outcomes relative to direct-choice methods, but the evidence as to when and if subjects will appear to be more pro-social is less clear. Cason and Mui (1998) study a sequential dictator game and find that the strategy method does not alter choices made using the direct-response method. However, Brandts and Charness (2000) report that the percentage of responders who sacrifice in order to reciprocate generous behavior in a binary-choice sequential-move Prisoner's Dilemma game is 47% for the strategy method versus 37% for the direct-response method.

If the focus of one's study is in exploring the role of social preferences, then it follows that subjects must see distributional information on the payoffs earned by others. Increasingly, researchers are also seeking to understand the extent of individuals' social preferences by directly eliciting information about such preferences using, e.g., the Social Values Orientation task (Murphy *et al.*, 2011). This task provides an incentivized means of measuring the magnitude of concerns that subjects have for others, with such data often helping to identify subjects with pro-social preferences and distinguishing them from those without such preferences.

Chapter 9

Auction Experiments

Auctions are a common means by which goods or services are sold. For instance, to finance the public debt, the U.S. Treasury sells bills, notes, bonds, Floating Rate Notes (FRNs), and Treasury Inflation-Protected Securities (TIPS) to institutional and individual investors through public auctions. Google, meanwhile, sells most of its advertising using automated auctions among advertisers that sell key words and phrases to the highest bidders in a matter of nanoseconds when you click the search button. The rights to transmit signals over specific bands of the electromagnetic spectrum have been auctioned off by the governments of many countries. These are just some of the many examples of the use of auctions.

In this chapter, we will focus on single-unit auctions, that is, auctions for a single unit of an item, as such settings comprise the bulk of experimental testing of auction formats. Multi-unit auctions are common in practice but challenging to study experimentally, meaning there are comparatively few such experimental studies.

Auctions are conducted because sellers often feel uncertain about buyers' willingness to pay for an item. At the same time, buyers or "bidders" also face uncertainty about the behavior of other bidders. The setting clearly involves strategic interaction and is properly modeled using the tools of game theory (see, e.g., Krishna (2010) for an introduction to auction theory).

An important distinction in the auction literature is whether bidders have different *private values* for an item being auctioned or whether there is a common-to-all but possibly unknown value of the item being auctioned; the latter is referred to as a *common-value* auction.[1]

In the private values case, we assume that each individual bidder i has their own private value, v_i, for a unit of the item being auctioned that only he or she knows. This private valuation represents bidder i's maximum willingness to pay for the item being auctioned. A further common assumption is that each bidder's valuation v_i is an independent draw from some known probability distribution having support $[\underline{v}, \overline{v}]$, such that $v_i \geq 0$ for all i. This distribution could be, for instance, a uniform random distribution over this interval. This case is referred to as an independent private values (IPV) auction. In the field, the distribution of such private values and the support of valuations is not generally known. Thus, an advantage of using experimental methods to study auctions is that these values can be *induced* on subjects in the role of bidders, enabling the experimenter to observe bidding behavior relative to these induced values.

In the case where the value of an item is common to all, the item has a common value (CV), V, but each individual i may receive only a noisy signal of that common value, $v_i = v + \epsilon$, where ϵ is typically a random, mean zero-noise term.

The experimental auction literature has primarily focused on *bidders'* behavior, with the experimenter assuming the role of the seller. In procurement auctions where there are typically multiple sellers and a single buyer, these roles are reversed, with the experimenter playing the role of the buyer and subjects playing the role of sellers.

Much of the experimental research has focused on bidding behavior in light of auction rules and in relation to equilibrium predictions. In the next sections, we discuss some of the main findings from such research. For a more detailed description of experimental auction implementation and design issues, the reader is encouraged to consult Lusk and Shogren (2007).

9.1   Private-Value Auctions

Assume N bidders and one item for sale. Bidder i is randomly assigned some private value, v_i, and makes a bid of b_i. The payoff to player (bidder)

---

[1]A third case that we will not discuss is that of *affiliated values*, which is a hybrid of the private and common value settings where bidders have some shared affiliation/ common interest with other bidders and thus consider not only their own individual value for an item but also the value that the item will bring to affiliated group members.

i is given by

$$\pi_i = \begin{cases} v_i - p & \text{if } b_i = \max\{b_1, b_2, \ldots, b_N\}, \\ 0 & \text{otherwise,} \end{cases}$$

where p is the price paid and is determined by the auction rules. For instance, in a first-price auction, p is equal to the maximum bid, but in a second-price auction, p is equal to the bid of the second-highest bidder. Thus, subjects' earnings, π_i, are the surplus, $v_i - p$ or 0, per replication of the auction market.

In making these bids, subjects face certain budget constraints. Typically, experimenters allow b_i to exceed v_i in order to account for the possibility of *bankruptcy*. However, since it can be awkward to demand that bankrupt subjects pay the experimenter for losses, subject/bidders are often provided with an endowment or show-up payment that is adequate to cover any potential negative earnings.

There are four main types of independent private value auctions that have been studied experimentally:

1. **Open-cry ascending "English" auctions:** Starting from some reserve price level, either bidders shout out prices, or, more typically, a clock is used to steadily raise prices at a set increment per period. Bidders decide at each period/increment whether they want to remain in the bidding (active) or exit the bidding (inactive). Exiting is irreversible. The winner is the last bidder who remains active; in the Japanese "button version", the last bidder is the individual who, at the end of the auction, still pushes a button, indicating a desire to remain active.

2. **Open-cry descending price "Dutch" auctions:** Starting from a very high reserve price, the auctioneer or a clock steadily lowers the price at a set increment per period and the first bidder to agree to a given price wins the item and pays the price at which they stopped the clock.

3. **Sealed-bid "first-price" auctions:** Bidders simultaneously place bids for an item. After all bids have been entered, the highest bidder is declared the winner and pays his bid, which corresponds to the highest or first bid price.

4. **Sealed-bid "second-price" or Vickrey auctions:** These follow the same design as the first-price sealed-bid auction except that the

winner (who places the highest bid) pays a price, p, that is equal to the second-highest bid.[2]

A key reason for studying private-value auction formats has been to test whether subjects bid in a manner that is incentive-compatible with the auction rules and whether the auction generates the maximum revenue for sellers. Furthermore, the ascending English auction and second-price auction formats are strategically equivalent—that is to say, it is a weakly dominant strategy for bidders in both of these types of auctions to bid their true valuations for an item:

$$b_i = v_i$$

for all i. In this case, the winning price $p = v^*$, where v^*, is the maximum of all valuations. Notice that this prediction is independent of the number of bidders or the risk attitudes of subjects.

The Dutch and first-price auction formats are also strategically equivalent, but bidding behavior under these auction rules will generally depend on risk attitudes and the number of bidders while also typically involving some *bid shaving*. For instance, if valuations are uniformly drawn over the interval $[\underline{v}\ \overline{v}]$ and bidders are risk-neutral expected payoff maximizers, then the symmetric, risk-neutral Nash equilibrium (RNNE) bid function for the first-price auction will be as follows:

$$b_i = \underline{v} + \frac{N-1}{N}(v_i - \underline{v})$$

or in the case where $\underline{v} = 0$,

$$b_i = \frac{N-1}{N}v_i.$$

Notice that the extent of bid shaving (i.e., player i bidding below her valuation, v_i) depends on the total number of bidders, N, and, as this increases, bid shaving goes down. In the case where $\underline{v} = 0$, the winning price $p = \frac{N-1}{N}v^*$, where v^* is the maximum of all valuations.

Assuming risk-neutral bidders, the expected price paid under all four auction formats is the same, meaning the seller's revenue is equivalent across these four auction formats (Vickrey (1961), Myerson (1981)).[3] This *revenue equivalence theorem* has been the subject of much experimental testing.

---

[2] Vickrey (1961) proposed such an auction mechanism in looking for a sealed bid auction format that would be strategically equivalent to the English auction and hence the second price sealed bid auction is sometimes called a "Vickrey auction".

[3] In essence, the bid-shaving of the winning bidder in the first-price and Dutch auctions on average approximates the second-highest valuation and price paid by the winning bidder in the second-price and English auctions, assuming the play of equilibrium bid strategies by all N players.

A comparison of all four auction formats was first conducted by Coppinger *et al.* (1980) and Cox *et al.* (1982). Coppinger *et al.* (1980) studied groups of $N = 8$ bidders and found price differences between the oral Dutch auction and the first-price sealed-bid auctions when valuations for subjects were the same in both treatments. Specifically, prices in the first-price sealed-bid auction were found to be significantly higher than equilibrium predictions, while prices in the Dutch auction (conducted orally) were lower and not significantly different from equilibrium predictions. First-price and Dutch auctions were thus found to not be strategically equivalent. English and second-price auction predictions also did not differ significantly from equilibrium predictions, and were found to be strategically equivalent. The authors conclude that, from the seller's perspective (and in contrast to the revenue equivalence theorem), the first-price sealed-bid auction should be preferred as it yields the highest prices for sellers.

Cox *et al.* (1982) report on first-price and Dutch auctions for groups of various sizes ($N = 3$, 4, 5, 6, and 9). Their design is within-subjects and involves sequences of play of both first-price and Dutch auctions in various orders. They also report higher prices in the first-price sealed-bid auction as compared with the Dutch auction for each different value of N and using the same induced distribution of valuations. However, they report that bids are significantly in excess of the RNNE bid function predictions for both the first-price and the Dutch auctions when $N > 3$.

A further comparison between the English and second-price auction formats was conducted by Kagel *et al.* (1987) and Kagel and Levin (1993). These authors relaxed the constraint that Coppinger *et al.* (1980) imposed, which prohibited subjects from bidding above their induced value. The English and second-price auction formats have a dominant bidding strategy of bidding one's valuation that does not depend on the number of bidders, N, or on whether bidders are risk-averse (as opposed to risk-neutral) or on the distribution of valuations. Intuitively, in both auction formats, the winning bidder pays the second-highest price (=valuation) and thus maximizes her chances of winning by bidding her own valuation. (In the English clock version, the last bidder pays the price on the clock when the next-to-last bidder drops out).

Kagel and Levin (1993) find that prices in the second-price auction are significantly higher than prices in English ascending auctions. This is because the majority of bidders, approximately 62% on average, in those auctions are bidding significantly more than their valuation (over bids), as

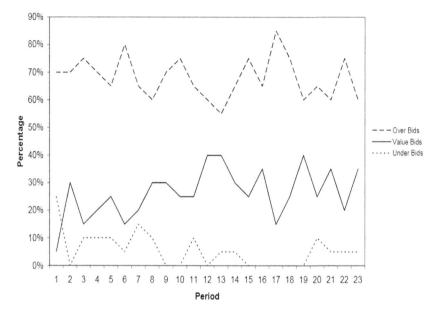

Figure 9.1: Percentage of over, under, and value bids ($b_i = v_i$) in 23-second-price auctions with 5 bidders.
Source: Data from Kagel and Levin (1993), figure by Garratt and Wooders (2010), reprinted under the terms of a Creative Commons license.

illustrated in Figure 9.1. By contrast, only around 30%, on average, are bidding their valuations as predicted, while the remaining 8% are under-bidding on average.

One possible explanation for these results is that the English open-cry or clock auction structure provides greater transparency regarding the disadvantage of bidding above one's own value—indeed, winning the English clock auction with a bid exceeding your valuation inevitably leads to financial losses. This appears to be less evident to subjects in a *simultaneous-move* second-price auction. Repeated experience with the second-price auction leads only to a small reduction in the overbidding tendency, as reported by Kagel and Levin (1993) and Harstad (2000). Cooper and Fang (2008) point out that the persistence of overbidding is most likely due to the limited opportunities to learn about the costs of overbidding, as only the winner incurs a cost for such behavior. This limited learning environment in auction experiments contributes to the continuation of overbidding tendencies.

An important issue in auction (and other) experiments is that giving subjects an endowment of money to bid may encourage them to spend it since they may not perceive it as being their own money or because they wish to please the experimenter (an experimenter demand effect). Concerns with this "house money effect" have led to experimental designs in which subjects have to earn some or all of their endowment by completing simple "real effort" tasks like adding up numbers or counting the number of zeros in a matrix that do not require any specialized knowledge (see, e.g., Drichoutis *et al.* (2017)). Alternatively, one can give subjects money and explicitly ask them to make bids using this endowment.

For instance, Rosenboim and Shavit (2012) pre-paid one group of students two weeks prior to an experiment. The control group, meanwhile, was given the same endowment of money but only as the experiment was about to begin, as is usual. They found that the pre-paid group bid significantly lower in a second-price auction as compared with those who were paid "on the spot." Zhang *et al.* (2019) compared prepaid and deferred payment schemes in laboratory second-price auctions where participants received a cash endowment either two weeks before or after the experiment and used personal funds for immediate losses at the time of the experiment. They found that when subjects faced liquidity constraints, both prepaid and delayed payment methods curbed overbidding. However, in situations without liquidity constraints, only the delayed compensation mechanism led to reduced overbidding.

Of course, external validity can be further increased by conducting real auction experiments in the *field* with real bidders who have actively chosen to participate in such auction markets and who may have greater experience than the convenience sample of student subjects. The main cost of such field experiments is a loss of control or internal validity, e.g., control over the number of bidders who choose to participate and knowledge of those bidders' private valuations for an item.

For example, Lucking-Reiley (1999) conducted real internet auctions of "Magic: The Gathering" cards, a real good, under different auction formats in order to test the revenue equivalence theorem of Vickrey (1961). Vickrey demonstrated that under risk-neutral Nash equilibrium bidding behavior, the seller's expected revenue under the four main auction formats—the English, Dutch, first-price, and second-price sealed-bid auctions—should all be the same.

Lucking-Reiley advertised his auctions to real bidders for the game cards. Specifically, he offered these potential bidders the opportunity to bid in pairs of auctions for the same game card. The only difference across auction pairs were in the auction rules: In one pairing, he compared first-price sealed-bid and the Dutch auction formats as these are strategically equivalent. He also auctioned off matched pairs of game cards under second-price sealed-bid and English auction formats as these two are also strategically equivalent.

The experimental results revealed a violation of the revenue equivalence prediction. First, Dutch auctions raised significantly more revenue (roughly 30% more) than did the first-price sealed-bid auctions—the opposite outcome to what is found in laboratory settings. Lucking-Reiley suggests that this result may be due to greater participation by bidders in the Dutch internet auctions that he conducted, as this was a more novel auction mechanism for bidders in this market. The greater participation in the Dutch auctions appears to have driven up bids and thus revenues. Second, regarding strategic equivalence, Lucking-Reiley, while not privy to bidders' true valuations for the items, observed that bidders tended to place higher bids in the Dutch auctions than in the comparable first-price auctions. Finally, there was no difference in bidding behavior or seller revenue in the second-price sealed-bid and English auctions of the same cards. In particular, unlike in laboratory studies, he did not find that bids in the second-price format were higher than in the English auction format. While the results from field experiments speak more practically to the empirical relevance of theories such as revenue equivalence, they also shed light on the possible shortcomings of more theory-oriented laboratory experiments, such as in the presumption that all bidders in a laboratory experimental auction are motivated to participate or to maximize their expected earnings.

9.2   Common-Value Auctions and the Winner's Curse

Another important auction format that has been widely studied experimentally is the *common-value* auction. In a common-value auction, the value of the item being bid for is common to all bidders, i.e., $v_i = v$ for all i. However, this common value v is typically unknown at the time of bidding. Instead, prior to bidding, each bidder can obtain a noisy signal, s_i, of the item's common-to-all-valuation, v. With this estimate in hand, bidding then proceeds.

Examples of common-value auctions include government auctions of bonds, the allocation of rights to transmit over the electromagnetic spectrum, or the leasing of areas for timber cutting, oil drilling, or gas exploration. Private sector examples include the takeover of troubled firms by venture capitalists or the auctioning off of book distribution rights or the contents of abandoned self-storage lockers.

While common-value and private-value auctions are treated as distinct settings, in many private-value auctions, there can be common-value elements. For example, individuals who place bids for famous artworks may be motivated in part by their own private valuation of the artwork, but they may also bid for investment and resale prospects, which would reflect common-value concerns.

The rules of common-value auctions usually follow the open-cry ascending English auction format or the sealed-bid first-price format. The payoff to the winner is $v - p$, where v is the true but unknown value and p is the price paid by the winning bidder. All other bidders earn 0.

The noisy signal that bidders in common-value auctions receive prior to bidding is some function of the true but unknown common value. For example, in the experimental studies of Kagel and Levin (1986) and Kagel *et al.* (1989), the true common value v for an item being auctioned is first drawn from a uniform random distribution over $[\underline{v}, \overline{v}]$. Then, each subject is given a private signal, s_i, which is a random draw from a uniform distribution centered at v with a lower bound $v - \epsilon$ and an upper bound $v + \epsilon$.

The risk-neutral, symmetric Nash equilibrium bid function for first-price common-value auctions (Wilson (1977)) is of the following form:

$$b_i = \gamma s_i.$$

Like the first-price private-value auction, the common-value version again involves some shaving, as γ is less than 1. Note here that one is shaving not the private valuation for the item but the signal s_i of the common value for the item.

Here the interesting behavioral finding is that the winning bidder is usually the one who has the highest signal. If the bid is not sufficiently discounted relative to this high signal, the winning bidder will experience negative profits—the so-called winner's curse outcome. The winner's curse is the failure to recognize the adverse-selection problem inherent in winning the auction; if you win the auction, then your noisy signal is likely to be an over-estimate of the true common value of the item.

Early experimental tests of the winner's curse phenomenon did not control the signal(s) that subjects received. For example, Bazerman and Samuelson (1983) had subjects bid on a variety of objects (jars of pennies, jars of nickels, jars of large paper clips worth 4 cents per clip, etc.) all of which, unbeknownst to the subjects, were worth $8. They also elicited subjects' estimates for the items' values. The average value estimated by subjects was $5.13, but the average winning bid was $10.01. In other words, the average winner actually lost slightly more than two dollars. However, Bazerman and Samuelson (1983) acknowledge that their findings are to a significant extent contingent on a limited subset of participants who consistently engage in overbidding. This implies that the winner's curse could potentially be mitigated with more seasoned subjects, owing to their enhanced grasp of auction dynamics and potential bankruptcy. Moreover, the degree of uncertainty associated with the objects being auctioned was an uncontrolled element in the Bazerman and Samuelson study. This makes it hard to precisely define irrational behavior or equilibrium behavior.

As noted, Kagel *et al.* (1989) and Kagel and Levin (1986) sought to reduce this uncertainty by randomly assigning subjects noisy signals centered on the true value of the item, v, and considering their bids relative to these signals. Using this design, Kagel *et al.* (1989) studied bidding behavior in first-price sealed-bid common-value auctions with 6 inexperienced subjects. To cover possible losses, subjects were given starting balances large enough to allow them to make some bidding mistakes. However, if their balance dropped below zero, they were no longer permitted to bid; instead, they were paid their show-up fee and asked to exit the experiment.

The 11 experiments they conducted varied the support of the common value, $[\underline{v}, \overline{v}]$, and the value of ϵ. Some results from these experiments are presented in Table 9.1. Over the nine periods of these auctions, average profits were −$2.57, as compared with average risk-neutral Nash equilibrium (RNNE) payoffs of $1.90. In only 17.2% of auctions did the winner earn positive profits. Unlike in the case of Bazerman and Samuelson's research, these results cannot be attributed to a small number of irrational subjects. Almost half of all subjects had gone bankrupt (41.1%) and 59.4% of subjects bid an amount that was greater than the expected value of the item given the signal and information about the signal process.

Kagel and Levin (1986) studied bidding by *experienced* subjects in first-price common-value auctions (subjects who had previously participated in one or more common-value auction experiments). They found that profits

Table 9.1: Profits and bidding behavior in the first-price common-value
auctions of Kagel *et al.* (1989).

Exp. No.	% Auctions with Pos. Profits	Avg. Predicted Profits with RNNE Bidding (st. err.)	Avg. Actual Profits (*t*-stat)	% All Bids $b_i > E[v\|s_i]$	% Subjects Going Bankrupt
1	0.0	0.72 (0.21)	−4.83 (−3.62)**	63.4	50.0
2	33.3	2.18 (1.02)	−2.19 (−1.66)	51.9	16.7
3	11.1	1.12 (1.19)	−6.57 (−2.80)*	74.6	62.5
4	11.1	0.85 (0.43)	−2.26 (−3.04)**	41.8	16.7
5	33.3	3.60 (1.29)	−0.84 (−1.00)	48.1	50.0
6	22.2	2.55 (1.17)	−2.65 (−1.53)	67.3	33.3
7	11.1	0.57 (0.25)	−2.04 (−2.75)*	58.5	50.0
8	11.1	1.59 (0.34)	−1.40 (−2.43)*	51.9	16.7
9	44.4	2.37 (0.76)	0.32 (0.30)	35.2	16.7
10	0.0	3.53 (0.74)	−2.78 (−3.65)**	77.2	20.0
11	11.1	1.82 (0.29)	−3.05 (−3.53)**	81.5	37.5
Avg.	17.2	1.90	−2.57	59.4	41.1

Note: *(**) statistically significant at the 5 (1)% level, two-tailed test.
Source: Kagel *et al.* (1989), copyrighted material reproduced with the
permission of John Wiley and Sons.

earned by winning, experienced bidders were closer to risk-neutral predictions in auctions with small numbers of bidders (3–5), but in larger groups
of 6–7 experienced bidders, profits were consistently negative, in line with
the winner's curse.

The results of Kagel *et al.* (1989) and Kagel and Levin (1986) are relatively robust and have been replicated in a number of different studies using
a variety of treatment modifications and subject pools (see, e.g., Lind and
Plott (1991); Goeree and Offerman (2002)).

Toward an understanding of the winner's curse phenomenon,
Charness and Levin (2009) study the adverse selection problem that lies
at the heart of the winner's curse phenomenon, but they use an individual
choice set-up that enables abstraction from complicating factors, such as
uncertainty about the signals of other bidders. Specifically, they study the

"takeover game" of Samuelson and Bazerman (1985) (and a game-theoretic representation of the famous "lemons problem" proposed by Akerlof (1970)). In this game, a bidder seeks to take over a company with a known value of between 0 and 100. If the bidder is successful in acquiring the company, he is certain to increase its value by 50%. The seller alone knows the true value, v, of the company, whereas the bidder does not. The seller will agree to sell the company to the bidder if the bid is at least as great as the true value of the firm. To further simplify the setting, the seller's decision to buy or sell was automated by a computer program. Thus, in effect, each bidder placed a bid in the interval [0,150], with 0 meaning no bid was made. Then, the true value of the firm v was determined by a uniform random draw from [0, 100]. The bidder's payoff was $\frac{3}{2} \times v - b_i$.

The optimal strategy in this game is to bid 0. The rationale behind this strategy is that if a positive bid $b > 0$ is made and accepted, then the true (but unknown) value of the company, v, is less than or equal to that accepted b. In terms of expectation, conditional on acceptance, this true value is $\frac{b}{2}$ (since values are continuously distributed over the interval $[0, b]$). The acquired firm is thus worth $\frac{3}{2}\frac{b}{2}$ or $\frac{3b}{4}$, which is less than b, so *in expectation*, the bidder's payoff, $\frac{3b}{4} - b < 0$. Thus, the optimal, expected payoff-maximizing bid is $b = 0$. Charness and Levin consider a variety of different treatments of this individual choice game. One treatment involved different levels of instruction detail, ranging from detailed instructions with examples to less detailed ones. Despite the detailed instructions eliminating the need to speculate about the behavior of other players, the winner's curse phenomenon persisted in this individual choice experiment. In the less detailed treatment, the mean bid was 33.47 and only 18.23% of subjects submitted 0 bids. Similar results are obtained with more detailed instructions, although the percentage of subjects making zero bids rises to between 25–40%. Still, the majority of subjects tended to overbid, resulting in negative payoffs. Charness and Levin conclude that the winner's curse is an individual, bounded rationality phenomenon in which the majority of subjects are unable to comprehend that a future contingency (acceptance of their bid and acquiring the firm) can impact their current bidding behavior.

9.3 All-pay Auctions

Economic allocations in various contexts are often determined through competitive processes where individuals or entities engage in costly activities to vie for a coveted prize. These competitions encompass a wide range of scenarios, including political elections, races to secure patents, efforts to win contracts, such as the exclusive rights for local garbage collection, and many others. These settings can all be viewed as *all-pay* auctions where each of N players bids an amount b_i and the winner is the player who places the maximum bid, but *all* participants must pay the amount of their bid. This means that even if a bidder does not win the auction, they still have to pay the amount of their bid, which can make this type of auction more expensive for bidders than auctions where only the winner pays.

Consider a complete information, all-pay auction where there is a known common value, v, to the item that the N players are bidding for and the auction is of the first-price format so that the highest bidder wins and pays their bid, b_i. Since all bids are paid, the payoff to bidder i in this type of all-pay auction is given by the following:

$$\pi_i = \begin{cases} v - b_i & \text{if } b_i = \max\{b_1, b_2, \ldots, b_N\}, \\ -b_i & \text{otherwise.} \end{cases}$$

A player can guarantee a 0 payoff by not participating, i.e., by bidding 0. In this setting, the risk-neutral symmetric Nash equilibrium prediction is that players will follow a mixed strategy in determining the amounts that they bid. The more readily testable equilibrium prediction is that total bids, or the expected revenue to the seller, are equal to the prize value, v (see Baye *et al.* (1996)).

This common-value complete-information setting has been studied experimentally by Davis and Reilly (1998), Potters *et al.* (1998), Gneezy and Smorodinsky (2006), and Lugovskyy *et al.* (2010), among others. For instance, Gneezy and Smorodinsky (2006) consider the setting where $v = 100$ and subjects participated in 10 all-pay auctions. The treatments varied the group size: $N - 4$, 8, or 12. Since payoffs can be negative, they gave subjects an endowment of 1,000 points and instructed them that their bids could never exceed their remaining point balance. Then, in each of the 10 rounds, they auctioned off 100 points using the all-pay auction rules. One of the primary observations in all-pay auctions is the phenomenon known as "overdissipation", where the total bids submitted by participants exceed the actual value of the item being auctioned.Gneezy and Smorodinsky (2006) report strong evidence for the overdissipation phenomenon even when subjects repeatedly interacted in such auctions. As Figure 9.2 reveals, the seller's revenue consistently exceeded 100, which is the value of the item

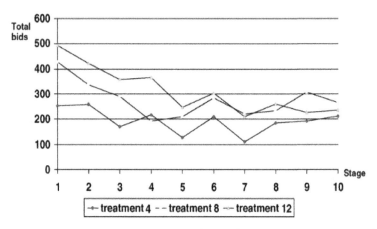

Figure 9.2: Total bids over 10 rounds (stages) in the 4-, 8-, and 12-player all-pay auction experiments of Gneezy and Smorodinsky (2006), where $v = 100$.
Source: Gneezy and Smorodinsky (2006), copyrighted material reproduced with the permission of Elsevier.

being auctioned, in nearly all rounds across various treatments. Furthermore, the likelihood of revenues surpassing this value increased in line with the number of bidders, N, which was either 4, 8 or 12.

Lugovskyy *et al.* (2010) focus on understanding the overdissipation phenomenon in a complete-information common-value setting where the prize is $v = 1000$. To do this, they considered several treatment changes relative to Gneezy and Smorodinsky (2006). First, they increased the number of rounds played from 10 to 60 to determine whether greater experience reduced the amount of overdissipation. Second, they considered partner-versus-stranger matching protocols while keeping the group size fixed at $N = 4$. Finally, they considered a change in the admissible bid space. Instead of setting the minimal bid to 0, they set it to -1000, while keeping the all-pay auction rules the same. In the case where negative bids are allowed, overdissipation requires that the total bids among the $N = 4$ bidders must exceed -3000. They report that greater repetition or stranger matching by themselves do not eliminate overdissipation, though they do diminish it. Aggregate overdissipation was effectively eliminated only when negative bidding was combined with partner matching and the increased repetition of rounds in the experimental design. This is a good example of the effective use of experimental design changes to better understand the sources of behavioral departures from the rational actor model.

The prospect of overdissipation in all-pay auctions has not gone unnoticed by those interested in raising money for charities. Goeree *et al.* (2005), for instance, compared lotteries and auctions in situations where bidders have independent private values for a prize object and all proceeds from the fundraising mechanism go to a public good (charity) that benefits all bidders. The prize object is predetermined and not influenced by the amounts bid. The authors found that although lotteries may be preferred over winner-pay auctions, they are always inefficient and may generate less revenue than k-price all-pay auctions. In the latter, the highest bidder wins the prize, and the kth highest bidders pay the kth highest bid, while all other bidders pay their bids. The authors also identified conditions where the lowest-price all-pay auction is the best fundraising mechanism as it generates the most revenue and ensures that the prize goes to the bidder with the highest valuation. Schram and Onderstal (2009) conducted an experimental study comparing lotteries, winner-pay auctions, and all-pay auctions and found that all-pay auctions were the more effective mechanism for charitable fundraising in terms of charitable funds raised.

9.4 Summary

Auctions are an important mechanism by which buyers and sellers engage in trade.

In private-value auctions, where each bidder's valuation for an item remains private information, there are four primary auction formats, each of which have been the subject of experimental study. English and second-price auction formats have a dominant strategy of bidding one's valuation that does not depend on the number of bidders, risk preferences, or the distribution of valuations. Nevertheless, a common finding in experiments is that participants tend to overbid relative to their induced private valuations. While Dutch auctions and first-price sealed-bid auctions are also strategically equivalent, the experimental evidence is mixed as to whether this is in fact the case. Field experiments using all four auction formats, meanwhile, have raised doubts about the revenue equivalence theorem's prediction that sellers earn the same revenues across all four types of private-value auction formats.

In some settings, the value of the item being auctioned is not private but, rather, is common to all bidders, although not always known for certain. In experimental designs, this uncertainty is captured by a private signal of the common but unknown value that is given to each bidder. While the optimal bidding strategy is to bid less than this signal, experimental evidence suggests that there is a substantial winner's curse phenomenon wherein the winning bidder bids too much so that their net payoff considering the true common value of the item can be negative.

Finally, we also considered all-pay auctions, which is a format that is designed to capture patent races or lobbying efforts. Here, the behavioral phenomenon uncovered by experimenters is again over-bidding relative to optimal bidding strategies. This over-bidding can be so great that the amount of total bids exceeds the value of the object of bidding, a phenomenon known as overdissipation.

As this chapter has made clear, the rules of auctions are readily testable in the laboratory, with experimental economics solidifying itself as a method used to testbed many auction formats before they are put into practice, e.g., government spectrum auctions of rights to transmit signals over specific bands of the electromagnetic spectrum. Although this chapter predominantly focuses on single-unit auction experiments, which facilitate revenue and strategic comparisons, it is worth noting that *multi*-unit auctions are more common in practice and there is a growing literature on multi-unit auction experiments as well (see, e.g., Engelmann and Grimm (2009)).

Chapter 10

Market Experiments

A market is a *venue* that allows buyers and sellers to interact in order to trade goods and services, usually in exchange for money. There are many specialized markets, including for various goods and services, labor, and commodities. There is also a larger variety of different market venues, including wholesalers, retailers, eBay, Craigslist, and Tinder.

Market behavior depends on a number of factors, including the thickness of the market (the number of participants), the market rules (e.g., decentralized or centralized trading), and institutional features (such as information on bids and asks and improvement rules for submitting such bids and asks).

Market experiments generally consider the case with large (for experiments) numbers of both buyers and sellers, e.g., more than 1 buyer/seller on each side of the market. In this sense, market experiments differ from auction experiments where there is typically just one agent on one side of the market and many on the other, such as when there is a single seller and multiple buyers.

In the perfectly competitive markets of economic theory, the price of a good or service is determined by the interaction of market demand and market supply. The theoretical equilibrium market price is that for which market demand becomes equal to market supply. A question for experimental research is how to *operationalize* the process by which a market or markets achieve such an equilibrium.

10.1   Double Auctions and Competitive Equilibrium

An early first effort to understand price determination in competitive markets was a series of classroom experiments designed and reported on by Chamberlin (1948). In these experiments, subjects were randomly given cards with either the label "B" for buyer or "S" for seller in addition to a number chosen from the interval 18–104 representing the subject's reservation value for a unit of some good. Sellers were also endowed with one unit of that good. Thus, as Chamberlin explained to subjects, a buyer with the card "B-36" should be willing to pay a price of up to 36 for a unit of the good, while a seller with "S-20" should be willing to accept a price as low as 20 for her unit of the good. In other words, Chamberlin was *inducing* different subjects to hold different reservation values, v, for the good, and he further instructed them to try to maximize their surplus from trades. For the buyers, this meant maximizing $v_b - p$, where v_b is the buyer's induced reservation value (or maximum willingness to pay) and p is the price paid. For sellers, the objective is to maximize $p - v_c$, where v_c is the seller's reservation value (or cost). The trading mechanism was a kind of pit market, where buyers mingled with sellers and attempted to reach an agreement on a price within a ten-minute time period. If a price agreement was reached, then the pair went to the trading desk, reported their agreed-upon price and surrendered their cards so that the seller's unit was no longer available for trade. Those who did not reach agreement by the end of the market simply surrendered their cards but earned no payoff. This was expected since some buyers and sellers were intentionally assigned values outside the market equilibrium, with their valuations (costs) being lower (higher) than the equilibrium price.

Sorting each buyer's reservation values from highest to lowest and each seller's reservation values from lowest to highest yields the market demand and supply curves, respectively, as shown in Figure 10.1. The equilibrium price is predicted to lie in the small window between 56–58 where demand equals supply, which is associated with an equilibrium quantity traded of 15 units. Chamberlin conducted this experiment and reported that the average actual price, 52.63, was lower than predicted, while the trading volume of 19 units was greater than predicted. He conducted 45 repetitions of this same experiment, though with different numbers each time, and always found consistent results: prices were typically below equilibrium

Market Experiments 185

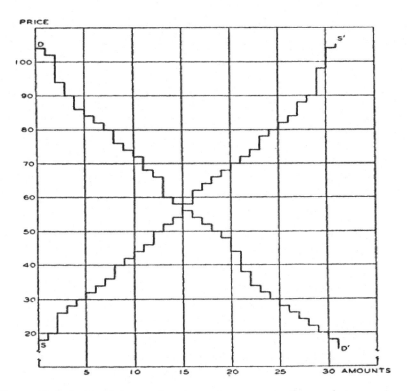

Figure 10.1: Induced demand and supply curves in the market experiment of Chamberlin (1948).
Source: Chamberlin (1948). Copyright: University of Chicago Press; reprinted with permission.

while quantity traded was above. Chamberlin referred to these results as "imperfect" since some players who should not have been able to trade (extra-marginal players) were able to trade while other players who should have been able to trade (infra-marginal traders) were unsuccessful. He attributed this tendency of underpricing and overtrading to the students' personal experiences as buyers rather than sellers. As buyers, they were more inclined to negotiate for favorable deals, and their experiences with sellers primarily involved price negotiations, leading them to emulate such behavior by setting and accepting lower prices. Chamberlin argued that market professionals would get market prices and trading volume correctly.

Vernon Smith, who was a participant in one of Chamberlin's experiments, saw things a little differently (based on his own account: Smith

(1981)). Smith agreed with the notion that trades should be based on an individual's own private information concerning their valuation or cost for a good. However, he thought the problem with obtaining competitive equilibrium did not lie with the student subjects but rather with the market institution as well as the amount of experience subjects had and the feedback they were given. He therefore proposed replacing Chamberlin's pit market with the double-oral auction market institution that was used in stock and commodity exchanges at the time (electronic versions of the double auction are still in use) along with their bid and ask improvement rules. Furthermore, he decided to conduct the experiment repeatedly, in a sequence of trading "days" for which supply and demand were continually renewed in order to give players experience with maximizing their surplus from trade. Finally, he proposed the use of centralized feedback on bids and asks through an order book that all subjects could consult.

The double auction (DA) market institution allows buyers and sellers to interact with one another over some finite period of time with the aim of trading at least two goods, one of which is typically an (indivisible) good or commodity while the other "numeraire" good is typically divisible money (there can be more than one non-numeraire good or commodity).[1] The DA institution admits simultaneous bids (orders to buy) from multiple buyers and asks (orders to sell) from multiple sellers which are presented for all to see in a market "order book." To be admissible for inclusion in this order book, new bids typically have to improve upon (that is, exceed) current existing bids in the order book, while new asks have to improve upon (that is, undercut) existing asks in the order book; these improvement rules help to facilitate equilibration. Trades automatically occur when a new bid exceeds an existing ask or a new ask lies below an existing bid, in which case those bids/asks disappear from the order book and the trades are settled between the pair of buyers and sellers.

Smith (1962) reported on an experiment that used the induced, private-value approach of Chamberlin's market experiments, but Smith used an oral DA institution in place of the pit market. In an oral DA, the best bids and asks are communicated orally to the experimenter, who writes those bids and asks on a chalkboard, proxying the order book, for all experimental participants to see. Sellers were typically endowed with a single unit of the good and buyers were endowed with an amount of money equal to their

---

[1]See Friedman (1993) for an overview of the double auction market mechanism.

induced valuation for a single unit of the good.[2] Buyer i seeks to maximize $v_i - P$, where v_i is i's induced valuation for a unit of the good and P is the price paid, while seller j seeks to maximize $P - c_j$, where P is the price paid and c_j is seller j's induced cost of producing a unit.

A further modification of Smith's study was that subjects repeated the same 5–10 minute market trading scenario involving the same induced values or costs several times in order to gain experience, akin to that of market professionals. The induced demand and supply schedules for a

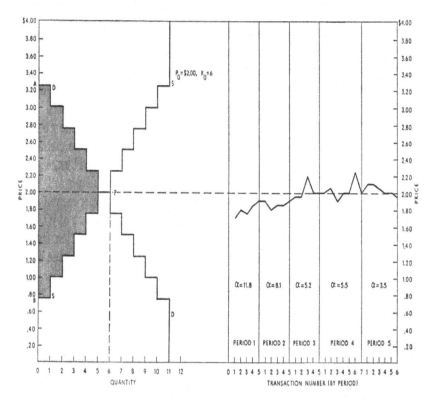

Figure 10.2: Experimental evidence of equilibration to competitive market equilibrium.
Source: Smith (1962): Copyright: University of Chicago Press; reprinted with permission.

---

[2]Thus, buyers were not allowed to overbid, nor were sellers allowed to sell below cost in Smith's experiment. Smith also considered environments where buyers and sellers could trade more than one unit of the good.

representative session of Smith's study are shown in the left part of Figure 10.2. The shaded area refers to the potential gains from trade and includes both the consumer's and producer's surplus. The theoretical equilibrium price was $2.00 and the equilibrium quantity was 6 units. The right part of Figure 10.2 shows the evolution of traded prices and quantities in the 5 replications (or "periods") of each market, lasting up to 10 minutes. At the end of each market, the market conditions were renewed once more so that subjects had the same induced demand and supplies and endowments of goods and money as in previous periods. As this figure reveals, and as Smith found in other replications of this same type of experiment, traded prices and quantities under the DA market institution with common order flow feedback and repetition do eventually converge quite closely if not precisely to the market equilibrium prediction. This is an important demonstration of the fundamental concept of market equilibration that would be difficult to comprehend and document without the control provided by induced values and the implementation of an experimental methodology. Smith was recognized for this achievement by being awarded the Nobel Prize in Economics in 2002.

The DA market institution remains a workhorse, price determination mechanism, but in modern usage, this market institution is fully computerized. In the computerized user interface, subjects can submit bids and asks within some finite time limit. Subject's commodity holdings, cash balances, the order book of all current bids and asks, and the transacted trade prices all appear on their computer screens and are updated in real time. An example of such a programmed DA user interface, as formulated by Chapkovski and Kujansuu (2019), can be seen in Figure 10.3. The screen depicted in this figure is for a buyer, but the screen for a seller is similar. In the upper-left portion, participants can submit their bids along with the corresponding quantities they wish to transact. Directly below this trading window, the display provides information about the best current ask and bid prices available in the market. Moving to the bottom-left and center of the screen, one can see the complete order book listing of asks and bids (including those made by the specific bidder using the screen). The buyer's own trades are shown in the upper-right corner, while the valuations of each of the buyer's units can be found in the bottom-right corner. In the example shown here, the buyer has so far transacted one unit, valued at 9 for a price of 4, and therefore earned a net profit of 5 points. This is a fairly typical trading screen layout. In general, programming a real-time continuous double auction is a difficult task and so it is best to use pre-programmed

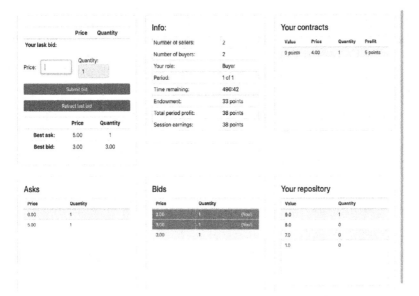

Figure 10.3: Double auction trading screen illustration (for a buyer). *Source*: Chapkovski and Kujansuu (2019), copyrighted material reproduced with the permission of Elsevier.

versions of this market mechanism that have already been subjected to extensive testing or used by other experimentalists. The one shown here is programmed in oTree (Chen *et al.* (2016) and is freely available.

Another practical concern regarding implementation of the double auction mechanism concerns the numeraire good, or "money," that buyers are endowed with to make bids for a good or service. This numeraire good is often given a name such as "cash," "francs," "talers," experimental currency units (ECUs), or simply points, to distinguish it from the main good(s) or service(s) of interest. Furthermore, the surpluses obtained in trade by buyers (b) and sellers (s), $v_b - P$ and $P - c_s$, respectively, are also typically denominated in units of this numeraire good (that is, linear utility—risk-neutral preferences—is typically assumed). To keep the focus of the analysis on the surplus generated by actual trades and not on endowments of the numeraire good, a standard practice is to provide bidders with a "loan" of amount, L, of the numeraire good that must be repaid at the end of each trading period (or at the end of a market, in dynamic, multi-period trading markets). In practice, this loan amount should be more than enough for each buyer to achieve the equilibrium quantity of trades at the equilibrium market price, meaning that liquidity constraints do not play any role in the outcome. A further standard practice is to convert points/ECUs earned in trade exchanges into money at a fixed and known conversion rate. Alternatively, and more simply, the ECU could be directly expressed in terms of a certain monetary unit.

10.2   Call Markets

A call market is another, simpler means of implementing a double auction market institution which has also attracted considerable attention from experimental researchers. The call market (CM) differs from a continuous double auction (CDA) mechanism in that bids and asks in a call market accumulate anonymously (as in a sealed-bid auction) until a call is made to clear the market. The CM mechanism then clears the market at a single market price. By contrast, in the CDA, market orders are submitted asynchronously and clear at different times over the course of a trading period.

Practically speaking, a CM works as follows. First, buyers and sellers privately submit bids and asks, respectively, along with the number of units they wish to purchase for those bids and asks within some period of time. In doing so, their aim is again to maximize their surpluses from any trades, given their induced values and costs. Once the call is made to clear the market (i.e., the time for submitting bids/asks ends), a computer program sorts the bids from highest to lowest, generating a decreasing left-continuous step function; similarly, all asks are sorted from lowest to highest, generating an increasing left-continuous step function. The intersection of the sorted, downward sloping bid (demand) function with the sorted upward sloping ask (supply) function determines the single market clearing price and quantity traded. All buyers whose bids were strictly above the market clearing price get to buy their units at the market clearing price P, while all sellers whose asks were below the market clearing price get to sell their units at the market clearing price P. That is, unlike a CDA, in a CM there is a single market clearing price. The players who get to trade are often referred to as "infra-marginal" players. By contrast, the "extra-marginal" players, those whose bids (asks) were less (greater) than the single market clearing price, P, do not get to trade. Buyers/sellers at the margin who submit a bid or ask exactly equal to P *may* get to trade depending on whether they are on the short or the long side of the market; if on the short side, they do get to trade, but if on the long side, the determination of who gets to trade at price P is typically random.

Some of the earliest efforts to study the call market mechanism experimentally were undertaken by McCabe *et al.* (1990, 1993). They termed this mechanism the uniform price double auction (UPDA). In their investigations, they explored various aspects of this mechanism, which included considerations such as the trading of multiple units, the choice between open and closed order books, the ability to modify or cancel orders, and the distinction between endogenous and exogenous rules for a market clearing call. They found that, relative to a CDA, the CM generated slower convergence of prices to the competitive equilibrium price (where demand aligns with supply in terms of induced values and costs) and slightly lower but comparable allocative efficiency.

To get a better handle on the price formation process under the CM institution, Cason (1993), Cason and Friedman (1997), and Kagel (2004) have modified the basic setup so that buyers and sellers could only trade a single unit per period and, as in one-sided auction experiments, the induced values and costs are randomly drawn anew and independently each period from known (e.g., uniform) distributions. This approach allows for a single observation of the price determination process each period, as opposed to the extended series of repeated periods with the same induced values. Furthermore, the order book is closed until the market clearing price is determined. These design changes enable testing of a Bayesian Nash equilibrium (BNE) model of the associated pricing game. The results from these experiments yielded mixed outcomes. While the results are closer to the BNE predictions than to the competitive equilibrium, subjects are less efficient and responsive to changes in the pricing rule than the BNE would predict. The efficiency reduction relative to the CDA seems to come from subjects shaving their offers (bids less than valuations and asks above costs) more than they should, so that realized market efficiency falls short of the competitive equilibrium or BNE predictions. Plott and Pogorelskiy (2017) consider multiple unit CMs to increase market thickness, with two calls per period with a continuous and public flow of bid and ask orders. They find that prices, trading volume, and efficiency approach competitive equilibrium levels and are responsive to shifts in market demand and supply.

A clear advantage of the CM mechanism is that it may be easier to explain and implement than a CDA. The user interface only needs to collect a buyer or seller's bids and asks and then report back to them the market clearing price and whether they are able to trade or not. The disadvantage of the mechanism, though, is that information flow is (typically) less continuous and, perhaps as a result of this, subjects engage in too much order shading.

One effort to further simplify the call market mechanism is a version of that mechanism known as a bid-only call market (BOCM) (see, e.g., Duffy *et al.* (2022)). In this variant of the CM there are no asks, only bids. Traders are asked to submit bids for different quantities of units. As in the standard CM mechanism, these bids are made all at once. After all bids have been submitted, they are sorted from highest to lowest and the *median* bid price is determined. Traders whose bids are greater than the median bid are classed as "buyers," while those whose bids are below the median bid are classed as "sellers." The market clearing price is the median bid price and all transactions take place at this market price. Buyers acquire those units for which their bids were strictly greater than the median bid, paid for at the market price per unit. Sellers give up the units for which their bids were strictly below the median bid and receive the market price per unit in exchange. If there are multiple bids exactly at the market (median) price, then bidders may be randomly assigned the role of buyers or sellers for these units. The main advantage of this method is that it condenses the bid/ask elicitation of traders to a single dimension.

10.3   Sunspots and Market Prices

The CM and CDA differ in the amount of information that traders have about prices in real time. To illustrate the implications of these differences, consider the experimental study by Duffy and Fisher (2005) in which they explored the role of extraneous market information for price determination using both the CDA and CM mechanisms. In their study, 10 subjects were divided up equally between buyers (B1, B2, B3, B4, and B5) and sellers (S1, S2, S3, S4, and S5). Each buyer and seller could buy or sell up to two units of a good in each period. Buyers and sellers were informed that there were two possible states of the world, "high" or " low", and they were provided with state-dependent induced values or costs as shown in Figure 10.4. Thus, for example, in the low state of the world, buyer B1's induced value for her first unit on the low demand curve was 140 and her induced value for the second unit was 60. However, in the high state of the world, buyer B1 had the same induced value for the first and second unit on

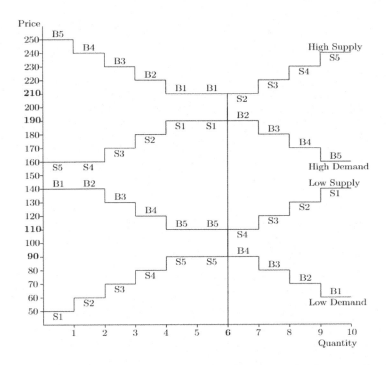

Figure 10.4: Induced high and low demand and supply, buyers: B1–B5, sellers: S1–S5.
Source: Duffy and Fisher (2005). Copyright: American Economic Association; reproduced with the permission of *American Economic Review*.

the high demand curve, namely 210 each. Similarly, in the low state, seller S3's induced cost for the first unit on the low supply curve was 70 and his induced cost for the second unit was 120, but in the high state, seller S3's cost for the first unit on the high supply curve was 170 and his cost for the second unit was 220. For buyer i, the aim was to maximize the surplus on each purchase equal to $v_{ij} - P$, where v_{ij} is the buyer i's valuation of the jth unit, $j = 1, 2$, and P is the price paid. Similarly, for seller i, the aim was to maximize the surplus $P - c_{ij}$, where c_{ij} is the cost to seller i of the jth unit, $j = 1, 2$.

The market mechanism was either a call market or a continuous double auction. In the call market, each buyer submits bids for each of the two units that she can buy, while each seller submits asks for each of the two units he can sell. The bids are then sorted from highest to lowest and the asks are sorted from lowest to highest. The point at which the bid demand schedule intersects the ask supply schedule determines the unique market price for a period. All buyers with bids above this market price get to buy at the market price, while all sellers with asks below the market price get to sell at the market price. By contrast, in the double auction market, buyers and sellers submit up to two bids or asks using an interface such as that shown in Figure 10.3. If a new bid crosses an existing ask or a new ask crosses an existing bid, then trade occurs at the ask or bid price in the order book. This process continues for a matter of minutes (typically 3–5) or until trading activity ceases. Notice that trades may occur at different prices under this institution.

In the study by Duffy and Fisher (2005), in the first three periods of each session, only the high values and costs were in effect, resulting in a unique equilibrium. In both the CM and CDA, subjects quickly coordinated on the high price equilibrium with a price in the range of 190–210 and a quantity bought and sold of 6 units in total. During the next three periods, only the low values and costs were in effect, producing a unique equilibrium yet again. In both the CM and CDA, subjects quickly coordinated on the low price equilibrium with a price in the range of 90–110 and a quantity bought and sold of 6 units in total. Note that the two equilibria are not Pareto rankable; some subjects prefer the high price equilibrium as their surplus is higher in that equilibrium, while other subjects prefer the low price equilibrium for the same reason.

After subjects had gained some experience of both equilibrium possibilities in the first 6 rounds, the subsequent 10 rounds introduced an element of uncertainty regarding the prevailing state of the world—whether it would be characterized by high or low demand and supply. Subjects were informed that the true state of the world would be endogenously determined. The low state, involving low valuations and costs, would prevail if the end-of-period median transaction price in the CDA or the market price in the CM was less than 150; the high state, with its attendant high costs and valuations, would occur otherwise. To help subjects coordinate, the experimenters made some announcements based on coin flips. In one treatment, if the flipped coin landed heads, the announcement made to all was that the "forecast is high," whereas if it landed tails, the announcement made was the "forecast is low." The idea here was to study whether non-fundamental factors (known in economics as "sunspots" or "animal spirits")—in this case, price forecasts that were (clearly) determined by flipping a coin—could play an important role in the economic decisions made by human subjects. In other words, could these forecasts determined by exogenous coin flips have real economic consequences? The main finding is that the exogenous random forecasts played a strong coordinating role under the CM institution, where the forecasts were always followed: if the forecast was high (low), the market clearing price turned out to be high (low). However, in the CDA, this was not often the case. In the CDA, subjects who preferred the high or low state could try to influence the endogenous state of the world by trading in the early minutes of each trading period at high or low prices, which served as a signal to others regarding the likely state of the world. The contrast between the two market institutions is illustrated in Figure 10.5. The figure shows, for the same sequence of coin flips (drawn in advance),

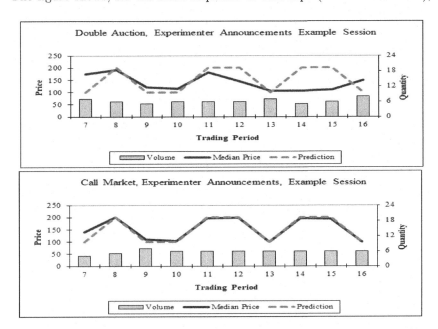

Figure 10.5: Median prices and volume from representative sessions of the CDA and CM market treatments of Duffy and Fisher (2005)

that median prices are at odds with predictions of 100 or 200 (if the coin flip was low or high, respectively) in the CDA treatment but not in the CM treatment. In the CM treatment, there is only one, centralized market price, and it cannot be known until all trading has taken place. Hence, the announced forecasts can play an important coordinating role. By contrast, the CDA is more decentralized, and, as noted, subjects have more opportunity to try to manipulate the price; in the case of multiple equilibria, as studied here, this manipulation affects selection and coordination on a particular market equilibrium high or low.

10.4   Shapley–Shubik Market Game Mechanism

The CDA and CM are the most widely used market institutions in experimental research, but experimenters do use other centralized market mechanisms. One such mechanism that has been used by experimenters is the market game mechanism of Shapley and Shubik (1977). This market mechanism has the advantage of being explicitly game-theoretic in nature, as it respects the finite number of subjects used in experimental social science research. A further advantage is that it is relatively simple to explain to subjects. Using the market game approach, one can implement a equilibrium outcome as a Nash equilibrium.

Specifically, the Shapley–Shubik market game approach assumes that there are n traders and k goods, where the $k + 1^{th}$ good is assumed to be the numeraire good, or money, which is denoted by m. Under this market mechanism, the strategic variables are all expressed in terms of *quantities* of the $k + 1$ goods and not in terms of prices, as in the bids and asks of the CDA and CM market mechanisms.

Each trader i is initially endowed with some bundle of the $k + 1$ goods,

$$e^i = (e_1^i, e_2^i, \ldots, e_k^i, m^i)$$

Furthermore, traders typically have some preference/payoff function over final (post-trade) quantities (x_j) of these goods $u^i = (x_1^i, x_2^i, \ldots, x_k^i, x_{k+1}^i)$ that they are seeking to maximize.

With this objective in mind, each player i decides how many units of good $j = 1, 2, \ldots k$ she wishes to offer for sale and simultaneously how many units of the numeraire good m^i she wishes to give up in order to buy additional units of each of the k goods. These trades are made according to prices that are determined by market-wide demand and supply for each good. These prices are not known in advance.

Specifically, for each of the m goods, there is a "trading post" for that specific good. At the trading post for good j, each player i offers an amount $q_j^i \in [0, e_j^i]$ that she is willing to sell of good j; this amount cannot exceed his endowment. Then, the total amount of good j offered for sale at trading post j is the sum, $\sum_{i=1}^{n} q_j$. Simultaneously, while deciding on their supply, traders are also tasked with deciding how many units of m they are willing to bid in order to acquire more units of good j. This bid is represented by b_j^i and signifies player i's bid of money holdings m^i to acquire further units of good j. If no borrowing is allowed, then it must be the case that

$$\sum_{j=1}^{k} b_j^i \leq m^i$$

for every player i. Moreover, we assume that $b_j^i \geq 0$ for all i and j. Then demand for good j is given by $\sum_{i=1}^{n} b_j^i$.

Finally, the market prices for each good j are determined as follows. The market-clearing price of the jth good:

$$p_j = \frac{\sum_{i=1}^{n} q_j}{\sum_{i=1}^{n} b_j^i},$$

provided that $\sum_{i=1}^{n} b_j^i > 0$. If the latter condition does not hold, then $p_j = 0$. The post-market quantity that player i ends up with of good $j = 1, 2, \ldots, k$ is given by

$$x_j^i = e_j^i - q_j^i + b_j^i / p_j,$$

where b_j^i / p_j are additional units bought of good j. The net amount of money that player i holds post trade is given by the following:

$$x_m^i = m^i + \sum_{j=1}^{k} p_j q_j^i - \sum_{j=1}^{k} b_j^i$$

where $\sum_{j=1}^{k} p_j q_j^i$ represents the money earned from all sales. Note that sales or purchases of goods precede prices under this market mechanism.

The Shapley Shubik quantity-based market mechanism has been used experimentally by Duffy *et al.* (2011), Duffy and Puzzello (2014, 2022), Ding and Puzzello (2020), and Jiang *et al.* (2023), among others.

A general finding from these studies is that prices do eventually converge to Nash equilibrium market game predictions, though they can be quite volatile along the path to convergence. As with the CM, no-trade outcomes seem more common, at least compared with CDA mechanisms and, as a result, market efficiency tends to be lower than in the CDA. Nevertheless, the Shapley–Shubik market game has the same general equilibrium properties associated with the competitive market paradigm while being a full-fledged non-cooperative game with clear predictions as to how the number of players should matter for price determination. Duffy *et al.* (2011) have shown that, as the number of players n increases, the Nash equilibrium of this non-cooperative game approaches the allocations predicted by the Walrasian competitive equilibrium of the associated endowment economy.

10.5   Decentralized Markets

Finally, we discuss several experiments involving decentralized market mechanisms. These take the form of posted offer markets or over-the-counter (OTC) markets and are relatively common in retail and financial markets. These markets differ from the centralized market mechanisms that we have discussed thus far in that they are *decentralized* non-exchange-based markets, where traders must visit a particular market in order to engage in trade in that market. These visits may involve costly search or matching frictions. What is more, these markets do not typically involve any bid/ask improvement rules or the sorting of bids and asks in order to determine market clearing prices. Instead, traders trade in small groups or with a single dealer and not in all-with-all auctions. As Robert Lucas observed (paraphrasing the opening line of Tolstoy's novel *Anna Karenina*), "all centralized markets are the same, but each OTC market is unique in its own way" ((Lucas, 2012, p. 272)).

A posted offer mechanism works as follows. There are n sellers and m buyers. Each seller simultaneously and independently posts a selling price at the start of a trading period. These prices are then displayed to all buyers and sometimes to all sellers and the buyers can then choose to visit sellers to conclude purchases. If a seller sells all her units, she must indicate that such a "stock out" event has occurred. Otherwise, the period continues until no more trades are demanded or a time limit is reached. This type of posted offer market mechanism is common in retail and service markets and has been the subject of some experimental studies (see, e.g., Ketcham *et al.* (1984) and Plott (1986, 1989)).

For instance, Ketcham *et al.* (1984) report on an experiment comparing the posted offer and CDA market institutions. They induce values and costs to buyers and sellers following the induced values approach of Chamberlin–Smith. Sellers first choose a common selling price and then choose the quantity of units they want to sell at that price (under some constraints based on induced marginal costs). After that, buyers are randomly ordered, and one buyer at a time can visit a seller to buy units. Buyers and sellers are prevented from making trades that result in negative surpluses, and buyers cannot buy from sellers who experience a stockout. To make the posted-offer institution more comparable to the CDA, Ketcham *et al.* (1984) allowed all sellers and buyers to see the prices being offered. However, unlike the CDA, in the posted offer market, there is no opportunity for buyers to signal their willingness to pay with a low or high bid.

This difference in signalling opportunities for buyers likely explains the slower convergence of prices to equilibrium predictions and the lower market efficiency observed under the posted price institution relative to the CDA. Indeed, the problem gets worse if there are shifts in demand conditions over time. As Davis and Holt (1996b) document, in cases where demand decreases, sellers in posted-offer markets tend to respond sluggishly to such information. This is primarily because they do not receive signals from buyers' bids that would reveal a reduction in demand, as would occur in a centralized market like the CDA. They show that, by contrast, prices in CDAs do respond to changes in demand or supply conditions much more efficiently.

Another type of decentralized market institution involves costly buyer (or consumer) search. In this setting, sellers, much like in posted-offer markets, present prices for their goods. However, there is a crucial difference: these prices are not made public knowledge. Instead, buyers are tasked with actively searching for sellers, and this search process carries its own costs for buyers. A common challenge associated with markets having such search frictions is known as the Diamond paradox (Diamond, 1971). This posits that in a market for a homogeneous good, if posted price information is not publicly available, and there exist positive search costs for buyers, the unique equilibrium price will be the monopoly price, even if there are many sellers. The paradox is that if search costs are zero, prices should converge to competitive equilibrium levels.

An experimental test of the Diamond paradox was conducted by Davis and Holt (1996a), who compared a posted offer price institution with publicly displayed prices to a search treatment where posted prices were not public. To make the treatments comparable, buyers had to pay a small search cost each time they visited a different seller. The experimental design and mean prices from the two treatments and both treatment orders are shown in Figure 10.6. The experiment involved the use of induced values/costs with the objective of surplus maximization. There were 3 buyers and 3 sellers per session and a clear distinction between the competitive

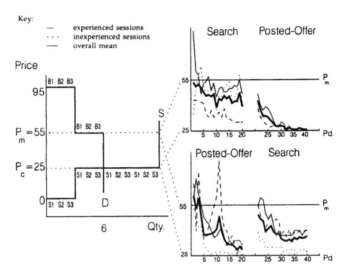

Figure 10.6: Induced values/costs and mean price outcomes in the posted-offer versus search treatments of Davis and Holt (1996a).
Source: Davis and Holt (1996a), copyrighted material used with the permission of John Wiley and Sons.

market price, P_c, where price equals the sellers' marginal cost, and the monopoly price, P_m, where the quantity is the same but the sellers extract all of the surplus. They also employed a within-subjects design where 20 rounds of the search treatment were conducted first, followed by 20 rounds of the posted-offer treatment, after which they considered the reverse order.

As Figure 10.6 reveals, mean traded prices in the search treatment are not equal to the monopoly price, P_m, as predicted by the Diamond paradox. However, they are also generally greater than under the posted-offer institution. Furthermore, the posted-offer market institution generally results in convergence to the competitive market price P_c, albeit slowly as in other posted-offer market experiments. Finally, the treatment order does not significantly affect these findings. The authors conclude that the Diamond paradox is too extreme a prediction; it breaks down because sellers do not fully appreciate their market power in the search treatment setting.

Finally, another notable experiment that investigates the dynamics of posted-offer market institutions explores the impact of matching frictions between buyers and sellers, rather than focusing on search costs. In this experiment, conducted by Cason and Noussair (2007) and based on a model by Burdett *et al.* (2001), sellers have a single unit of a homogeneous good for sale and they simultaneously post price offers. Buyers then observe these prices but have to choose a seller to visit in order to complete a transaction. The matching friction is that if more than one buyer visits a given seller, only one of the buyers gets to purchase the item; buyer must commit to visiting a seller without knowing the decisions of other buyers. Symmetrically, if no buyers visit a seller, that seller does not get to sell her unit even if her posted price was lower than that of other sellers.

In Cason and Noussair's study, all buyers have a valuation $v = 1$ and all sellers have a cost of $c = 0$. Thus, if a trade occurs at a seller's posted price p_s, the buyer gets $1 - p_s$ and the seller gets p_s. If no trade occurs, then both the buyer and seller get 0. The unique subgame perfect Nash equilibrium for the n buyer, m seller setting is that all sellers set the same price and buyers visit each seller with an equal probability $1/m$. Cason and Noussair consider treatments with 2 sellers and 3 buyers and with 3 sellers and 2 buyers, with the price being predicted to be greater in the former case than in the latter. They find that while there is some price dispersion among sellers, median prices are generally consistent with theoretical predictions, higher with 2 sellers than with 3. Buyers do not always exploit price differences among sellers to the extent they should in the 2-seller treatment, where they face some risk of not transacting, but they do respond to such differences in prices in the 3-seller treatment, consistent with equilibrium predictions.

10.6 Summary

In this chapter we have provided a small taste of the many different centralized and decentralized market mechanisms used by experimentalists to determine market prices. We have seen how Chamberlin's imperfect pit market design was transformed by Smith's double-oral auction market mechanism to yield reliable and consistent convergence to competitive equilibrium outcomes despite limited information on the part of any single market participant. A variety of other market mechanisms have been used and studied for their own sake by experimentalists, including centralized mechanisms such as call markets and Shapley–Shubik-type market games, as well as decentralized mechanisms, such as posted-offer markets and search models.

We note that the need for the development and use of such market mechanisms to determine prices in experimental economies is often borne out of the absence of any clear guidance from economic theory as to how

prices are actually determined. Thus, the design and evaluation of centralized and decentralized market institutions has become an important part
of the experimentalists's toolkit, and new innovations in the construction
of such markets continue to be made and evaluated using the experimental
methodology.

In the next chapter we will see how the use of such market mechanisms
has been applied in finance to the study of asset pricing.

Chapter 11

Asset Market Experiments

Financial markets generate volumes of data on the behavior of real financial market participants on a daily basis. Thus, it may seem curious to use experimental methods to address questions in finance. However, using experiments to address questions in finance offers several key advantages. First, experimental methods afford a high degree of control. For instance, using experiments, one can induce subjects' valuations for assets, making it possible to determine the true fundamental value of those assets and to understand whether there are departures of asset prices from those fundamental values. Control also enables the researcher to make causal inferences such as whether changes to fundamental values affect prices. A second reason to conduct experiments in finance is that they help us to better understand the impact of different market institutions on financial participants' behavior. In the field, the institutions have to be taken as given, and so experiments with alternative institutional features can inform policymakers of potential improvements. Finally, experiments in finance provide an important window, at the individual level, into what behaviors might be driving aggregate financial market behavior. In this chapter, we provide a review of some finance experiments, with a particular focus on experimental studies of asset pricing.

An **asset** is a resource with some economic value that an individual, corporation, or government owns or controls, with the expectation that the asset will provide some future flow of benefits, e.g., a stock provides dividends; a bond provides interest payments; a house provides housing services or rental income. Assets are often traded between buyers and sellers using some centralized market mechanism, which will be our focus, though there are also decentralized financial markets such as over-the-counter markets as well.

11.1 Informational Efficiency of Asset Prices

According to the efficient markets hypothesis (EMH), asset markets are informationally efficient. This means that it is not possible for investors to purchase undervalued assets or sell assets at inflated prices. Some of the earliest work in experimental finance explored whether in fact asset prices are informationally efficient in line with the EMH.

Informational efficiency means that all relevant information is properly incorporated into asset prices. If everyone has the same information, then there is no reason to trade, but if there is heterogeneity/asymmetry in information, then this can provide a motivation for trade and the trades themselves reveal information. Accordingly, prices will adjust as the information diffuses (see, e.g., Grossman and Stiglitz (1980), Shiller (1981)).

As a representative example of experiments exploring the informational efficiency of asset prices, consider the study of Plott and Sunder (1982). Their design uses what is known as the "Arrow–Debreu" approach to induce different valuations for shares of the single asset across subjects.[1] In this approach, subjects are assigned to one of several types. There are also two states of the world, X and Y, which are ex-ante equally likely. Payoffs (dividends) from holding shares of the asset differ across the three player types in the different states. This heterogeneity in valuations provides a reduced-form rationale for trade in the asset. Plott and Sunder's induced valuations are shown in Table 11.1.

Table 11.1: Types and asset valuations in the experimental design of Plott and Sunder (1982).

Player type	Dividend Value in	
[Number]	State X	State Y
I [4]	400	100
II [4]	300	150
III [4]	125	175

---

[1]This approach is based on Arrow and Debreu's concept of generalizing commodities so that they have different values in different states of the world. A standard "Arrow–Debreu security" is one that pays off 1 unit of some numeraire good if a particular state of the world is reached and yields zero otherwise.

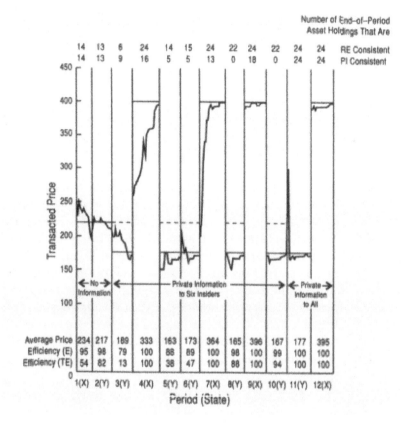

Figure 11.1: Experimental market prices in Plott and Sunder (1982).
Source: Plott and Sunder (1982). Copyright: University of Chicago Press;
reprinted with permission.

The experiment involves 12 subjects playing the role of traders. Each
trader—type I, II, and III—is endowed with two asset shares. Initially,
no subjects are informed about the state of the world. Then, half of the
traders (6/12), or two of each type, are privately informed of the state of
the world, X/Y, while the others are not. Finally, all traders are informed
about the state of the world. Trading of asset shares was implemented via a
continuous double auction (CDA) with each trading period lasting several
minutes.

As shown in Figure 11.1, in the first two periods when there is no information about the state, prices are close to the rational expectation prediction. In periods 3-8, while only half the subjects are informed about
the true state of the world, trading information reveals this information

quickly. Prices converge rapidly to 400 in state X and to 175 in state Y, which represent the maximum valuation for the asset across the three trading types. This is clear evidence in support of the informational efficiency of asset prices. There is also considerable allocative efficiency as well (the right traders are buyers and sellers of the asset).

11.2   Asset Price Bubbles

After the efficient markets hypothesis gained considerable momentum (and garnered a certain amount of experimental support as well), attention turned to understanding potential departures, particularly the phenomenon of asset price bubbles and crashes. An asset price bubble is notoriously difficult to define. It is a seemingly irrational, sustained departure of asset prices from the fundamental valuations of those same assets. Shiller (2000) defines a speculative bubble as "a situation in which temporarily high prices are sustained largely by investors' enthusiasm rather than by consistent estimation of real value." While bubbles are typically viewed as unsustainable, examples of stationary bubbles do exist. For instance, Tirole (1985) makes the case that government-issued fiat money provides such an example of a sustained bubbly asset.

The idea that asset price bubbles are inherently irrational has been a subject of intense scrutiny and debate, as it poses a challenge to the efficient markets hypothesis. While there exist theories of "rational" bubbles, it is important to note that these rational bubbles are quite fragile and cannot generally exist in finite horizon economies (Tirole (1982), Diba and Grossman (1988)). By contrast, there is considerable evidence from finite-horizon experimental markets that asset prices can depart from fundamentals in sustained and systemic ways. These "non-rational" bubble experiments have led to a new *experimental finance* literature that challenges the conventional rational choice approach to asset pricing.

The canonical experimental asset pricing environment that reliably generates asset price bubbles and crashes, at least among inexperienced subjects, was proposed by Smith *et al.* (1988). They employ a *finite-horizon* economy, meaning that they rule out any *rational bubbles*.

Specifically, in the Smith *et al.* (1988) design, there are T (typically 15) trading periods and 9–12 subjects. Subjects are initially endowed with different amounts of cash and assets. The assets generate a common-to-all dividend realization in each of T periods and then cease to exist. Endowments in terms of asset shares and cash are all ex-ante identical in expected value, so, unlike in the Arrow–Debreu induced-value approach, there is no reason for trade in the asset; if there are trades, they should all occur at the fundamental value.

In each trading period, agents are free to buy or sell the asset. Trade takes place through a continuous double auction, and bids and asks must obey standard improvement rules. For each unit of the asset held at the end of a trading period, the asset owner earns a dividend payment that is a uniform random draw from a known distribution with mean $\overline{d}$. It is public knowledge that the fundamental value (FV) of an asset at the start of period t with a horizon of T periods is given by the following:

$$FV_t^T = \overline{d}(T - t + 1) + R_{T+1}$$

where R_{T+1} is the final redemption or continuation value of the asset paid out after the completion of the final round, T. Figure 11.2 shows a representative session of the SSW experiment, where the FV of the asset in the first period is $3.60 per share and this value decrements each period t by the mean dividend amount $\overline{d} = \$0.24$, while the redemption value R_{16} in this case is set to 0. In the figure, we can clearly observe a pattern in which the mean traded asset prices, represented by the connected line, initially start below the fundamental value. They then rapidly increase and soar above the fundamental value during periods 3–8. However, as trade volume diminishes, the prices gradually decline and eventually fall below the fundamental values in the final periods. This pattern of a bubble followed by a crash, as observed in the SSW experimental design, has been replicated numerous times using inexperienced subjects. Interestingly, though, groups of subjects who have experienced this bubble crash phenomenon are less likely to repeat such behavior in further replications of the 15-round market.

Smith *et al.* (1988) analyze a price adjustment dynamic of the form:

$$\overline{P}_t - \overline{P}_{t-1} = \alpha + \beta(B_t - O_t)$$

where $\overline{P}_t$ is the mean traded price in period t, B_t is the number of bids in period t, and O_t is the number of asks in period t. The rational, efficient markets hypothesis is that $\alpha = -\overline{d}$ and $\beta = 0$, i.e., that subjects are trading according to fundamentals. Empirically, Smith *et al.* report that they cannot reject the hypothesis that $\alpha = -\overline{d}$ but they do find that β is

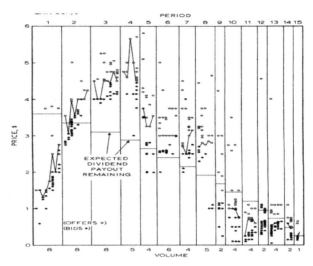

Figure 11.2: Asset price bubble and crash using the SSW design.
Source: Smith et al. (1988), copyrighted material used with the permission
of John Wiley and Sons.

significantly positive: variations in $B_t - O_t$ reflecting variations in aggregate
demand or supply for the asset (or order book imbalances) also affect asset
prices. SSW conclude that a common dividend and common knowledge
of that dividend are insufficient to generate common expectations among
inexperienced subjects.

The bubble-crash phenomenon using the SSW design attracted much
attention, with many studies focused on changes that might eliminate the
phenomenon among inexperienced subjects or further our understanding
of what is going on. For instance, Noussair et al. (2001) and Holt et al.
(2017) consider the case where there is a constant fundamental value for the
asset, which might be easier for subjects to price relative to an asset with
a downward sloping fundamental value as in SSW. Holt et al. pay interest
on cash holdings at the rate i and set $R_{T+1} > 0$. In such a case, $FV_1 =$
$\frac{E[d]}{1+i} + \frac{E[d]}{(1+i)^2} + \cdots + \frac{E[d]}{(1+i)^{T-1}} + \frac{E[d]}{(1+i)^T} + \frac{R}{(1+i)^T}$. Setting the redemption value,
R, of the asset in period $T + 1$ to $R = E[d]/i$, i.e., the present value of an
asset paying $E[d]$ in perpetuity, the asset has a constant $FV_t = R = E[d]/i$
for all t. Nevertheless, this change to a constant FV does not eliminate
asset price bubbles among inexperienced subjects; rather, prices continue
to exhibit the bubble crash pattern among inexperienced subjects. It is
also worth noting that there are several alternative experimental designs

and approaches that have replicated the bubble-crash pattern observed in the SSW experiments.

For instance, Lei *et al.* (2001) address the possibility that agents are subject to the "greater fool hypothesis": that investors buy assets at inflated prices with the expectation that they will be able to sell those same assets later at an even higher price to "a greater fool" than themselves. They also study the possibility that asset price bubbles are caused by subject boredom. To address the greater fool hypothesis, they eliminate speculative activity by restricting players to being either buyers or sellers of the asset but not both (i.e., resale is not possible.) Then, to address the boredom hypothesis, they allow subjects to participate in two markets—the asset pricing market and a less exciting, repeated static commodity market. Ultimately, they find that bubbles and crashes in the asset market continues to arise in both of these treatments.

Dufwenberg *et al.* (2005) mix in experienced traders with inexperienced traders, and report that bubble-crash pricing patterns are much less prominent in groups with as few as $1/3$ experienced subjects.

Haruvy *et al.* (2007) elicit long-term forecasts for prices, and find that subjects' beliefs about prices mirror actual traded prices—that is, subjects expect the price to rise over time. Furthermore, the act of eliciting beliefs does not eliminate bubbles, though beliefs gradually adjust in line with experience of the bubble-crash pattern.

Hussam *et al.* (2008) note that bubbles are a recurrent phenomenon. They employ an experimental design in which they re-shuffle experienced subjects together with changes to endowments and dividend payoffs in order to "rekindle" the bubble-crash pattern even among experienced subjects.

Kirchler *et al.* (2012) point out that in the SSW design, dividend payments accrue to each trader's cash balance, so that over time there is more cash in the economy while the number of assets available for trade does not change. Taking this into account, it may not be so surprising that the prices of assets rise over time. The solution they propose is to put the dividend payments that subjects earn into a *separate account* that cannot be used for trade but which is still paid out to subjects at the end of the experiment. In this manner, the cash-to-asset ratio C/A is kept constant. In a 2×2 design, they consider asset prices when the C/A ratio is increasing or constant and when the FV is decreasing or constant. The mean price outcomes from various sessions of the four cells of their experiment are illustrated in Figure 11.3. As is clear, there is no bubble-crash pattern when the C/A ratios is held constant along with the FV of the asset as in their Treatment 4.

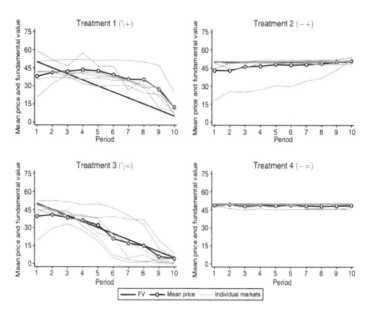

Figure 11.3: Mean asset price path relative to fundamental value from Kirchler *et al.* (2012). Top-left is the treatment with downward-sloping FV and increasing C/A ratio (SSW design); top-right is constant FV and increasing C/A ratio; bottom-left is decreasing FV and constant C/A ratio; and bottom-right is constant FV and constant C/A ratio.
Source: Kirchler *et al.* (2012). Copyright: American Economic Association; reproduced with the permission of *American Economic Review*.

Akiyama *et al.* (2017) study environments where a single subject trades against robot traders programmed to make asset trades in line with the asset's FV in each period of the SSW experimental design. Their aim is to assess the role of confusion versus strategic uncertainty regarding what other subjects will do. The robot trading environment isolates the role of confusion, and the difference between the robot trader and the standard all-human subject trader environment provides a measure of the role of strategic uncertainty. They elicit price forecasts as in Haruvy *et al.* (2007) and report that strategic uncertainty accounts for around 50% of the median initial forecast deviation from the fundamental value; the remaining 50% is due to confusion.

Bosch-Rosa *et al.* (2018) show that the magnitude and incidence of bubble formation is correlated with cognitive ability measures. Specifically, they use cognitive reflection test (CRT) scores from subjects to find that groups with lower mean CRT scores are more likely to exhibit the bubble-crash patter in SSW asset market experiments. When they sort subjects according to CRT scores, they find no bubbles in groups of subjects with high CRT scores and bubbles in groups of subjects with low CRT scores.

Weitzel *et al.* (2020) and Cipriani *et al.* (2020) study how real financial professionals behave in SSW-type asset markets. They consider environments with constant or increasing C/A ratios. A general finding is that financial professionals are less likely to mis-price the asset than are student subjects. Still, students and professionals have similar CRT scores, which suggests again that experience is an important determinant of whether bubbles and crashes arise in SSW-type laboratory asset markets.

Finally, Duffy *et al.* (2023) study an *indefinite horizon* version of the SSW model. In this version, the asset pays a constant dividend per period of d. The asset continues to yield dividends and be tradeable from one period to the next with a constant probability δ; with probability $1 - \delta$, the asset ceases to exist/pay dividends. Thus, the FV of the asset at any date t is as follows:

$$FV_t = d + \delta d + \delta^2 d + \cdots = \frac{d}{1 - \delta}.$$

In this case, the experimental finding from sessions with subjects who trade the asset in a continuous double auction is that the asset is *under*-priced relative to the constant fundamental value of the indefinite horizon—that is, there is a *negative* bubble, as illustrated in Figure 11.4. One possible explanation for this finding is that subjects have to be paid a risk premium for holding the risky asset, and this risk premium takes the form of a traded price that is below the fundamental value.

11.3 Learning-to-Forecast Experiments

An alternative approach to asset pricing experiments is to focus on the role that *expectations* of future prices plays in determining current period asset prices. This "learning to forecast" approach involves no trade in the asset at all. Specifically, suppose the supply of assets is exogenously fixed and that traders have mean-variance preferences. Suppose further that investors are risk-neutral and can invest in either a long-lived risky asset by paying an expected dividend next period of d_{t+1} and having a future price of p_{t+1} or a safe asset with a fixed and known one period rate of return $R = 1 + r$

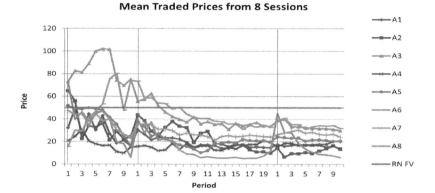

Figure 11.4: Mean asset prices in 8 sessions of an indefinite horizon asset pricing experiment. Here, $d = 5$, $\delta = 0.9$, and so the FV is 50. There are 3 indefinite horizon markets; the starting period of each is indicated by the vertical line.
Source: Duffy *et al.* (2023), reproduced with permission of the authors.

(e.g., a one-period bond). Through arbitrage, we can determine that the rate of return on the risky asset should be as follows:

$$R_{t+1} = \frac{E_t \left[p_{t+1} + d_{t+1} \right]}{p_t} = 1 + r$$

where p_t is the time t price of the risky asset. Rewriting this expression, we get

$$p_t = \frac{E_t p_{t+1} + d_{t+1}}{1 + r}.$$

In the first learning-to-forecast asset pricing experiment, Hommes *et al.* (2005) fixed the dividend amount on the risky asset to be a constant d for all periods. Furthermore, in place of $E_t p_{t+1}$, they elicited the forecasts of 6 subjects, using time t information, as to what those subjects thought the next period's price, p_{t+1}, would be. Thus, in place of $E_t p_{t+1}$ they used the average forecast of these 6 subjects, $\frac{1}{6} \sum_{i=1}^{6} p_{i,t+1}^e$, where $p_{i,t+1}^e$ is subject i's expected value for p_{t+1}. Note that since these expectations determine p_t, the information available to subjects at date t does not include p_t but does include all previous prices, $p_1, p_2 \cdots p_{t-1}$, each of which are shown on subjects' decision screens. Thus, the actual price p_t is determined by

$$p_t = \frac{1}{1 + r} \left(\frac{1}{6} \sum_{i=1}^{6} p_{i,t+1}^e + \overline{d} + \epsilon_t \right),$$

where ϵ_t is a mean zero-noise term. Payoffs to each individual subject i are a decreasing function of their own forecast errors alone $(p^e_{i,t+1} - p_{t+1})$ and are not realized until the next period $t + 1$. Note the self-referential nature of this system; if agents expect higher future prices, then current prices will increase, whereas if agents expect lower future prices, this too will have a self-fulfilling effect. The rational expectation prediction is $p^{RE}_t = d/r$ (ignoring a possible rational bubble term, which is ruled out by a finite guessing interval for the price forecast of [0,100]). However, the RE prediction requires that all agents coordinate their expectation on this fundamental value.

The experiment is repeated for 50 periods, typically with a constant dividend of $d = 3$ and with $r = .05$, so that the FV of the asset is 60. For 3 groups, the dividend was lowered to $d = 2$, with no other changes so that the FV of the asset was 40. Note that the choice of $r = 0.05$ means that the coefficient multiplying the expectations term is 20/21, which is close to being a unit root; the unit root case would be unlikely to be stable under adaptive learning dynamics, making this an extreme test of whether agents can learn the REE. The results from 10 different groups of this learning-to-forecast asset pricing experiment, each with 6 subjects, are shown in Figure 11.5.

As Figure 11.5 reveals, there is either monotonic or oscillatory convergence/divergence to the REE, $p^{RE} = d/r + \epsilon_t/r$. A further finding is that there is excess volatility relative to exogenous noise term ϵ, which is very small; this finding is also consistent with the excess volatility found in actual asset prices. In some treatments, the researchers add a certain fraction of robot fundamentalist traders who always forecast p^{RE}. The presence of these fundamentalist traders works to further stabilize prices. Still, it is apparent from Figure 11.5 that asset prices in this expectations-based approach to understanding pricing can also exhibit bubbles, crashes, and volatility.

11.4 Consumption-Based Asset Pricing Models

As discussed in Section 11.1, employing the Arrow–Debreu framework to generate varying asset values for different traders across various states of the world results in efficient pricing of such assets over time (after a few periods when agents accumulate experience). By contrast, in the SSW design, there

214 Lecture Notes in Experimental Economics

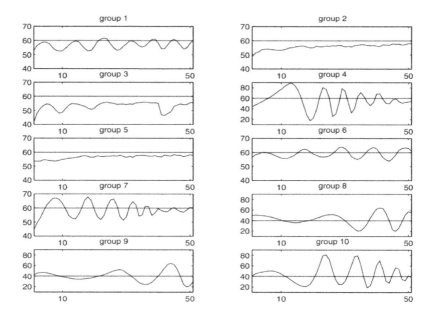

Figure 11.5: Asset prices in the learning-to-forecast experiment of Hommes *et al.* (2005). Mean prices in each of 50 periods relative to the FV of 60 or 40.
Source: Hommes *et al.* (2005), copyrighted material used with the permission of Oxford University Press.

is no real reason to trade assets because all agents have the same initial endowments in expected terms and the dividend realization is common to all. Nevertheless, agents do engage in trade, leading to mispricing of assets for an extended period, although this tends to diminish with experience.

An important difference between the two approaches is the presence or absence of a motivation to trade the asset. The Arrow–Debreu framework introduces a motivation for trading, but it lacks a comprehensive explanation for why different agents would have different valuations for the asset in different states or moments in time. When considering the motivations behind asset trading, one potentially vital incentive for buying and selling assets is the need to intertemporally smooth consumption in the face of potential income fluctuations, either in the short term or over the lifecycle. While a person's income can be highly variable, long-lived assets provide a means of saving to smooth out fluctuations in income, thereby facilitating consumption smoothing as well. The idea that agents use assets to intertemporally smooth their consumption is known as the consumption-based asset pricing approach, and this model is a workhorse of modern macro-finance models starting with Lucas Jr. (1978) and Breeden (1979). Several experimental tests of this model have been performed by Asparouhova *et al.* (2016), Crockett *et al.* (2019), and Carbone *et al.* (2021). Here we report on the research design and results of the study by Crockett *et al.* (2019).

In the experiment, agents are of two types $i = 1, 2$, which distinguishes their variable income amount of a perishable good called "francs" in each period. These agents can save by investing in a long-lived asset that pays a common dividend d, also measured in francs. Any francs not used to buy assets are considered "consumed", meaning they are converted into dollar earnings via the induced utility function and then cease to exist. The conventional model is an infinite horizon model, but in the experiment this is translated into an indefinite horizon model with a constant probability of continuing a sequence of trading periods (where the asset retains its value).

Subjects are induced to maximize a utility function (the franc-to-dollar exchange rate), which is either concave or linear. In the concave utility case, there is an induced smoothing incentive for asset trade; the concave utility function implies diminishing marginal utility, where each additional unit of consumption provides less additional satisfaction. Agents facing variable income and who seek to maximize their overall well-being will want to distribute their consumption more evenly over time. However, if the induced utility function is linear, then there is no induced incentive for an agent facing income variability to want to consumption smooth or to use asset trades for that purpose, as in the SSW approach.

In the theory, the representative agent of type i seeks to maximize:

$$\max_{\{c_t^i\}_{t=1}^{\infty}} E_1 \sum_{t=1}^{\infty} \beta^{t-1} u^i(c_t^i),$$

subject to

$$c_t^i = y_t^i + ds_t^i - p_t \left(s_{t+1}^i - s_t^i\right), \quad y_t^i + ds_t^i - p_t(s_{t+1}^i - s_t^i) \geq 0, \quad s_t^i \geq 0.$$

where c_t^i denotes' player i's consumption at time t, y_t^i denotes i's time t, s_t^i is i's time t shareholding position, and p_t is the time t price paid for shares. Shares yield a common dividend of d francs, which is distributed to all shareholders, assuming that the asset economy continues, a scenario that occurs with probability β (representing the discount factor). In the alternative scenario, which occurs with a probability of $1 - \beta$, the economy comes to an end and all shares are rendered worthless. As in other asset market experiments, no borrowing is allowed in this context.

The first-order condition for each time period $t \geq 1$, suppressing agent superscripts for notational convenience is as follows:

$$p_t = \beta E_t \left[\frac{u'(c_{t+1})}{u'(c_t)} (p_{t+1} + d) \right].$$

The steady-state equilibrium price is $p^* = \frac{\beta}{1-\beta} d$, which is the same for both the concave and linear treatments. One aim of the experiment is to determine, given knowledge of β and d alone, whether the steady-state price prediction of the theory is achieved and whether agents use the asset to intertemporally smooth their consumption.

To address the latter question, subjects are divided into two types: even and odd. Even types have a high income in even-numbered periods and a low income in odd-numbered periods, while odd types have a high income in odd-numbered periods and a low income in even-numbered periods. This two-cycle process for income y_t^i is known to all. Given this process and an induced consumption smoothing motivation (a concave utility function), even type agents should buy the asset in even-numbered periods and sell the asset in odd-numbered periods, while odd type agents should do the opposite. Furthermore, the prices at which these exchanges take place should be equal to p^*. By contrast, if the induced utility function is linear, there is no reason to buy or sell the asset to smooth consumption.

The experimental design was 2×2: the treatment variables are the common dividend value, $d = 2$ or $d = 3$, which affects p^* and the induced utility function, which was either concave or linear. Trading was implemented via a continuous double auction (CDA) with each trading period lasting 3 minutes. Then subjects rolled a die to determine whether the experiment would continue with another period. The experiment involved multiple indefinite sequences—that is, when a sequence ended, a new sequence would begin, depending on the time available.

The experimental results, depicting deviations of median traded prices from steady-state equilibrium predictions are shown in Figure 11.6. The figure reveals that in the induced concave utility treatment, observed

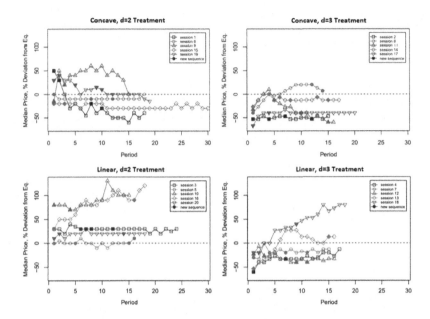

Figure 11.6: Deviations of median traded prices from p^*. Top panels: Concave treatments with $d = 2, 3$; Bottom panels Linear treatments with $d = 2, 3$. A solid dot indicates the first period of a new indefinite horizon. *Source*: Crockett *et al.* (2019), copyrighted material used with the permission of Oxford University Press.

transaction prices by the end of the session are generally less than or equal to p^* (represented in the figure by a deviation of 0) while in the induced linear utility treatment, transaction prices toward the end of the treatment are generally greater than or equal to p^*.

An additional finding is that in the concave utility treatments there is strong evidence that subjects are using the asset to intertemporally smooth their consumption across periods. By contrast, in the linear treatments there is significantly less consumption smoothing, with some subjects immediately selling their assets, while others hoard the asset and accumulate large shareholdings. Overall, the evidence suggests that a consumption smoothing motivation for asset trades may help agents to better price indefinitely lived assets—or at least avoid overpricing them—as the asset serves as a means to the end of consumption smoothing.

11.5   Asset Market Experiments with Multiple Assets

Thus far, we have considered asset pricing experiments where agents trade in markets for a *single* dividend-paying asset. Of course, in actual financial markets, many different types of dividend-bearing assets are traded simultaneously by many traders who may be more concerned about the portfolio of the assets that they hold.

Fisher and Kelly (2000) study an asset market with *two* SSW-type assets that can be traded simultaneously with the aim of studying cross-asset arbitrage and foreign exchange markets. Their assets markets all have both a *red* asset and a *blue* asset, whose dividends are either perfectly positively correlated with one another or are independently drawn from a known distribution of possible values. The market mechanism is a continuous double auction. Each session is composed of 15 six-minute trading rounds. While there were six treatments conducted overall, we focus here on just three of these. In the first treatment, the dividend support for both assets was equiprobable and independently distributed. In the second treatment, dividends for both assets were positively correlated, but the dividend value for the blue asset was twice that of the red asset. The third treatment had the same structure as the second, except that dividends were independently distributed. All subjects started with different amounts of assets and cash, but these endowments were equivalent in expected value. Fisher and Kelly find bubbles in both assets, but show that there are only small deviations in relative pricing between the red and blue assets in all of their treatments, which suggests that subjects do trade to eliminate arbitrage opportunities.

Similarly, Charness and Neugebauer (2019) use a two-asset market experiment to empirically evaluate the Modigliani–Miller theorem, which states that, independent of its debt structure, the market value of a firm equals the present value of its future earnings and its underlying assets. They use a continuous double auction asset market with two SSW-type assets to study the pricing of shares issued by two identical firms that have different debt structures (leveraged and unleveraged firms). In their experiment, asset returns of the two firms are either perfectly positively correlated or independently drawn.

Charness and Neugebauer (2019) report a significantly higher price discrepancy when asset dividends are independently drawn relative to the case where there is perfect correlation in asset returns. They conclude that for the value indifference prediction of the Modigliani–Miller theorem to hold, perfect correlation may be essential.

Finally, we note that there is experimental research using a multi-asset framework to study the *disposition effect*, which is investors' tendency to sell assets that have gained value (winners) and hold on to assets that have lost value (losers) (see Shefrin and Statman (1985)). While there is considerable field evidence documenting the disposition effect (see Odean (1998)), a laboratory setting offers better control in determining which stocks are true winners to be retained and which are losers to be sold.

Consider, for instance, the experimental study by Weber and Camerer (1998). In this study, subjects had the opportunity to buy and/or sell six risky assets whose prices were determined by a random process, rather than being endogenously determined by the trading actions of all subjects as in the other asset market experiments discussed in this chapter. Specifically, the six assets had different and independent chances of rising or falling over the 14 trading rounds of an experimental session. While subjects knew the probability of all six assets rising and/or falling, they did not know which share, labeled A–F, had which particular probability of rising or falling. A Bayesian subject would update the probabilities for each share's likelihood of rising or falling based on the history of past prices. Thus, with this design, winner and loser stock shares can be carefully identified. Shares with the highest (lowest) historical price rises were most likely to have the highest (lowest) probability of continuing to rise (fall), indicating that these assets should not be (should be) sold. Subjects were endowed with a large amount of cash and could buy or sell shares of each of the 6 assets in the 14 periods of the experiment. The main finding from this experiment is that subjects sell fewer shares when the share price is falling as compared with when the share price is rising. They also use the purchase price as a reference point, selling fewer shares when the price is below the purchase price as compared to when the price is above the purchase price.

11.6 Summary

In this chapter, we have discussed just some of the asset pricing questions that experimental methods can address. While there exists considerable field data on asset prices, the additional control provided by experimental methods enables additional insights into asset prices and trading behavior. For instance, in the laboratory, the fundamental value of an asset can be perfectly determined; this information is not always available in the field. Having said this, experimental evidence suggests that even if the fundamental value of an asset is perfectly known (and reported) to subjects (truly ideal conditions), it is possible for there to be mispricing of that asset, though such mispricing does tend to diminish or even disappear with experience. The apparent complexity of asset pricing has caused some researchers to considerably simplify the setting or to focus on the forecasting problem alone, while other researchers have sought to focus greater attention on the usefulness of assets as a means of smoothing consumption over time to enable better pricing behavior.

There are many avenues for future research in this area, including the relaxation of borrowing constraints, short-selling constraints and other limits to arbitrage. There is also a need for research on derivative assets such as options, futures, and swaps that derive their value from an underlying asset. Testing the pricing of such complex assets would require further developments in multi-asset market experiments, which are of interest in their own right. In multi-asset market experiments, disparities in the pricing of different assets and the profit opportunities these disparities entail may be more readily observed by subjects and acted upon accordingly.

Chapter 12

Macroeconomic Experiments

Thus far, we have primarily considered experiments that have addressed topics with a *microeconomic* flavor or focus, e.g., game theory experiments, public economic experiments, and auction experiments. In this chapter, we consider some experiments designed to test questions of relevance to *macroeconomists*. Of course, one might immediately object and argue that it is not possible to conduct experiments that would be of relevance to the large-scale aggregate outcome variables that macroeconomists study, as one would need impossibly high numbers of subjects to generate any relevant data. However it is possible to evaluate the micro-foundational assumptions that macroeconomists use (e.g., intertemporal optimization) and rational expectations for their empirical relevance. If these micro-foundational assumptions do not hold, then one may question the predictions of macroeconomic models that build upon these assumptions. Moreover, many macroeconomic phenomenon are modelled as *games*, such as bank runs and other coordination problems and these are settings that *can* be effectively tested in the laboratory. Indeed, a common issue in macroeconomic modeling is that there are often multiple equilibrium outcomes. An understanding of which of these equilibrium outcomes is the most empirically relevant one is a task that well-designed experiments can often address. Finally, experimental methods are increasingly being used to understand private sector reactions to various macroeconomic policies, in particular to *monetary policies*. Instead of conducting experiments on the entire macroeconomy, policymakers can test and analyze reactions to new policies or tools on a much smaller scale in laboratories first, before implementing such policy changes in the field. This approach has been likened to wind-tunnel testing of jet engines or the creation of architectural models for buildings before implementation, as it enables a better understanding of effective policies.[1]

12.1   Intertemporal Optimization

Households and firms in modern macroeconomic models are typically modelled as inter-temporal optimizers. For instance, households are often modelled as making consumption and savings decisions over their lifecycle taking into account lifecycle earnings and how their savings decisions will contribute to their future wealth. In a full-blown macroeconomic model, interest on savings, prices for consumption goods, and wages for labor income would all be endogenously determined as part of a dynamic general equilibrium model. By contrast, laboratory studies have focused on subjects' ability to inter-temporally optimize in a *partial equilibrium* framework where prices, interest rates, and wage income are exogenously given. While this is a simpler problem, it is still of interest to understand whether and how subjects behave relative to the full rational actor, intertemporal optimization approach; if subjects cannot intertemporally smooth consumption in a partial equilibrium setup, they may have even more trouble in the full-blown general equilibrium environment.

Specifically, consider the following finite T period horizon intertemporal optimization problem of a representative household:

$$\max_{\{c_{i,t},a_{i,t+1}\}_{t=1}^T} \sum_{t=1}^T u(c_{i,t})$$

subject to:

$$c_{i,t} + \frac{a_{i,t+1}}{1+r} = \underbrace{e_{i,t} + a_{i,t}}_{\text{cash on hand}} , \tag{12.1}$$

where a "no borrowing" constraint, $a_{i,t+1} \geq 0$, is typically imposed along with the assumption that initial wealth, $a_{i,1} = 0$. Here, u is a concave utility function, $c_{i,t}$ is household i's time t, consumption choice, $a_{i,t+1}$ is their time t augmentation (savings) to cash on hand (or wealth), $e_{i,t} + a_{i,t}$ and β is the period discount factor. In this setting, everything is in real

---

[1]For a longer introduction to macroeconomic experiments, the reader is referred to Duffy (2016) and Duffy (2022). This chapter draws upon material from those two sources.

terms (there are no prices) and r is the exogenous real interest rate earned on savings. With full knowledge of endowment income over the lifecycle $\{e_{i,t}\}_{t=1}^{T}$, this problem is solvable: one combines $T-1$ Euler equations of the form,

$$u'(c_t) = \beta(1+r)E_t u'(c_{t+1}),$$

together with the budget constraint (12.1) and the fact that $a_{T+1} = 0$ to obtain a sequence of consumption amounts, $\{c_{i,t}\}_{t=1}^{T}$ for household i. The concave utility function implies that inter-temporal consumption smoothing is desirable, with most experiments focusing on subjects' ability to achieve this goal.

Versions of this intertemporal optimization task have been studied in a number of different laboratory experiments (see, e.g., Hey and Dardanoni (1988), Anderhub *et al.* (2000), Carbone and Hey (2004), Ballinger *et al.* (2003), Ballinger *et al.* (2011), Carbone (2006), Brown *et al.* (2009), Carbone and Duffy (2014), Meissner (2016), and Duffy and Li (2019)).

These versions have involved either stochastic or known deterministic processes for income, $\{y_t\}$, and have typically involved an induced concave utility function, u, to map consumption choices to the monetary payoffs made to subjects. Discounting is not usually considered (i.e., $\beta = 1$) due to the short time horizons of most experiments. However, in the infinite horizon case, where $T \to \infty$, the discount factor represents the constant probability that a sequence of consumption decisions continues from one round to the next. In finite settings, T is typically set to many periods, e.g., 20–30, so as to simulate a lifecycle setting, with each period representing some length of time, e.g., 1–2 years.

For example, Duffy and Li (2019) consider the case where $T = 25$ and u is an induced logarithmic function. They further varied the endowment profile over the lifecycle. In one of the profiles studied, shown in Figure 12.1, endowment income is constant for the first 17 periods and then drops in period 18, thereby simulating retirement (here, each period reflects 2.3 years). Relative to the optimal consumption path (or even the conditionally optimal consumption path), mean subject behavior exhibits a consistent pattern of over-consumption in the first 17 working periods, resulting in lower accumulation of wealth. As a consequence, there is under-consumption relative to the optimal path in the retirement phase of life. The over- and under-consumption relative to the optimal path is shown in the right panel of Figure 12.1. This pattern has been replicated in other experiments as well Several explanations have been proposed to account

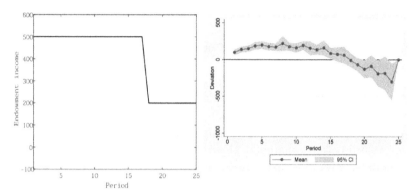

Figure 12.1: Lifecycle endowment profile (left panel) and mean deviation from optimal consumption path (right panel).
Source: Duffy and Li (2019), copyrighted material used with the permission of Elsevier.

for the phenomenon of over-consumption in youth and under-consumption in old age. One explanation posits that this pattern is a result of type heterogeneity. Following Campbell and Mankiw (1989), some agents are "hand to mouth" consumers, consuming their endowments in every period, while others are more rational, consuming less than their endowments and accumulating savings for their retirement periods. Indeed, Duffy and Li (2019) find in lab experiments that there is a mix of hand-to-mouth and conditionally optimal subject types and they propose a rational inattention model to explain this. Another explanation is that subjects employ shorter-than-optimal planning horizons when making consumption/savings decisions, e.g., Carbone and Hey (2004) find that consumption choices are excessively sensitive to current income and Carbone (2006) estimates that subjects' planning horizons are much shorter than the $T-t$ periods remaining as of period t. A further bias that has been uncovered is "exponential growth bias." Levy and Tasoff (2016) present experimental evidence for this bias, which involves individuals failing to account for the compounding of interest income over time and instead using a linear model. This misjudgment leads to a reduction in the present value of future wealth and results in subjects wanting to save less. Finally, in experiments where subjects are allowed to borrow and not just save, Meissner (2016) provides experimental evidence that laboratory subjects are *debt-averse*. He considers two main treatments. In one, income is stochastically trending upward over the lifecycle, while in another, income is stochastically trending downward over the lifecycle. In the former case, subjects should borrow when young in order to intertemporally smooth their lifecycle consumption, while in the latter case, they should save when young because income in later periods will be lower. While subjects have comparatively little trouble saving when that is the optimal policy, they seem quite averse to borrowing in the setting where they should do so; instead, they primarily consume their income in that setting. These are just some examples of the many interesting anomalies and explanations for the heterogeneity that we observe in intertemporal consumption decision-making experiments.

12.2 Rational Expectations

A second important building block in modern macroeconomic models is the notion that agents have *rational expectations* with regard to realizations of future endogenous variables. Under the rational expectations hypothesis (REH), subjects use correctly specified models and all available information to make such forecasts; thus, they do not succumb to making systematic forecast errors. Given these expectations, subjects then make optimal intertemporal decisions. However, if the expectations are not rational, then the model predictions may not be valid. As expectations play such a crucial role in macroeconomic models and since expectations data is generally not available, experimental evidence has been brought to bear on the question of how agents form expectations and assess the reasonableness of the REH.

One approach to testing the REH is to have subjects forecast exogenous time series variables, either taken from the historical record (e.g., Schmalensee (1976) and Bernasconi *et al.* (2009)) or generated by a computer program (e.g., Dwyer Jr. *et al.* (1993) and Beshears *et al.* (2013)). Subjects in these experiments are incentivized to minimize their forecast error relative to the actual data they are asked to forecast. The evidence from these experimental studies is mixed. For instance, Dwyer Jr. *et al.* (1993) report that subjects have no difficulty learning to forecast a variable following a random walk, e.g.,

$$y_t = y_{t-1} + \epsilon_t,$$

where $\epsilon \sim (N, \sigma^2)$. Stock prices and other financial market data often follow random walk processes that can appear to generate various patterns. However, the forecast consistent with the REH in the random walk case is naïve expectations, which may come rather naturally to many subjects. In more complicated settings, subjects have more difficulty forecasting in a manner that is consistent with the REH. For instance, Beshears *et al.* (2013)

generate more general, autoregressive integrated moving average (ARIMA) time series processes that exhibit short-run momentum and long-run mean reversion, which refers to the tendency of a variable to move back toward its historical average or mean over time following a deviation. Such dynamic properties are often found in the time series data of important macroeconomic variables like GDP and unemployment. In Beshears *et al.*'s "fast" ARIMA(0,1,10) treatment, the dynamics resolve in response to a shock within 10 periods, while in their "slow" ARIMA(0,1,50) treatment, the dynamics are not fully resolved until 50 periods. In their experiment, Beshears *et al.* find that most subjects forecasts in the fast treatment are well approximated by the ARIMA(0,1,10) model consistent with the REH and with only a small minority following an ARIMA(0,1,0) or random walk model. By contrast, in the slow treatment, only 6% of subjects' forecasts are well approximated by the ARIMA(0,1,50) model (the RE prediction) while 29% of subjects' forecasts are well approximated by the simpler ARIMA(0,1,0) model, reflecting naïve and irrational expectations.

These exogenous time series forecasting experiments abstract from the *self-referential* nature of rational expectations models. In such models, forecasts matter for optimal choices which affect the realizations of the outcome variables subjects are trying to forecast. Those realizations, in turn, affect future forecasts, so that there is *belief-outcome interaction*. This belief-outcome interaction is well captured by learning-to-forecast experiments (discussed briefly in the previous chapter), which were first introduced by Marimon and Sunder (1994, 1995). This experimental design uses a self-referential forecasting model but removes the need for subjects to solve any optimization problems, given their forecasts. Instead, subjects simply concentrate on the forecasting problem. There are many such learning-to-forecast experiments including those of Hommes *et al.* (2005, 2008).

As an example, consider the following first-order dynamic stochastic self-referential system for determination of the price level, p_t

$$p_t = \mu + \alpha E_t[p_{t+1}] + \epsilon_t,$$

where $\mu > 0$, $\alpha < 1$ are known constants and ϵ_t is a mean zero error term. This type of forward-looking expectational difference equation lies at the heart of many macroeconomic models, though it may involve many more variables or the inflation *rate* rather than the price *level*.[2] If, as under the REH, agents *know* the model (and they are given this information in the

---

[2]It is also clearly related to the beauty contest game of Nagel (1995).

experiment), then they should be able to immediately solve for the rational expectations equilibrium value:

$$p_t^{RE} = \frac{\mu}{1 - \alpha} \text{ for all } t.$$

Bao and Duffy (2016) use the simple model described above and elicit subject forecasts, $E_t p_{t+1}$ given full knowledge of the model. In one "monopoly" treatment they elicit individual price forecasts and in another "oligopoly treatment" they use the average forecast of N subjects, so that $E_t[p_{t+1}] = N^{-1} \sum_{i=1}^{N} E_{i,t}[p_{t+1}]$. In the latter case, subjects are paid based on the accuracy of their own forecast, but must consider how the forecasts made by others will affect the average forecast. These forecasts were elicited over the course of 50 periods, and the mean number of periods it took to reach the REE prediction, P_t^{RE}, was recorded. Figure 12.2 shows CDFs of these convergence times for various values of α, the coefficient on $E_t[p_{t+1}]$ and for the monopoly (left panel) versus the oligopoly (right panel) treatments.

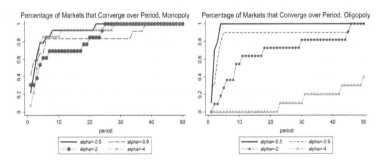

Figure 12.2: Percentage of markets converging to rational expectations predictions. Monopoly treatment (left) and Oligopoly treatment (right). *Source*: Bao and Duffy (2016), copyrighted material used with the permission of Elsevier.

We observe that individuals and groups require time to grasp the concept of REE and that the duration of this learning process depends on the model's parameters and whether it involves a single representative agent or multiple heterogeneous agents. For some values of α, full convergence to the REE does not occur within the experiment's allotted 50 periods. We may conclude that bounded rationality and/or *strategic uncertainty* regarding the forecasts of others may play important roles in the process by which agents form rational expectations in self-referential models.

It is natural to ask how to best characterize bounded rationality in forecasting behavior. While many approaches have been suggested, the consensus view seems to be that no single model of boundedly rational forecasting
will suffice. Instead, what seems necessary is to allow for *heterogeneity* in
boundedly rational forecasting rules. For instance, Anufriev and Hommes
(2012) posit that agents consider several different *heuristic rules-of-thumb*
and switch among these based on the relative performance of each rule over
time. The specific rules they find to be a best fit to the learning-to-forecast
experimental data of Hommes *et al.* (2005, 2008) are as follows:

Adaptive rules	$E_t[p_{t+1}] = \lambda p_{t-1} + (1 - \lambda)E_{t-1}[p_t],$
Trend-following rules	$E_t[p_{t+1}] = p_{t-1} + \gamma(p_{t-1} - p_{t-2}),$
Anchor and Adjust type rules	$E_t[p_{t+1}] = \phi\left(p_{t-1}^{avg} + p_{t-1}\right) + (p_{t-1} - p_{t-2})$

Subjects are found to switch between such rules over the periods in which
they participate in learning-to-forecast experiments; sometimes one rule
comes to dominate while, in other cases, there remain a substantial portion
of subjects using different types of rules. Economists have only just begun
the process of understanding the various ways in which agents may depart
from REH in making forecasts, meaning that, as yet, there is no consensus
on the most reasonable approach to use.

12.3 Inflation in an Overlapping Generations Economy

Macroeconomic models are complex, dynamical systems that frequently
give rise to a multiplicity of equilibria, the so-called indeterminacy problem.
The experimental method enables an empirical approach to resolving such
equilibrium selection problems. As Robert Lucas noted (Lucas (1986)), no
amount of theorizing helps to resolve the question of which equilibrium path
subjects will coordinate upon. There is simply no substitute for putting
people in the situation of interest, incentivizing them to behave as in the
model, and observing which equilibria or equilibrium is the most empirically
relevant.

The equilibrium selection problem that Lucas was referring to concerned the path of inflation in the overlapping generations model of money
(Samuelson (1958)). In this context, when applying perfect foresight and
rational expectations dynamics, there are a multiplicity of paths for inflation, where, depending on the monetary policy that is in place, the limiting

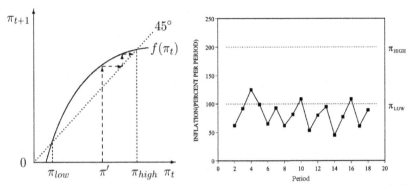

Figure 12.3: Inflation dynamics in the overlapping generations model (left) and inflation (right) from a representative session of Marimon and Sunder (1993).

Source: Marimon and Sunder (1993), copyrighted material used with the permission of John Wiley and Sons.

rational expectations outcome is either a hyperinflation or a stationary but high inflation rate, with the latter case illustrated in the left panel of Figure 12.3. In this figure, the dynamics of the perfect foresight model are governed by an equation of the form $\pi_{t+1} = f(\pi_t)$, where π_t denotes inflation at time t. Note that there are two steady-state inflation rates (where the dynamical system intersects the 45-degree line). However, unless the economy starts at the low inflation steady state, π_{low}, that low inflation steady state will be *unstable*; for an arbitrary initial inflation rate such as π', the inflationary dynamics converge to the high inflation steady state π_{high}. By contrast, under adaptive learning dynamics, as Lucas pointed out, the low inflation steady state is the predicted outcome. This is because adaptive, backward-looking behavior for inflation (e.g., $\pi_t = g(\pi_{t-1})$ effectively flips the perfect foresight dynamics as depicted in Figure 12.3 over the 45-degree line, making the low inflation steady state the attractor under those non-RE adaptive dynamics. Lucas thought the question of equilibrium selection would make for an interesting experiment and Marimon and Sunder (1993, 1994, 1995) undertook the challenge to observe how people behave in such a setting.

The environment is complicated to study experimentally, as subjects live for two periods, young and old, and at any moment in time, there is a mix of both young and old agents in the population. Still, the economy endures for far more than 2 periods, as it is an infinite horizon model. Marimon and

Sunder solved these problems by allowing subjects to be reborn after cycling through a two-period lifetime. The infinite horizon was implemented using the random termination procedure.

In this experiment. young agents are endowed with an amount of goods (chips) that yields them utility if consumed. However, they have little or no endowment of chips in old age and the induced concave utility function defined over both periods of life can only be maximized if they intertemporally smooth their consumption. The old hold the entire stock of fiat money, which is a token object with no utility redemption value. The old can utilize the "social contrivance" of fiat money to buy goods from the young. The government (the experimenter) also purchases a known and fixed amount of goods (chips) each period, which it finances by printing some more fiat money.

Subjects can smooth consumption over both periods by selling some of their chip endowment when young to "old subjects" in exchange for fiat money. Then, when the young agents become old, they can use their holding of the fiat money object to buy goods from the next young generation. In practice, the young agents provided a supply schedule, indicating their reservation price for quantities of chips traded. An aggregate supply schedule is then created. As the old simply give up all their money holdings inelastically so as to acquire chips at the market price, a market clearing price is easily determined.[3] Once the market clearing price is determined, the young sell the quantity defined by their supply schedule and both the young and old realize their utility payoff for the round. The young age a period and the old die and the economy continues, unless the random draw indicates otherwise. The inflation rate π_t is the ratio of market prices in adjacent periods, i.e., p_t/p_{t-1}.

Marimon and Sunder find that, by contrast, with the predicted rational expectations path for inflation, in all of their experimental sessions inflation always lies in a neighborhood of the *low* inflation steady state, π_{low} and *not* the high steady state, π_{high}. The right panel of Figure 12.3 provides a representative example of the actual inflation path from one of Marimon and Sunder's experimental sessions. This is an effective illustration of the use of the experimental method to resolve questions of equilibrium selection

---

[3]In a later "learning to forecast" design (Marimon and Sunder (1994, 1995), the authors elicited subjects' inflation forecasts and the computer program used that forecast to determine the optimal quantity of chips that each young agent should sell for fiat money. Then market clearing happens as in the Marimon and Sunder (1993) study.

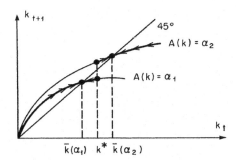

Figure 12.4: Multiple equilibrium possibilities in the poverty trap model of Azariadis and Drazen (1990).
Source: Azariadis and Drazen (1990), copyrighted material used with the permission of Oxford University Press.

and it further validates the use of adaptive learning models for making such predictions.

12.4 Poverty Traps

A second type of macroeconomic coordination problem that has been studied experimentally comes from the literature on economic development. The poverty trap model, developed by Azariadis and Drazen (1990), seeks to explain how some economies may get stuck in a low-level equilibrium of poverty, while others manage to break out and achieve sustained economic growth. This scenario can be generated by a simple model with a non-convexity in production, as shown in Figure 12.4

For low levels of the capital stock k, the economy produces output according to the production function with the lower scale factor, α_1. For higher levels of the capital stock, those above k^*, the economy produces output according to the production function with the higher scale factor, α_2. A key aspect of the poverty trap model is the idea of multiple equilibria. As shown in Figure 12.4, depending on initial conditions and savings behavior, there are two steady-state levels for the capital stock. For example, an economy with a high savings rate and high levels of investment may grow rapidly and achieve the high steady-state capital stock $\bar{k}(\alpha_2)$ and its associated higher income level. An economy with a low savings rate and low levels of investment may be stuck in a poverty trap equilibrium with a low steady-state level for the capital stock $\bar{k}(\alpha_1)$. The poverty trap outcome results from a vicious cycle of low investment, low productivity, low wages, and thus low savings.

In an experiment, Lei and Noussair (2007) have subjects start in an economy where the aggregate capital stock lies below or above k^*. In their decentralized treatment, groups of 5 subjects begin by transforming their share of the aggregate capital stock into output according to the relevant production technology. These agents are then able to engage in the trading of output for a numeraire good in the goods market. Subsequently, they are required to make decisions regarding the allocation of their output between consumption and savings, with the saved portion designated as the capital input for the following period. Lei and Noussair also considered a social planner treatment, where subjects make a collective consumption-savings decision, i.e., playing the role of a social planner. The main experimental finding is that the poverty-trap equilibrium is frequently the final outcome from repeated play. In the decentralized treatment, it is the outcome in all sessions where the initial aggregate capital stock is below k^* as well as in some sessions where the initial aggregate capital stock lies above k^*. There are some instances of convergence to the high steady-state equilibrium, $\bar{k}_h$, but only in the decentralized setting where the initial capital stock lies above k^*. In the social planner treatment, neither of the two stationary equilibria were ever achieved; instead there was either convergence to a capital stock close to the threshold level k^*, or to the "golden rule" level of the capital stock that maximizes consumption. Lei and Noussair (2007) conclude that additional institutional features might be needed to help subjects in these economies escape from the poverty trap.

The idea that institutions could play a role was taken up in a follow-up experimental study by Capra *et al.* (2009). They point out that experimental tests of the efficacy of exogenously induced institutions avoid endogeneity issues that are encountered in field data studies on the role of institutions for economic growth. The institutions they study are (1) free-form communication among subjects prior to each round of decisions, which they term "freedom of expression"; (2) "democratic voting" in which subjects vote on proposals for how to divide up consumption and savings (future capital) at the end of each period; and (3) a hybrid institution combining both communication and voting.

The baseline treatment is similar to the low initial capital stock treatment of Lei and Noussair (2007), where five subjects begin with capital stocks that aggregate up to a level below k^*. The main findings are revealed in Figure 12.5. In the baseline treatment, most economies (groups of 5

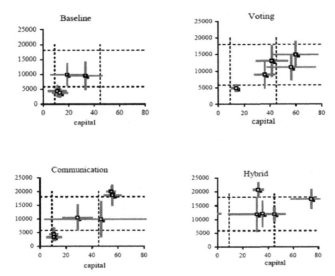

Figure 12.5: Mean aggregate welfare (vertical axis) and capital (horizontal axis) for each session (squares) of the four treatments of Capra *et al.* (2009). Line segments report 95% confidence intervals. The poverty trap equilibrium is the lower-left intersection of the two dashed lines and the efficient equilibrium is the upper-right intersection of the two dashed lines. *Source*: Capra *et al.* (2009), copyrighted material used with the permission of John Wiley and Sons.

subjects) are in a neighborhood of the poverty trap equilibrium outcome. Communication or voting helps some but not all economies to escape this outcome. A hybrid of both communication and voting leads to the highest average capital stocks and welfare. While this is a very stylized setting, it nicely illustrates how one can use experimental methods to address questions of economic development and the role of institutions.

12.5 Bank Runs

Another example of a macroeconomic coordination problem is the bank run model of Nobel laureates Diamond and Dybvig (1983). These authors model a bank run as an equilibrium possibility in a simultaneous-move coordination game involving two types of depositors: impatient types, who have immediate liquidity needs, and patient types, who are willing to keep their funds deposited in the bank for a longer period of time. Initially, all customers deposit funds with a bank, and only later do they learn their true type. The bank uses these deposits to make illiquid loans that take time to pay off. The bank provides its depositors with a risk-sharing deposit contract that allows depositors to share in the returns to intermediation, but which also allows them to withdraw funds early if they learn that they are an impatient type. The model has an efficient, separating equilibrium where only the impatient depositors withdraw early and the patient wait to withdraw their deposits and share in the larger returns from doing so, but there is also a pooling equilibrium where the patient depositors join the impatient depositors in withdrawing early, which is the bank run outcome.

The experimental literature extensively explores the bank run coordination model of Diamond and Dybvig (1983) as an n-player game (see Kiss *et al.* (2022) for a survey). As the interesting strategic players are the *patient types* who can either wait or withdraw early, most bank run experiments ignore or automate the impatient types and study only the patient player types. For example, Arifovic *et al.* (2013) focus on the behavior of 10 such patient players. They vary payments to early withdrawals in a way that affects the amount of coordination necessary for agents who choose to wait to receive a higher payoff than those who choose to withdraw early. This coordination parameter η varies from 0.10 to 0.90, where in the first case just 1 out of 10 depositors need to wait in order for those who wait to earn a higher return, whereas in the latter case 9 out of 10 must keep their deposits in the bank (wait) in order to earn a higher return from waiting. Subjects experienced multiple periods of 7 different values for η. As Figure 12.6 reveals for a representative session, when $\eta \leq 0.50$, the number choosing to wait was high and there were no bank runs. When $\eta \geq 0.80$, the run equilibrium where no one waits to withdraw is common. In the intermediate region where $0.50 < \eta < 0.80$, both run and no-run outcomes are observed.

The bank runs documented by Arifovic *et al.* do not arise from any fundamental problems with the bank; they are due to the fragility of the coordination problem alone. Other researchers have studied the role of *fundamental factors* for the incidence of bank runs and also considered the case where agents make decisions sequentially as opposed to simultaneously. For instance, Schotter and Yorulmazer (2009) consider groups of 6 subjects who have deposits in 1 of 5 possible banks that differ in the quality of their investments and thus in their susceptibility to bank runs (premature withdrawals). In a symmetric information treatment, no depositor knows the type of the bank. In an asymmetric information treatment, 1/3 of

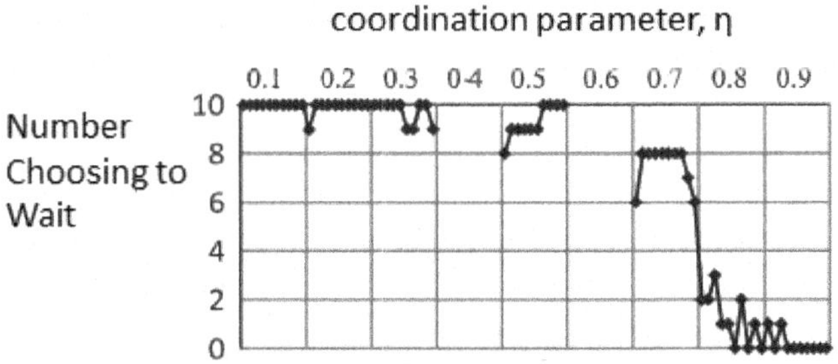

coordination parameter, η

Figure 12.6: Equilibrium selection as a function of the coordination parameter η in a representative session of the bank run experiment of Arifovic *et al.* (2013).
Source: Arifovic *et al.* (2013), copyrighted material used with the permission of Elsevier.

depositors are insiders and know the type of the bank, while others do not. A third treatment variable was whether depositors can observe the withdrawal decisions of other depositors over the four periods for which they make withdrawal decisions. Finally, they considered treatments with the addition of partial (50 and 20%) deposit insurance to assess whether that affected subjects' early withdrawal decisions.

Schotter and Yorulmazer report that when the bank's fundamentals are strong (weak), early withdrawals are less (greater). Interestingly, in the case of good fundamentals, the presence of insiders is found to enhance welfare as subjects tend to withdraw later in that case relative to the case of no insiders. Finally, they report that partial deposit insurance is effective in reducing the frequency of early withdrawals.

Other researchers have also explored the role of deposit insurance (Madies (2006), Kiss *et al.* (2012)) as well as other policy interventions to mitigate bank runs including suspension of convertibility (Madies (2006)), the renegotiation of contract considerations Davis and Reilly (2016)), and liquidity regulations designed to ensure that banks have sufficient funds on hand to meet liquidity needs in a crisis (Davis *et al.* (2020)).

12.6 Monetary Policies

The Banks of England, Japan, the European Central Bank, and the U.S. Federal Reserve have all experimented with approaches to monetary policy over time, from control of monetary aggregates, to interest rate targeting, inflation targeting, quantitative easing, and forward guidance, among other policies. Evaluation of the effects of different monetary policies is typically done using dynamic stochastic general equilibrium (DSGE) models instead of natural or laboratory experiments. The idea is that, as in natural or laboratory experiments, micro-founded models provide greater control over causal mechanisms that are at work in the real world. However, this greater control requires that the model micro-structure and assumptions are valid. A complementary approach is to conduct monetary policy experiments in laboratory settings that are simplified versions of complex DSGE models.

Consider, as an example, the Friedman Rule (Friedman (1969)), which specifies that the optimal monetary policy is to set the nominal interest rate to 0, ensuring that the opportunity costs of holding money are equal to the social costs of creating money. Duffy and Puzzello (2022) implement the Friedman rule within a micro-founded economy with money, as initially proposed by Lagos and Wright (2005). In this experiment, participants engage in pairwise interactions and negotiate trades involving goods and money. In one treatment, the experimenters acting as the central bank gradually decrease the money supply in the economy at a rate equivalent to the induced rate of time preference, denoted as ρ. If we define the nominal interest rate as $i = \pi + \rho$, where π represents inflation, then in accordance with Friedman's recommendation to achieve $i = 0$, inflation must be set to $\pi = -\rho$. This specific inflation rate corresponds to the pace at which the money supply is reduced in the experiment. Duffy and Puzzello compare the Friedman Rule with a constant money supply regime as well as with a regime where the money supply grows at a constant positive rate $k = \rho$ over time. Their main finding is that the Friedman rule is no better in welfare terms than the constant money supply regime and that both of those regimes are dominated in welfare terms by the constant, inflationary k-percent money growth rule. One reason for this is that inflation helps to stimulate economic exchange; in the deflationary regime of the Friedman rule, some subjects tend to hoard money, which is appreciating in value, and this behavior reduces economic activity.

A more modern approach to monetary policy involves the management of short-term interest rates. According to the famous rule of Taylor (1993), nominal interest rates should adjust to deviations of inflation π_t and possibly the output gap y_t from the central bank's target values π^* and y^*. That is, the central bank should adjust interest rates as follows:

$$i_t = \alpha_\pi(\pi_t - \pi^*) + \alpha_y(y_t - y^*),$$

where α_π and α_π reflect the weights given to the two types of deviations. Experimental tests of this model typically employ New Keynesian DSGE models where expectations of future values of inflation π_t and the output gap y_t matter for the realizations of these variables. See, e.g., Pfajfar and Žakelj (2018), Cornand and M'baye (2018), Assenza *et al.* (2021), and Mokhtarzadeh and Petersen (2021), among others. Subjects in these experiments simply forecast inflation and/or the output gap as in learning-to-forecast experiments. The accuracy of their forecasts is the key determinant of their payoffs. These forecasts are subsequently integrated into the underlying New Keynesian model to generate real-world outcomes for variables like actual inflation and the output gap.

One policy question that has been studied using this framework relates to the weights α_π, α_y that central banks should use in the Taylor interest rate policy rule in order to stabilize expectations regarding inflation and the output gap. For instance, the Taylor policy is that α_π should be greater than 1; that is, interest rates should respond more than proportionally to deviations of inflation from target levels. Similarly, an inflation targeting policy would set $\alpha_y = 0$ and focus on the achievement of the inflation target, π_t^*. Assenza *et al.* (2021) set $\alpha_y = 0$, and the target levels $\pi^* = 2$ and $y^* = 0$. They then consider four treatments, T1–T4, where they set α_π from 1.0 to 1.005, to 1.015, and finally to 1.5, with the latter three treatments being consistent with the Taylor principle. For each regime, they elicit subjects' forecasts for inflation and the output gap and feed those through a New Keynesian model under different weights for the policy rule. As shown in Figure 12.7, they find that the weight α_π matters for the stabilization of both inflation and the output gap. Low weights that are consistent with the Taylor principle may not suffice; what is needed are sufficiently large policy weights as in their treatment with $\alpha_\pi = 1.5$; interestingly, this value happens to be the weight that Taylor (1993) himself proposed.

Kostyshyna *et al.* (2022) have used experimental learning-to-forecast experiments in combination with the New Keynesian DSGE model to evaluate a wider variety of different monetary policy rules for setting interest rates. The set of rules includes an inflation targeting regime, a dual mandate (where some weight is given to the output gap), an average inflation targeting rule (where 4- and 10-period horizons are considered), and both price-level and nominal-GDP-level targeting rules. Contrary to theoretical predictions based on rational expectations, the study found that rate-targeting regimes, such as those targeting inflation or the output gap, outperformed level-targeting regimes, including price-level or nominal GDP targeting. The reason is that many subjects employ trend-extrapolation

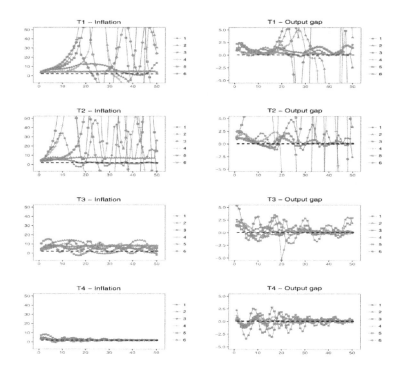

Figure 12.7: Dynamics of inflation (left) and the output gap (right) over time from six sessions each of four treatments varying α_{pi} as conducted by Assenza *et al.* (2021). Across all treatments, the inflation target is 2% and the output gap target is 0.
Source: Assenza *et al.* (2021), copyrighted material used with the permission of Elsevier.

heuristics as their forecast rules. Given the use of such rules, rate targeting rules such as inflation targeting, provide a better means of controlling expectations than do more history dependent, level-targeting regimes. This insight is an important example of how experimental methods can be a useful tool for central bank policy-making.

Finally, what can be said about the external validity of these monetary policy experiments? How useful are expectations data collected in laboratory settings for evaluating the effectiveness of monetary policies? Cornand and Hubert (2020) take a first step toward answering this question. They compare the inflationary expectations data gathered in laboratory experiments of the type discussed above with the inflationary expectations of households, firms, professional forecasters, and central bankers taken from surveys. They consider both the frequency of forecast revisions and the extent of disagreement among forecasters in the experimental data with the same metrics using data on inflationary expectations from the field. They report that in terms of revisions and disagreement, the laboratory subjects' expectations are more in line with the behavior of professional forecasters or policymakers and less similar to those of firms or households. This seems to be an artefact of the incentivized nature of experimental forecasts. Still, it is reassuring to note that there is some relationship between experimental inflationary expectations and inflationary expectations found in field data, among professionals. While experiments testing monetary policies are still in their infancy, further research along these dimensions seems promising and certainly provides a less costly way of evaluating changes in monetary policies than experiments in the field.

12.7 Summary

Macroeconomics is the study of the overall economy, focusing on how consumption, investment, and government spending choices and government policies affect aggregate activity. While it is not possible (nor ethical) to perform aggregate experiments designed to evaluate macroeconomic theories or policies, as discussed in this chapter, it *is* possible to evaluate the empirical relevance of the micro-foundational assumptions that macroeconomists use, e.g., intertemporal optimization and rational expectations. Furthermore, as we have seen, there are some important questions of equilibrium selection and coordination that experimental evidence can be used to address. For instance, whether subjects prefer to coordinate on low or high inflation steady states, or the determinants of bank runs, or the factors that may enable economies to escape from poverty traps. Finally, experimental evidence has been used to evaluate the efficacy of various monetary policies without the need to actually implement these policies in the field. Future research in this area will undoubtedly leverage technological advances in experimenting with larger, more representative subject samples in order to provide even clearer predictions regarding the impact of government policies on macroeconomic activity.

References

AHN, T.-K., R. M. ISAAC, AND T. C. SALMON (2008): "Endogenous group formation," *Journal of Public Economic Theory*, 10, 171–194.

AKERLOF, G. A. (1970): "The market for 'lemons': Quality uncertainty and the market mechanism," *Quarterly Journal of Economics*, 84, 488–500.

AKERLOF, G. A. AND R. E. KRANTON (2000): "Economics and identity," *Quarterly Journal of Economics*, 115, 715–753.

AKIYAMA, E., N. HANAKI, AND R. ISHIKAWA (2017): "It is not just confusion! Strategic uncertainty in an experimental asset market," *Economic Journal*, 127, F563–F580.

ALIPRANTIS, C., G. CAMERA, AND D. PUZZELLO (2007): "Bilateral matching with Latin squares," *Journal of Mathematical Economics*, 43, 99–114.

ALLINGHAM, M. G. AND A. SANDMO (1972): "Income tax evasion: A theoretical analysis," *Journal of Public Economics*, 1, 323–338.

ALM, J., K. M. BLOOMQUIST, AND M. MCKEE (2015): "On the external validity of laboratory tax compliance experiments," *Economic Inquiry*, 53, 1170–1186.

ALM, J. AND A. MALÉZIEUX (2021): "40 years of tax evasion games: a meta-analysis," *Experimental Economics*, 24, 699–750.

ALM, J., G. H. MCCLELLAND, AND W. D. SCHULZE (1992): "Why do people pay taxes?" *Journal of Public Economics*, 48, 21–38.

AMBRUS, A. AND P. A. PATHAK (2011): "Cooperation over finite horizons: A theory and experiments," *Journal of Public Economics*, 95, 500–512.

ANDERHUB, V., W. GÄUTH, W. MÄULLER, AND M. STROBEL (2000): "An experimental analysis of intertemporal allocation behavior," *Experimental Economics*, 3, 137–152.

ANDERSEN, S., S. ERTAÇ, U. GNEEZY, M. HOFFMAN, AND J. A. LIST (2011): "Stakes matter in ultimatum games," *American Economic Review*, 101, 3427–3439.

ANDERSEN, S., G. W. HARRISON, M. I. LAU, AND E. E. RUTSTRÖM (2008): "Eliciting risk and time preferences," *Econometrica*, 76, 583–618.

ANDREONI, J. (1995): "Cooperation in Public-Goods Experiments: Kindness or Confusion?" *American Economic Review*, 85, 891–904.

ANDREONI, J. AND B. D. BERNHEIM (2009): "Social image and the 50–50 norm: A theoretical and experimental analysis of audience effects," *Econometrica*, 77, 1607–1636.

ANDREONI, J. AND R. CROSON (2008): "Partners versus strangers: Random rematching in public goods experiments," in *Handbook of Experimental Economics Results Volume 1*, ed. by C. R. Plott and V. Smith, Elsevier, 776–783.

ANDREONI, J. AND C. SPRENGER (2012): "Estimating time preferences from convex budgets," *American Economic Review*, 102, 3333–3356.

ANGRIST, J. D. AND J.-S. PISCHKE (2008): *Mostly Harmless Econometrics: An Empiricist's Companion*, Princeton University Press.

ANUFRIEV, M., J. DUFFY, AND V. PANCHENKO (2022): "Learning in two-dimensional beauty contest games: Theory and experimental evidence," *Journal of Economic Theory*, 201, 105417.

ANUFRIEV, M. AND C. HOMMES (2012): "Evolutionary selection of individual expectations and aggregate outcomes in asset pricing experiments," *American Economic Journal: Microeconomics*, 4, 35–64.

ARECHAR, A. A., S. GÄCHTER, AND L. MOLLEMAN (2018): "Conducting interactive experiments online," *Experimental Economics*, 21, 99–131.

ARIFOVIC, J., J. H. JIANG, AND Y. XU (2013): "Experimental evidence of bank runs as pure coordination failures," *Journal of Economic Dynamics and Control*, 37, 2446–2465.

ARMANTIER, O. AND N. TREICH (2013): "Eliciting beliefs: Proper scoring rules, incentives, stakes and hedging," *European Economic Review*, 62, 17–40.

ASPAROUHOVA, E., P. BOSSAERTS, N. ROY, AND W. ZAME (2016): ""Lucas" in the Laboratory," *Journal of Finance*, 71, 2727–2780.

ASSENZA, T., P. HEEMEIJER, C. H. HOMMES, AND D. MASSARO (2021): "Managing self-organization of expectations through monetary policy: a macro experiment," *Journal of Monetary Economics*, 117, 170–186.

AXELROD, R. (1984): *The Evolution of Cooperation*, New York: Basic Books.

AZARIADIS, C. AND A. DRAZEN (1990): "Threshold externalities in economic development," *Quarterly Journal of Economics*, 105, 501–526.

AZRIELI, Y., C. P. CHAMBERS, AND P. J. HEALY (2018): "Incentives in experiments: A theoretical analysis," *Journal of Political Economy*, 126, 1472–1503.

BALLINGER, T. P., E. HUDSON, L. KARKOVIATA, AND N. T. WILCOX (2011): "Saving behavior and cognitive abilities," *Experimental Economics*, 14, 349–374.

BALLINGER, T. P., M. G. PALUMBO, AND N. T. WILCOX (2003): "Precautionary saving and social learning across generations: an experiment," *Economic Journal*, 113, 920–947.

BAO, T. AND J. DUFFY (2016): "Adaptive versus eductive learning: Theory and evidence," *European Economic Review*, 83, 64–89.

BAO, T., E. NEKRASOVA, T. NEUGEBAUER, AND Y. E. RIYANTO (2022): "Algorithmic trading in experimental markets with human traders: A literature survey," in *Handbook of Experimental Finance*, ed. by F. Sasha and E. Haruvy, Edward Elgar Publishing, 302–322.

BARDSLEY, N. (2008): "Dictator game giving: altruism or artefact?" *Experimental Economics*, 11, 122–133.

BARDSLEY, N., R. CUBITT, G. LOOMES, P. MOFFATT, C. STARMER, AND R. SUGDEN (2010): *Experimental Economics: Rethinking the Rules*, Princeton University Press.

BARTLETT, E. E. (2008): "International analysis of institutional review boards registered with the US Office for Human Research Protections," *Journal of Empirical Research on Human Research Ethics*, 3, 49–56.

BATTALIO, R., L. SAMUELSON, AND J. VAN HUYCK (2001): "Optimization incentives and coordination failure in laboratory stag hunt games," *Econometrica*, 69, 749–764.

BAYE, M. R., D. KOVENOCK, AND C. G. DE VRIES (1996): "The all-pay auction with complete information," *Economic Theory*, 8, 291–305.

BAZERMAN, M. H. AND W. F. SAMUELSON (1983): "I won the auction but don't want the prize," *Journal of Conflict Resolution*, 27, 618–634.

BECKER, G. M., M. H. DEGROOT, AND J. MARSCHAK (1964): "Measuring utility by a single-response sequential method," *Behavioral Science*, 9, 226–232.

BELOT, M., R. DUCH, AND L. MILLER (2015): "A comprehensive comparison of students and non-students in classic experimental games," *Journal of Economic Behavior & Organization*, 113, 26–33.

BERG, J., J. DICKHAUT, AND K. MCCABE (1995): "Trust, reciprocity, and social history," *Games and Economic Behavior*, 10, 122–142.

BERG, J. E., L. A. DALEY, J. W. DICKHAUT, AND J. R. O'BRIEN (1986): "Controlling preferences for lotteries on units of experimental exchange," *Quarterly Journal of Economics*, 101, 281–306.

BERNASCONI, M., O. KIRCHKAMP, AND P. PARUOLO (2009): "Do fiscal variables affect fiscal expectations? Experiments with real world and lab data," *Journal of Economic Behavior & Organization*, 70, 253–265.

BERTRAND, M. AND S. MULLAINATHAN (2004): "Are Emily and Greg more employable than Lakisha and Jamal? A field experiment on labor market discrimination," *American Economic Review*, 94, 991–1013.

BESHEARS, J., J. J. CHOI, A. FUSTER, D. LAIBSON, AND B. C. MADRIAN (2013): "What goes up must come down? Experimental evidence on intuitive forecasting," *American Economic Review*, 103, 570–574.

BINMORE, K., A. SHAKED, AND J. SUTTON (1985): "Testing noncooperative bargaining theory: A preliminary study," *American Economic Review*, 75, 1178–1180.

BINMORE, K. G. (1999): "Why Experiment in Economics?" *Economic Journal*, 109, F16–F24.

BINSWANGER, H. P. (1981): "Attitudes toward risk: Theoretical implications of an experiment in rural India," *Economic Journal*, 91, 867–890.

BLANCO, M., D. ENGELMANN, A. K. KOCH, AND H.-T. NORMANN (2010): "Belief elicitation in experiments: is there a hedging problem?" *Experimental Economics*, 13, 412–438.

BOCK, O., I. BAETGE, AND A. NICKLISCH (2014): "hroot: Hamburg registration and organization online tool," *European Economic Review*, 71, 117–120.

BOLTON, G. E. AND A. OCKENFELS (2000): "ERC: A theory of equity, reciprocity, and competition," *American Economic Review*, 91, 166–193.

BOSCH-ROSA, C., T. MEISSNER, AND A. BOSCH-DOMÈNECH (2018): "Cognitive bubbles," *Experimental Economics*, 21, 132–153.

BRANDTS, J. AND G. CHARNESS (2000): "Hot vs. cold: Sequential responses and preference stability in experimental games," *Experimental Economics*, 2, 227–238.

BREEDEN, D. T. (1979): "An intertemporal asset pricing model with stochastic consumption and investment opportunities," *Journal of Financial Economics*, 7, 265–296.

BROWN, A. L., Z. E. CHUA, AND C. F. CAMERER (2009): "Learning and visceral temptation in dynamic saving experiments," *Quarterly Journal of Economics*, 124, 197–231.

BURDETT, K., S. SHI, AND R. WRIGHT (2001): "Pricing and matching with frictions," *Journal of Political Economy*, 109, 1060–1085.

BURKS, S. V., J. P. CARPENTER, L. GOETTE, AND A. RUSTICHINI (2009): "Cognitive skills affect economic preferences, strategic behavior, and job attachment," *Proceedings of the National Academy of Sciences*, 106, 7745–7750.

CAMERER, C. F. (2011): *Behavioral Game Theory: Experiments in Strategic Interaction*, Princeton University Press.

CAMERER, C. F., T.-H. HO, AND J.-K. CHONG (2004): "A cognitive hierarchy model of games," *Quarterly Journal of Economics*, 119, 861–898.

CAMPBELL, J. Y. AND N. G. MANKIW (1989): "Consumption, income, and interest rates: Reinterpreting the time series evidence," *NBER Macroeconomics Annual*, 4, 185–216.

CAPRA, C. M., T. TANAKA, C. F. CAMERER, L. FEILER, V. SOVERO, AND C. N. NOUSSAIR (2009): "The impact of simple institutions in experimental economies with poverty traps," *Economic Journal*, 119, 977–1009.

CARBONE, E. (2006): "Understanding intertemporal choices," *Applied Economics*, 38, 889–898.

CARBONE, E. AND J. DUFFY (2014): "Lifecycle consumption plans, social learning and external habits: Experimental evidence," *Journal of Economic Behavior & Organization*, 106, 413–427.

CARBONE, E., J. HEY, AND T. NEUGEBAUER (2021): "An experimental comparison of two exchange economies: long-lived asset vs. Short-lived asset," *Management Science*, 67, 6946–6962.

CARBONE, E. AND J. D. HEY (2004): "The effect of unemployment on consumption: an experimental analysis," *Economic Journal*, 114, 660–683.

CARPENTER, J., D. S. DAMIANOV, AND P. H. MATTHEWS (2022): "Auctions for Charity: the Curse of the Familiar," *International Economic Review*, 63, 1109–1135.

CASEY, K., R. GLENNERSTER, AND E. MIGUEL (2012): "Reshaping institutions: Evidence on aid impacts using a preanalysis plan," *Quarterly Journal of Economics*, 127, 1755–1812.

CASON, T. N. (1993): "Seller Incentive Properties of EPA's Emission Trading Auction," *Journal of Environmental Economics and Management*, 25, 177–195.

CASON, T. N. AND D. FRIEDMAN (1997): "Price formation in single call markets," *Econometrica*, 65, 311–345.

CASON, T. N. AND V.-L. MUI (1998): "Social influence in the sequential dictator game," *Journal of Mathematical Psychology*, 42, 248–265.

CASON, T. N. AND C. NOUSSAIR (2007): "A market with frictions in the matching process: an experimental study," *International Economic Review*, 48, 665–691.

CHAKRAVARTY, S., M. A. FONSECA, S. GHOSH, AND S. MARJIT (2016): "Religious fragmentation, social identity and cooperation: Evidence from an artefactual field experiment in India," *European Economic Review*, 90, 265–279.

CHAMBERLIN, E. H. (1948): "An experimental imperfect market," *Journal of Political Economy*, 56, 95–108.

CHAPKOVSKI, P. AND E. KUJANSUU (2019): "Real-time interactions in oTree using Django Channels: Auctions and real effort tasks," *Journal of Behavioral and Experimental Finance*, 23, 114–123.

CHARNESS, G. AND U. GNEEZY (2000): "What's in a name? Anonymity and social distance in dictator and ultimatum games," UCSB Working paper, https://escholarship.org/uc/item/57q360q6, A later version was published in the *Journal of Economic Behavior & Organization*, 68(1), 2008, 29–35.

CHARNESS, G., U. GNEEZY, AND B. HALLADAY (2016): "Experimental methods: Pay one or pay all," *Journal of Economic Behavior & Organization*, 131, 141–150.

CHARNESS, G., U. GNEEZY, AND M. A. KUHN (2012): "Experimental methods: Between-subject and within-subject design," *Journal of Economic Behavior & Organization*, 1–8.

CHARNESS, G. AND D. LEVIN (2009): "The origin of the winner's curse: a laboratory study," *American Economic Journal: Microeconomics*, 1, 207–236.

CHARNESS, G. AND T. NEUGEBAUER (2019): "A test of the Modigliani–Miller invariance theorem and arbitrage in experimental asset markets," *Journal of Finance*, 74, 493–529.

CHARNESS, G. AND M. RABIN (2002): "Understanding social preferences with simple tests," *Quarterly Journal of Economics*, 117, 817–869.

CHAUDHURI, A., S. GRAZIANO, AND P. MAITRA (2006): "Social learning and norms in a public goods experiment with inter-generational advice," *Review of Economic Studies*, 73, 357–380.

CHEN, D. L., M. SCHONGER, AND C. WICKENS (2016): "oTree—An open-source platform for laboratory, online, and field experiments," *Journal of Behavioral and Experimental Finance*, 9, 88–97.

CHEN, Y. AND S. X. LI (2009): "Group identity and social preferences," *American Economic Review*, 99, 431–457.

CINYABUGUMA, M., T. PAGE, AND L. PUTTERMAN (2005): "Cooperation under the threat of expulsion in a public goods experiment," *Journal of Public Economics*, 89, 1421–1435.

CIPRIANI, M., R. DE FILIPPIS, A. GUARINO, AND R. KENDALL (2020): "Trading by professional traders: An experiment," *FRB of New York Staff Report*.

COCHARD, F., P. N. VAN, AND M. WILLINGER (2004): "Trusting behavior in a repeated investment game," *Journal of Economic Behavior & Organization*, 55, 31–44.

COFFMAN, L. C. AND M. NIEDERLE (2015): "Pre-analysis plans have limited upside, especially where replications are feasible," *Journal of Economic Perspectives*, 29, 81–98.

COHEN, J. (1992): "Statistical power analysis," *Current Directions in Psychological Science*, 1, 98–101.

COLLER, M. AND M. B. WILLIAMS (1999): "Eliciting individual discount rates," *Experimental Economics*, 2, 107–127.

COOPER, D. J. AND H. FANG (2008): "Understanding overbidding in second price auctions: An experimental study," *Economic Journal*, 118, 1572–1595.

COOPER, R., D. V. DEJONG, R. FORSYTHE, AND T. W. ROSS (1989): "Communication in the battle of the sexes game: some experimental results," *RAND Journal of Economics*, 568–587.

——— (1993): "Forward induction in the battle-of-the-sexes games," *American Economic Review*, 1303–1316.

——— (1996): "Cooperation without reputation: Experimental evidence from prisoner's dilemma games," *Games and Economic Behavior*, 12, 187–218.

COOPER, R. W., D. V. DEJONG, R. FORSYTHE, AND T. W. ROSS (1990): "Selection criteria in coordination games: Some experimental results," *American Economic Review*, 80, 218–233.

COPPINGER, V. M., V. L. SMITH, AND J. A. TITUS (1980): "incentives and behavior in English, Dutch and sealed-bid auctions," *Economic Inquiry*, 18, 1–22.

CORAZZINI, L., M. FARAVELLI, AND L. STANCA (2010): "A prize to give for: An experiment on public good funding mechanisms," *Economic Journal*, 120, 944–967.

CORNAND, C. AND P. HUBERT (2020): "On the external validity of experimental inflation forecasts: A comparison with five categories of field expectations," *Journal of Economic Dynamics and Control*, 110, 103746.

CORNAND, C. AND C. K. M'BAYE (2018): "Does inflation targeting matter? An experimental investigation," *Macroeconomic Dynamics*, 22, 362–401.

COSTA-GOMES, M., V. P. CRAWFORD, AND B. BROSETA (2001): "Cognition and behavior in normal-form games: An experimental study," *Econometrica*, 69, 1193–1235.

COSTA-GOMES, M. A. AND V. P. CRAWFORD (2006): "Cognition and behavior in two-person guessing games: An experimental study," *American Economic Review*, 96, 1737–1768.

COX, J. C., B. ROBERSON, AND V. L. SMITH (1982): "Theory and behavior of single object auctions," *Research in Experimental Economics*, 2, 1–43.

CROCKETT, S., J. DUFFY, AND Y. IZHAKIAN (2019): "An experimental test of the Lucas asset pricing model," *Review of Economic Studies*, 86, 627–667.

CROCKETT, S., R. OPREA, AND C. R. PLOTT (2011): "Extreme walrasian dynamics: The gale example in the lab," *American Economic Review*, 101, 3196–3220.

CROSETTO, P. AND A. FILIPPIN (2013): "The "bomb" risk elicitation task," *Journal of Risk and Uncertainty*, 47, 31–65.

CROSON, R. T. AND M. B. MARKS (2000): "Step returns in threshold public goods: A meta-and experimental analysis," *Experimental Economics*, 2, 239–259.

DAL BÓ, P., G. R. FRÉCHETTE, AND J. KIM (2021): "The determinants of efficient behavior in coordination games," *Games and Economic Behavior*, 130, 352–368.

DAL-RÉ, R., J. P. IOANNIDIS, M. B. BRACKEN, P. A. BUFFLER, A.-W. CHAN, E. L. FRANCO, C. LA VECCHIA, AND E. WEIDERPASS (2014): "Making prospective registration of observational research a reality," *Science Translational Medicine*, 6, 224cm1–224cm1.

DANA, J., R. A. WEBER, AND J. X. KUANG (2007): "Exploiting moral wiggle room: experiments demonstrating an illusory preference for fairness," *Economic Theory*, 33, 67–80.

DANIELSON, A. J. AND H. J. HOLM (2007): "Do you trust your brethren?: Eliciting trust attitudes and trust behavior in a Tanzanian congregation," *Journal of Economic Behavior & Organization*, 62, 255–271.

DANKOVÁ, K. AND M. SERVÁTKA (2015): "The house money effect and negative reciprocity," *Journal of Economic Psychology*, 48, 60–71.

DAVIS, D. D. AND C. A. HOLT (1996a): "Consumer search costs and market performance," *Economic Inquiry*, 34, 133–151.

——— (1996b): "Markets with posted prices: Recent results from the laboratory," *Investigaciones Económicas*, 20, 291–320.

DAVIS, D. D., O. KORENOK, J. P. LIGHTLE, AND E. S. PRESCOTT (2020): "Liquidity requirements and the interbank loan market: An experimental investigation," *Journal of Monetary Economics*, 115, 113–126.

DAVIS, D. D. AND R. J. REILLY (1998): "Do too many cooks always spoil the stew? An experimental analysis of rent-seeking and the role of a strategic buyer," *Public Choice*, 95, 89–115.

——— (2016): "On freezing depositor funds at financially distressed banks: An experimental analysis," *Journal of Money, Credit and Banking*, 48, 989–1017.

DECHENAUX, E., D. KOVENOCK, AND R. M. SHEREMETA (2015): "A survey of experimental research on contests, all-pay auctions and tournaments," *Experimental Economics*, 18, 609–669.

DELLAVIGNA, S., J. A. LIST, U. MALMENDIER, AND G. RAO (2022): "Estimating social preferences and gift exchange at work," *American Economic Review*, 112, 1038–1074.

DIAMOND, D. W. AND P. H. DYBVIG (1983): "Bank runs, deposit insurance, and liquidity," *Journal of Political Economy*, 91, 401–419.

DIBA, B. T. AND H. I. GROSSMAN (1988): "Explosive rational bubbles in stock prices?" *American Economic Review*, 78, 520–530.

DING, S. AND D. PUZZELLO (2020): "Legal restrictions and international currencies: An experimental approach," *Journal of International Economics*, 126, 103342.

DOWNS, A. (1957): "An economic theory of political action in a democracy," *Journal of Political Economy*, 65, 135–150.

DRICHOUTIS, A. C., S. KLONARIS, AND G. S. PAPOUTSI (2017): "Do good things come in small packages? Bottle size effects on willingness to pay for pomegranate wine and grape wine," *Journal of Wine Economics*, 12, 84–104.

DUFFY, J. (2016): "Macroeconomics: a survey of laboratory research," in *Handbook of Experimental Economics Volume 2*, ed. by J. Kagel and A. Roth, Princeton University Press, 1–90.

——— (2022): "Why macroeconomics needs experimental evidence," *Japanese Economic Review*, 73, 5–29.

DUFFY, J. AND N. FELTOVICH (2002): "Do actions speak louder than words? An experimental comparison of observation and cheap talk," *Games and Economic Behavior*, 39, 1–27.

—— (2006): "Words, deeds, and lies: strategic behaviour in games with multiple signals," *Review of Economic Studies*, 73, 669–688.

DUFFY, J. AND E. O. FISHER (2005): "Sunspots in the Laboratory," *American Economic Review*, 95, 510–529.

DUFFY, J., D. FRIEDMAN, J. P. RABANAL, AND O. RUD (2022): "Trade, Voting, and ESG policies: Theory and Evidence," *SSRN Working paper*.

DUFFY, J., J. HUA JIANG, AND H. XIE (2023): "Pricing Indefinitely Lived Assets: Experimental Evidence," *Management Science*.

DUFFY, J. AND T. KORNIENKO (2010): "Does competition affect giving?" *Journal of Economic Behavior & Organization*, 74, 82–103.

DUFFY, J. AND J. LAFKY (2016): "Birth, death and public good provision," *Experimental Economics*, 19, 317–341.

DUFFY, J., E. K. LAI, AND W. LIM (2017): "Coordination via correlation: An experimental study," *Economic Theory*, 64, 265–304.

DUFFY, J. AND Y. LI (2019): "Lifecycle consumption under different income profiles: Evidence and theory," *Journal of Economic Dynamics and Control*, 104, 74–94.

DUFFY, J. AND A. MATROS (2021): "All-Pay auctions versus lotteries as provisional fixed-prize fundraising mechanisms: Theory and evidence," *Journal of Economic Behavior & Organization*, 192, 434–464.

DUFFY, J., A. MATROS, AND T. TEMZELIDES (2011): "Competitive behavior in market games: Evidence and theory," *Journal of Economic Theory*, 146, 1437–1463.

DUFFY, J. AND F. MUÑOZ-GARCÍA (2015): "Cooperation and signaling with uncertain social preferences," *Theory and Decision*, 78, 45–75.

DUFFY, J. AND R. NAGEL (1997): "On the robustness of behaviour in experimental 'beauty contest'games," *Economic Journal*, 107, 1684–1700.

DUFFY, J. AND J. OCHS (2012): "Equilibrium selection in static and dynamic entry games," *Games and Economic Behavior*, 76, 97–116.

DUFFY, J. AND D. PUZZELLO (2014): "Gift exchange versus monetary exchange: Theory and evidence," *American Economic Review*, 104, 1735–1776.

——— (2022): "The Friedman rule: experimental evidence," *International Economic Review*, 63, 671–698.

DUFFY, J. AND M. TAVITS (2008): "Beliefs and voting decisions: A test of the pivotal voter model," *American Journal of Political Science*, 52, 603–618.

DUFWENBERG, M., P. HEIDHUES, G. KIRCHSTEIGER, F. RIEDEL, AND J. SOBEL (2011): "Other-regarding preferences in general equilibrium," *Review of Economic Studies*, 78, 613–639.

DUFWENBERG, M. AND G. KIRCHSTEIGER (2004): "A theory of sequential reciprocity," *Games and Economic Behavior*, 47, 268–298.

DUFWENBERG, M., T. LINDQVIST, AND E. MOORE (2005): "Bubbles and experience: An experiment," *American Economic Review*, 95, 1731–1737.

DWYER Jr., G. P., A. W. WILLIAMS, R. C. BATTALIO, AND T. I. MASON (1993): "Tests of rational expectations in a stark setting," *Economic Journal*, 103, 586–601.

ENGEL, C. (2011): "Dictator games: A meta study," *Experimental Economics*, 14, 583–610.

ENGELMANN, D. AND V. GRIMM (2009): "Bidding behaviour in multi-unit auctions—An experimental investigation," *Economic Journal*, 119, 855–882.

ENGELMANN, D. AND M. STROBEL (2004): "Inequality aversion, efficiency, and maximin preferences in simple distribution experiments," *American Economic Review*, 94, 857–869.

FAHR, R. AND B. IRLENBUSCH (2000): "Fairness as a constraint on trust in reciprocity: earned property rights in a reciprocal exchange experiment," *Economics Letters*, 66, 275–282.

FALK, A., A. BECKER, T. DOHMEN, D. HUFFMAN, AND U. SUNDE (2023): "The preference survey module: A validated instrument for measuring risk, time, and social preferences," *Management Science*, 69, 1935–1950.

FALK, A., E. FEHR, AND U. FISCHBACHER (2003): "On the nature of fair behavior," *Economic Inquiry*, 41, 20–26.

FALK, A. AND U. FISCHBACHER (2001): "Distributional consequences and intentions in a model of reciprocity," *Annales d'Economie et de Statistique*, 111–129.

FALK, A., S. MEIER, AND C. ZEHNDER (2013): "Do lab experiments misrepresent social preferences? The case of self-selected student samples," *Journal of the European Economic Association*, 11, 839–852.

FARAVELLI, M., K. KALAYCI, AND C. PIMIENTA (2020): "Costly voting: A large-scale real effort experiment," *Experimental Economics*, 23, 468–492.

FEHR, E. AND S. GÄCHTER (2000a): "Cooperation and punishment in public goods experiments," *American Economic Review*, 90, 980–994.

——— (2000b): "Fairness and retaliation: The economics of reciprocity," *Journal of Economic Perspectives*, 14, 159–182.

——— (2002): "Altruistic punishment in humans," *Nature*, 415, 137–140.

FEHR, E. AND K. M. SCHMIDT (1999): "A theory of fairness, competition, and cooperation," *Quarterly Journal of Economics*, 114, 817–868.

FEHRLER, S. AND M. KOSFELD (2014): "Pro-social missions and worker motivation: An experimental study," *Journal of Economic Behavior & Organization*, 100, 99–110.

FELTOVICH, N. (2003): "Nonparametric tests of differences in medians: comparison of the Wilcoxon–Mann–Whitney and robust rank-order tests," *Experimental Economics*, 6, 273–297.

FISCHBACHER, U. (2007): "z-Tree: Zurich toolbox for ready-made economic experiments," *Experimental Economics*, 10, 171–178.

FISCHBACHER, U., S. GÄCHTER, AND E. FEHR (2001): "Are people conditionally cooperative? Evidence from a public goods experiment," *Economics Letters*, 71, 397–404.

FISHER, E. O. AND F. S. KELLY (2000): "Experimental foreign exchange markets," *Pacific Economic Review*, 5, 365–387.

FISHER, R. A. (1935): *The Design of Experiments*, New York: Hafner/Macmillan.

FLOOD, M. M. (1952): "Some experimental games," *Rand Memorandum 789-1*.

FORSYTHE, R., J. L. HOROWITZ, N. E. SAVIN, AND M. SEFTON (1994): "Fairness in simple bargaining experiments," *Games and Economic Behavior*, 6, 347–369.

FRÉCHETTE, G. R. (2015): "Laboratory experiments: Professionals versus students," in *Handbook of Experimental Economic Methodology*, ed. by G. Fréchette and A. Schotter, Oxford University Press, 360–390.

FRÉCHETTE, G. R. AND A. SCHOTTER (2015): *Handbook of Experimental Economic Methodology*, Oxford University Press.

FRÉCHETTE, G. R. AND S. YUKSEL (2017): "Infinitely repeated games in the laboratory: Four perspectives on discounting and random termination," *Experimental Economics*, 20, 279–308.

FREDERICK, S. (2005): "Cognitive reflection and decision making," *Journal of Economic Perspectives*, 19, 25–42.

FRIEDLAND, N., S. MAITAL, AND A. RUTENBERG (1978): "A simulation study of income tax evasion," *Journal of Public Economics*, 10, 107–116.

FRIEDMAN, D. (1993): "The Double Auction Market Institution: A Survey," in *The Double Auction Market*, ed. by D. Friedman and J. Rust, Addison-Wesley, 3–25.

FRIEDMAN, M. (1969): *The Optimum Quantity of Money and Other Essays*, Aldine Publishing Co.

GARRATT, R. J. AND J. WOODERS (2010): "Efficiency in second-price auctions: a new look at old data," *Review of Industrial Organization*, 37, 43–50.

GILL, D. AND V. PROWSE (2016): "Cognitive ability, character skills, and learning to play equilibrium: A level-k analysis," *Journal of Political Economy*, 124, 1619–1676.

GLAZER, A. AND K. A. KONRAD (1996): "A signaling explanation for charity," *American Economic Review*, 86, 1019–1028.

GNEEZY, U. AND J. POTTERS (1997): "An experiment on risk taking and evaluation periods," *Quarterly Journal of Economics*, 112, 631–645.

GNEEZY, U. AND A. RUSTICHINI (2000): "Pay enough or don't pay at all," *Quarterly Journal of Economics*, 115, 791–810.

GNEEZY, U. AND R. SMORODINSKY (2006): "All-pay auctions—an experimental study," *Journal of Economic Behavior & Organization*, 61, 255–275.

GOEREE, J., C. HOLT, AND J. O. LEDYARD (2007): "An Experimental Comparison of Flexible and Tiered Package Bidding," Tech. rep., Federal Communications Commission.

GOEREE, J. K., C. A. HOLT, AND T. R. PALFREY (2016): *Quantal Response Equilibrium: A Stochastic Theory of Games*, Princeton University Press.

GOEREE, J. K., E. MAASLAND, S. ONDERSTAL, AND J. L. TURNER (2005): "How (not) to raise money," *Journal of Political Economy*, 113, 897–918.

GOEREE, J. K. AND T. OFFERMAN (2002): "Efficiency in auctions with private and common values: An experimental study," *American Economic Review*, 92, 625–643.

GREINER, B. (2015): "Subject pool recruitment procedures: organizing experiments with ORSEE," *Journal of the Economic Science Association*, 1, 114–125.

GROSSKOPF, B. AND R. NAGEL (2008): "The two-person beauty contest," *Games and Economic Behavior*, 62, 93–99.

GROSSMAN, S. J. AND J. E. STIGLITZ (1980): "On the impossibility of informationally efficient markets," *American Economic Review*, 70, 393–408.

GUALA, F. (2005): *The Methodology of Experimental Economics*, Cambridge University Press.

GÜTH, W., M. KOCHER, AND M. SUTTER (2002): "Experimental 'beauty contests' with homogeneous and heterogeneous players and with interior and boundary equilibria," *Economics Letters*, 74, 219–228.

GÜTH, W., R. SCHMITTBERGER, AND B. SCHWARZE (1982): "An experimental analysis of ultimatum bargaining," *Journal of Economic Behavior & Organization*, 3, 367–388.

HAKIMOV, R. AND D. KÜBLER (2021): "Experiments on centralized school choice and college admissions: a survey," *Experimental Economics*, 24, 434–488.

HAM, J. C., J. H. KAGEL, AND S. F. LEHRER (2005): "Randomization, endogeneity and laboratory experiments: The role of cash balances in private value auctions," *Journal of Econometrics*, 125, 175–205.

HARRISON, G. W. (1989): "Theory and misbehavior of first-price auctions," *American Economic Review*, 749–762.

HARRISON, G. W. AND J. A. LIST (2004): "Field experiments," *Journal of Economic Literature*, 42, 1009–1055.

HARRISON, G. W., J. MARTÍNEZ-CORREA, AND J. T. SWARTHOUT (2013): "Inducing risk neutral preferences with binary lotteries: A reconsideration," *Journal of Economic Behavior & Organization*, 94, 145–159.

——— (2015): "Reduction of compound lotteries with objective probabilities: Theory and evidence," *Journal of Economic Behavior & Organization*, 119, 32–55.

HARRISON, G. W. AND K. A. MCCABE (1996): "Expectations and fairness in a simple bargaining experiment," *International Journal of Game Theory*, 25, 303–327.

HARSANYI, J. C. AND R. SELTEN (1988): *A General Theory of Equilibrium Selection in Games*, MIT Press.

HARSTAD, R. M. (2000): "Dominant strategy adoption and bidders' experience with pricing rules," *Experimental Economics*, 3, 261–280.

HARUVY, E., Y. LAHAV, AND C. N. NOUSSAIR (2007): "Traders' expectations in asset markets: experimental evidence," *American Economic Review*, 97, 1901–1920.

HECKMAN, J. J. AND E. J. VYTLACIL (2007): "Econometric evaluation of social programs, part I: Causal models, structural models and econometric policy evaluation," in *Handbook of Econometrics Volume 6*, Elsevier, 4779–4874.

HENRICH, J., S. J. HEINE, AND A. NORENZAYAN (2010): "The weirdest people in the world?" *Behavioral and Brain Sciences*, 33, 61–83.

Lecture Notes in Experimental Economics

HENRICH, J. P. (2004): *Foundations of Human Sociality: Economic Experiments and Ethnographic Evidence from Fifteen Small-scale Societies*, Oxford University Press, USA.

HERRMANN, B. AND C. THÖNI (2009): "Measuring conditional cooperation: a replication study in Russia," *Experimental Economics*, 12, 87–92.

HERTWIG, R. AND A. ORTMANN (2008): "Deception in experiments: Revisiting the arguments in its defense," *Ethics & Behavior*, 18, 59–92.

HEY, J. D. AND V. DARDANONI (1988): "Optimal consumption under uncertainty: An experimental investigation," *Economic Journal*, 98, 105–116.

HO, T.-H., C. CAMERER, AND K. WEIGELT (1998): "Iterated dominance and iterated best response in experimental 'p-beauty contests'," *American Economic Review*, 88, 947–969.

HOFFMAN, E., K. MCCABE, K. SHACHAT, AND V. SMITH (1994): "Preferences, property rights, and anonymity in bargaining games," *Games and Economic Behavior*, 7, 346–380.

HOLT, C. A. (2019): *Markets, Games, and Strategic Behavior: An Introduction to Experimental Economics*, Princeton University Press.

HOLT, C. A. AND S. K. LAURY (2002): "Risk aversion and incentive effects," *American Economic Review*, 92, 1644–1655.

HOLT, C. A., M. PORZIO, AND M. Y. SONG (2017): "Price bubbles, gender, and expectations in experimental asset markets," *European Economic Review*, 100, 72–94.

HOLT, C. A. AND A. M. SMITH (2009): "An update on Bayesian updating," *Journal of Economic Behavior & Organization*, 69, 125–134.

HOMMES, C., J. SONNEMANS, J. TUINSTRA, AND H. VAN DE VELDEN (2005): "Coordination of expectations in asset pricing experiments," *Review of Financial Studies*, 18, 955–980.

——— (2008): "Expectations and bubbles in asset pricing experiments," *Journal of Economic Behavior & Organization*, 67, 116–133.

HOUSER, D. AND R. KURZBAN (2002): "Revisiting kindness and confusion in public goods experiments," *American Economic Review*, 92, 1062–1069.

HUSSAM, R. N., D. PORTER, AND V. L. SMITH (2008): "Thar she blows: Can bubbles be rekindled with experienced subjects?" *American Economic Review*, 98, 924–937.

ISAAC, R. M. AND J. M. WALKER (1988): "Group size effects in public goods provision: The voluntary contributions mechanism," *Quarterly Journal of Economics*, 103, 179–199.

ISAAC, R. M., J. M. WALKER, AND S. H. THOMAS (1984): "Divergent evidence on free riding: An experimental examination of possible explanations," *Public Choice*, 43, 113–149.

ISAAC, R. M., J. M. WALKER, AND A. W. WILLIAMS (1994): "Group size and the voluntary provision of public goods: Experimental evidence utilizing large groups," *Journal of Public Economics*, 54, 1–36.

JAKIELA, P. (2011): "Social preferences and fairness norms as informal institutions: Experimental evidence," *American Economic Review*, 101, 509–513.

JIANG, J. H., D. PUZZELLO, AND C. ZHANG (2023): "Inflation, Output, and Welfare in the Laboratory," *European Economic Review*, 152, 104351.

JOHN, O. P. (2021): "History, measurement and conceptual elaboration of the Big-5 trait taxonomy: The paradigm matures," in *Handbook of Personality: Theory and Research, Fourth ed.*, ed. by O. John and R. Robins, New York: Guilford Press, 35–82.

KAGEL, J. H. (2004): "Double auction markets with stochastic supply and demand schedules: Call markets and continuous auction trading mechanisms," in *Advances in Understanding Strategic Behaviour: Game Theory, Experiments and Bounded Rationality*, ed. by S. Huck, Palgrave Macmillan, 181–208.

KAGEL, J. H., R. M. HARSTAD, AND D. LEVIN (1987): "Information impact and allocation rules in auctions with affiliated private values: A laboratory study," *Econometrica*, 55, 1275–1304.

KAGEL, J. H. AND D. LEVIN (1986): "The winner's curse and public information in common value auctions," *American Economic Review*, 76, 894–920.

—— (1993): "Independent private value auctions: Bidder behaviour in first-, second-and third-price auctions with varying numbers of bidders," *Economic Journal*, 103, 868–879.

KAGEL, J. H., D. LEVIN, R. C. BATTALIO, AND D. J. MEYER (1989): "First-price common value auctions: Bidder behavior and the "Winner's Curse"," *Economic Inquiry*, 27, 241–258.

KAGEL, J. H. AND A. E. ROTH (1995): *The Handbook of Experimental Economics*, Princeton University Press.

—— (2000): "The Dynamics of Reorganization in Matching Markets: A Laboratory Experiment Motivated by a Natural Experiment," *Quarterly Journal of Economics*, 115, 201–235.

—— (2016): *The Handbook of Experimental Economics, Volume 2*, Princeton University Press.

KAHNEMAN, D. (1988): "Experimental Economics: A Psychological Perspective," in *Bounded Rational Behavior in Experimental Games and Markets. Lecture Notes in Economics and Mathematical Systems*, ed. by T. R., A. W., and S. R., Springer, vol. 314, 11–18.

—— (2011): *Thinking, Fast and Slow*, New York: Farrar, Straus and Giroux.

KAHNEMAN, D., J. L. KNETSCH, AND R. H. THALER (1990): "Experimental tests of the endowment effect and the Coase theorem," *Journal of Political Economy*, 98, 1325–1348.

KARLAN, D. AND J. A. LIST (2007): "Does price matter in charitable giving? Evidence from a large-scale natural field experiment," *American Economic Review*, 97, 1774–1793.

KARNI, E. (2009): "A mechanism for eliciting probabilities," *Econometrica*, 77, 603–606.

KENDALL, R. (2022): "Decomposing coordination failure in stag hunt games," *Experimental Economics*, 25, 1109–1145.

KESER, C. (1996): "Voluntary contributions to a public good when partial contribution is a dominant strategy," *Economics Letters*, 50, 359–366.

KESSLER, J. B., C. LOW, AND C. D. SULLIVAN (2019): "Incentivized resume rating: Eliciting employer preferences without deception," *American Economic Review*, 109, 3713–3744.

KETCHAM, J., V. L. SMITH, AND A. W. WILLIAMS (1984): "A comparison of posted-offer and double-auction pricing institutions," *Review of Economic Studies*, 51, 595–614.

KEYNES, J. M. (1936): *The General Theory of Employment, Interest and Money*, New York: Harcourt Brace and Company.

KIM, D. G. (2022): "Clustering Standard Errors at the "Session Level"," CESifo Working Paper.

KIRCHLER, M., J. HUBER, AND T. STÖCKL (2012): "Thar she bursts: Reducing confusion reduces bubbles," *American Economic Review*, 102, 865–883.

KISS, H. J., I. RODRIGUEZ-LARA, AND A. ROSA-GARCÍA (2012): "On the effects of deposit insurance and observability on bank runs: an experimental study," *Journal of Money, Credit and Banking*, 44, 1651–1665.

KISS, H. J., I. RODRIGUEZ-LARA, AND A. ROSA-GARCIA (2022): "Experimental bank runs," in *Handbook of Experimental Finance*, ed. by S. Füllbrunn and E. Haruvy, Edward Elgar Publishing.

KOCHER, M. G., T. CHERRY, S. KROLL, R. J. NETZER, AND M. SUTTER (2008): "Conditional cooperation on three continents," *Economics Letters*, 101, 175–178.

KOSTYSHYNA, O., L. PETERSEN, AND J. YANG (2022): "A horse race of monetary policy regimes: An experimental investigation," Tech. rep., National Bureau of Economic Research Working Paper No. 30530.

KRISHNA, V. (2010): *Auction Theory*, Academic Press, 2nd ed.

LAGOS, R. AND R. WRIGHT (2005): "A unified framework for monetary theory and policy analysis," *Journal of Political Economy*, 113, 463–484.

LAURY, S. K., M. M. MCINNES, AND J. TODD SWARTHOUT (2012): "Avoiding the curves: Direct elicitation of time preferences," *Journal of Risk and Uncertainty*, 44, 181–217.

LEDYARD, J. O. (1984): "The pure theory of large two-candidate elections," *Public Choice*, 44, 7–41.

———— (1995): "Public goods: A survey of experimental research," in *Handbook of Experimental Economics*, ed. by J. H. Kagel and A. E. Roth, Princeton University Press Princeton, NJ, USA, 111–194.

LEI, V. AND C. N. NOUSSAIR (2007): "Equilibrium selection in an experimental macroeconomy," *Southern Economic Journal*, 74, 448–482.

LEI, V., C. N. NOUSSAIR, AND C. R. PLOTT (2001): "Nonspeculative bubbles in experimental asset markets: Lack of common knowledge of rationality vs. actual irrationality," *Econometrica*, 69, 831–859.

LEVINE, D. K. AND T. R. PALFREY (2007): "The paradox of voter participation? A laboratory study," *American Political Science Review*, 101, 143–158.

LEVY, M. AND J. TASOFF (2016): "Exponential-growth bias and lifecycle consumption," *Journal of the European Economic Association*, 14, 545–583.

LI, Z., P.-H. LIN, S.-Y. KONG, D. WANG, AND J. DUFFY (2021): "Conducting large, repeated, multi-game economic experiments using mobile platforms," *PloS One*, 16, e0250668.

LIND, B. AND C. R. PLOTT (1991): "The winner's curse: experiments with buyers and with sellers," *American Economic Review*, 81, 335–346.

LIST, J. A. (2007): "On the interpretation of giving in dictator games," *Journal of Political Economy*, 115, 482–493.

LUCAS, Jr., R. E. (1986): "Adaptive Behavior and Economic Theory," *Journal of Business*, 59, S401–26.

———— (2012): "The Effects of Monetary Shocks When Prices are Set in Advance, (1989 Working paper)," in *Collected Papers on Monetary Theory*, ed. by R. L. Jr. and M. Gilman, Harvard University Press, 272–299.

LUCAS Jr., R. E. (1978): "Asset prices in an exchange economy," *Econometrica*, 1429–1445.

LUCKING-REILEY, D. (1999): "Using field experiments to test equivalence between auction formats: Magic on the Internet," *American Economic Review*, 89, 1063–1080.

LUGOVSKYY, V., D. PUZZELLO, AND S. TUCKER (2010): "An experimental investigation of overdissipation in the all pay auction," *European Economic Review*, 54, 974–997.

LUSK, J. L. AND J. F. SHOGREN (2007): *Experimental Auctions : Methods and Applications in Economics and Marketing Research*, Cambridge University Press.

MADIES, P. (2006): "An experimental exploration of self-fulfilling banking panics: their occurrence, persistence, and prevention," *Journal of Business*, 79, 1831–1866.

MARCH, C. (2021): "Strategic interactions between humans and artificial intelligence: Lessons from experiments with computer players," *Journal of Economic Psychology*, 87, 102426.

MARIMON, R. AND S. SUNDER (1993): "Indeterminacy of equilibria in a hyperinflationary world: Experimental evidence," *Econometrica*, 1073–1107.

———— (1994): "Expectations and learning under alternative monetary regimes: an experimental approach," *Economic Theory*, 4, 131–162.

———— (1995): "Does a constant money growth rule help stabilize inflation?: experimental evidence," in *Carnegie-Rochester Conference Series on Public Policy*, Elsevier, vol. 43, 111–156.

MARWELL, G. AND R. E. AMES (1979): "Experiments on the provision of public goods. I. Resources, interest, group size, and the free-rider problem," *American Journal of Sociology*, 84, 1335–1360.

———— (1980): "Experiments on the provision of public goods. II. Provision points, stakes, experience, and the free-rider problem," *American Journal of Sociology*, 85, 926–937.

———— (1981): "Economists free ride, does anyone else?: Experiments on the provision of public goods, IV," *Journal of Public Economics*, 15, 295–310.

MASCHLER, M., S. ZAMIR, AND E. SOLAN (2020): *Game Theory*, Cambridge University Press.

MCCABE, K. A., S. J. RASSENTI, AND V. L. SMITH (1990): "Auction institutional design: Theory and behavior of simultaneous multiple-unit generalizations of the Dutch and English auctions," *American Economic Review*, 80, 1276–1283.

———— (1993): "Designing a uniform-price double auction: An experimental evaluation," in *The Double Auction Market*, ed. by D. Friedman and J. Rust, Addison-Wesley, 307–332.

MCKELVEY, R. D. AND T. R. PALFREY (1992): "An experimental study of the centipede game," *Econometrica*, 60, 803–836.

———— (1995): "Quantal response equilibria for normal form games," *Games and Economic Behavior*, 10, 6–38.

———— (1998): "Quantal response equilibria for extensive form games," *Experimental Economics*, 1, 9–41.

MEISSNER, T. (2016): "Intertemporal consumption and debt aversion: an experimental study," *Experimental Economics*, 19, 281–298.

MILLNER, E. L. AND M. D. PRATT (1989): "An experimental investigation of efficient rent-seeking," *Public Choice*, 62, 139–151.

———— (1991): "Risk aversion and rent-seeking: An extension and some experimental evidence," *Public Choice*, 69, 81–92.

MOFFATT, P. G. (2016): *Experimetrics: Econometrics for experimental economics*, London: Red Globe Press/Macmillan.

MOKHTARZADEH, F. AND L. PETERSEN (2021): "Coordinating expectations through central bank projections," *Experimental Economics*, 24, 883–918.

MORGAN, J. (2000): "Financing public goods by means of lotteries," *Review of Economic Studies*, 67, 761–784.

MORGAN, J. AND M. SEFTON (2000): "Funding public goods with lotteries: experimental evidence," *Review of Economic Studies*, 67, 785–810.

MÜLLER, J. AND C. SCHWIEREN (2020): "Big five personality factors in the trust game," *Journal of Business Economics*, 90, 37–55.

MURPHY, R. O., K. A. ACKERMANN, AND M. J. HANDGRAAF (2011): "Measuring social value orientation," *Judgment and Decision Making*, 6, 771–781.

MYERSON, R. B. (1981): "Optimal auction design," *Mathematics of Operations Research*, 6, 58–73.

―――― (1997): *Game Theory: Analysis of Conflict*, Harvard university press.

NAGEL, R. (1995): "Unraveling in guessing games: An experimental study," *American Economic Review*, 85, 1313–1326.

NORMANN, H.-T. AND B. WALLACE (2012): "The impact of the termination rule on cooperation in a prisoner's dilemma experiment," *International Journal of Game Theory*, 41, 707–718.

NOUSSAIR, C., S. ROBIN, AND B. RUFFIEUX (2001): "Price bubbles in laboratory asset markets with constant fundamental values," *Experimental Economics*, 4, 87–105.

NOUSSAIR, C. N., D. VAN SOEST, AND J. STOOP (2015): "Cooperation in a dynamic fishing game: A framed field experiment," *American Economic Review*, 105, 408–413.

OCHS, J. (1995): "Games with unique, mixed strategy equilibria: An experimental study," *Games and Economic Behavior*, 10, 202–217.

ODEAN, T. (1998): "Are investors reluctant to realize their losses?" *Journal of Finance*, 53, 1775–1798.

OFFERMAN, T. AND J. SONNEMANS (2004): "What's causing overreaction? An experimental investigation of recency and the hot-hand effect," *Scandinavian Journal of Economics*, 106, 533–554.

OLSON, M. (1965): *The Logic of Collective Action*, Harvard University Press.

OOSTERBEEK, H., R. SLOOF, AND G. VAN DE KUILEN (2004): "Cultural differences in ultimatum game experiments: Evidence from a meta-analysis," *Experimental Economics*, 7, 171–188.

ORTMANN, A. (2019): "Deception," in *Handbook of Research Methods and Applications in Experimental Economics*, ed. by A. Schram and A. Ule, Edward Elgar Publishing, 28–38.

OXOBY, R. J. AND J. SPRAGGON (2008): "Mine and yours: Property rights in dictator games," *Journal of Economic Behavior & Organization*, 65, 703–713.

PAGE, T., L. PUTTERMAN, AND B. UNEL (2005): "Voluntary association in public goods experiments: Reciprocity, mimicry and efficiency," *Economic Journal*, 115, 1032–1053.

PALACIOS-HUERTA, I. AND O. VOLIJ (2009): "Field centipedes," *American Economic Review*, 99, 1619–1635.

PALFREY, T. R. AND J. E. PRISBREY (1996): "Altruism, reputation and noise in linear public goods experiments," *Journal of Public Economics*, 61, 409–427.

——— (1997): "Anomalous behavior in public goods experiments: How much and why?" *American Economic Review*, 87, 829–846.

PALFREY, T. R. AND H. ROSENTHAL (1983): "A strategic calculus of voting," *Public Choice*, 41, 7–53.

——— (1985): "Voter participation and strategic uncertainty," *American Political Science Review*, 79, 62–78.

PALFREY, T. R. AND S. W. WANG (2009): "On eliciting beliefs in strategic games," *Journal of Economic Behavior & Organization*, 71, 98–109.

PFAJFAR, D. AND B. ŽAKELJ (2018): "Inflation expectations and monetary policy design: Evidence from the laboratory," *Macroeconomic Dynamics*, 22, 1035–1075.

PIGOU, A. C. (1932): *The Economics of Welfare*, London: Macmillan.

PLOTT, C. R. (1991): "Will Economics Become an Experimental Science?" *Southern Economic Journal*, 57, 901–919.

——— (1997): "Laboratory Experimental Testbeds: Application to the PCS Auction," *Journal of Economics & Management Strategy*, 6, 605–638.

PLOTT, C. R. (1986): "Rational choice in experimental markets," *Journal of Business*, S301–S327.

——— (1989): "An updated review of industrial organization: Applications of experimental methods," in *Handbook of Industrial Organization Volume 2*, ed. by R. Schmalensee and R. D. Willig, Elsevier, 1109–1176.

——— (1996): "Rational individual behavior in markets and social choice processes: The discovered preference hypothesis," in *The Rational Foundations of Economic Behavior*, ed. by K. Arrow, E. Colombatto, M. Perlman, and C. Schmidt, Macmillan, 225–250.

PLOTT, C. R. AND K. POGORELSKIY (2017): "Call market experiments: Efficiency and price discovery through multiple calls and emergent Newton adjustments," *American Economic Journal: Microeconomics*, 9, 1–41.

PLOTT, C. R. AND V. L. SMITH (2008): *Handbook of Experimental Economics Results Volume 1*, Elsevier.

PLOTT, C. R. AND S. SUNDER (1982): "Efficiency of experimental security markets with insider information: An application of rational-expectations models," *Journal of Political Economy*, 90, 663–698.

PLOTT, C. R. AND K. ZEILER (2005): "The willingness to pay–willingness to accept gap, the "endowment effect," subject misconceptions, and experimental procedures for eliciting valuations," *American Economic Review*, 95, 530–545.

POPPER, K. (1957): *The Poverty of Historicism*, Routledge.

POTTERS, J., C. G. DE VRIES, AND F. VAN WINDEN (1998): "An experimental examination of rational rent-seeking," *European Journal of Political Economy*, 14, 783–800.

PRASNIKAR, V. (2002): "Do binary lottery payoffs measure deviations from expected utility?-An Experimental Study," Tech. rep., mimeo.

RABIN, M. (1993): "Incorporating fairness into game theory and economics," *American Economic Review*, 83, 1281–1302.

RANKIN, F. W., J. B. VAN HUYCK, AND R. C. BATTALIO (2000): "Strategic similarity and emergent conventions: Evidence from similar stag hunt games," *Games and Economic Behavior*, 32, 315–337.

RAVEN, J. C. (1936): "Mental tests used in genetic studies: The performances of related individuals in tests mainly educative and mainly reproductive," *Unpublished MSC thesis. University of London.*

ROMERO, J. AND Y. ROSOKHA (2019): "The evolution of cooperation: The role of costly strategy adjustments," *American Economic Journal: Microeconomics*, 11, 299–328.

ROSENBOIM, M. AND T. SHAVIT (2012): "Whose money is it anyway? Using prepaid incentives in experimental economics to create a natural environment," *Experimental Economics*, 15, 145–157.

ROTH, A. E. (1995): "Introduction to Experimental Economics," in *Handbook of Experimental Economics*, ed. by J. Kagel and A. Roth, Princeton University Press, 3–109.

ROTH, A. E. AND M. W. MALOUF (1979): "Game-theoretic models and the role of information in bargaining." *Psychological Review*, 86, 574.

ROTH, A. E. AND J. K. MURNIGHAN (1978): "Equilibrium behavior and repeated play of the prisoner's dilemma," *Journal of Mathematical Psychology*, 17, 189–198.

ROTH, A. E., V. PRASNIKAR, M. OKUNO-FUJIWARA, AND S. ZAMIR (1991): "Bargaining and market behavior in Jerusalem, Liubljana, Pittsburgh and Tokyo: an experimental study," *American Economic Review*, 81, 1068–1095.

SAIJO, T. AND H. NAKAMURA (1995): "The "spite" dilemma in voluntary contribution mechanism experiments," *Journal of Conflict Resolution*, 39, 535–560.

SAMUELSON, P. A. (1954): "The pure theory of public expenditure," *Review of Economics and Statistics*, 36, 387–389.

——— (1958): "An exact consumption-loan model of interest with or without the social contrivance of money," *Journal of Political Economy*, 66, 467–482.

SAMUELSON, W. F. AND M. H. BAZERMAN (1985): "Negotiation under the winner's curse," *Research in Experimental Economics*, 3, 105–138.

SCHMALENSEE, R. (1976): "An experimental study of expectation formation," *Econometrica*, 44, 17–41.

SCHOTTER, A. AND T. YORULMAZER (2009): "On the dynamics and severity of bank runs: An experimental study," *Journal of Financial Intermediation*, 18, 217–241.

SCHRAM, A. AND J. SONNEMANS (1996): "Voter turnout as a participation game: An experimental investigation," *International Journal of Game Theory*, 25, 385–406.

SCHRAM, A. AND A. ULE (2019): *Handbook of Research Methods and Applications in Experimental Economics*, Edward Elgar Publishing.

SCHRAM, A. J. AND S. ONDERSTAL (2009): "Bidding to give: An experimental comparison of auctions for charity," *International Economic Review*, 50, 431–457.

SEALE, D. A. AND A. RAPOPORT (2000): "Elicitation of strategy profiles in large group coordination games," *Experimental Economics*, 3, 153–179.

SELTEN, R. (1965): "Die Strategiemethode zur Erforschung des eingeschränkt rationalen Verhaltens im Rahmen eines Oligopolexperimentes," in *Beiträge zur experimentelle Wirtschaftsforschung*, ed. by H. Sauermann, Tübingen: Mohr, 136–168.

SELTEN, R., M. MITZKEWITZ, AND G. R. UHLICH (1997): "Duopoly strategies programmed by experienced players," *Econometrica*, 517–555.

SELTEN, R., A. SADRIEH, AND K. ABBINK (1999): "Money does not induce risk neutral behavior, but binary lotteries do even worse," *Theory and Decision*, 46, 213–252.

SHAPLEY, L. AND M. SHUBIK (1977): "Trade using one commodity as a means of payment," *Journal of Political Economy*, 85, 937–968.

SHEFRIN, H. AND M. STATMAN (1985): "The disposition to sell winners too early and ride losers too long: Theory and evidence," *Journal of Finance*, 40, 777–790.

SHEREMETA, R. M. (2010): "Experimental comparison of multi-stage and one-stage contests," *Games and Economic Behavior*, 68, 731–747.

——— (2018): "Impulsive behavior in competition: Testing theories of overbidding in rent-seeking contests," *Available at SSRN 2676419*.

SHILLER, R. J. (1981): "Do Stock Prices Move Too Much to be Justified by Subsequent Changes in Dividends?" *American Economic Review*, 71, 421–436.

——— (2000): *Irrational Exuberance*, Princeton University Press.

SIEGEL, S. AND N. J. CASTELLAN Jr. (1988): *Nonparametric Statistics for the Behavioral Sciences, 2nd Edition*, New York: McGraw-Hill.

SITZIA, S. AND R. SUGDEN (2011): "Implementing theoretical models in the laboratory, and what this can and cannot achieve," *Journal of Economic Methodology*, 18, 323–343.

SLONIM, R. AND A. E. ROTH (1998): "Learning in high stakes ultimatum games: An experiment in the Slovak Republic," *Econometrica*, 569–596.

SMITH, V. (1982): "Microeconomic Systems as an Experimental Science," *American Economic Review*, 72, 923–55.

SMITH, V. L. (1962): "An experimental study of competitive market behavior," *Journal of Political Economy*, 70, 111–137.

——— (1976): "Experimental economics: Induced value theory," *American Economic Review*, 66, 274–279.

——— (1981): "Experimental economics at Purdue," in *Essays in Contemporary Fields of Economics*, ed. by G. Horwich and J. Quirk, Purdue University Press, 369–373.

SMITH, V. L., G. L. SUCHANEK, AND A. W. WILLIAMS (1988): "Bubbles, crashes, and endogenous expectations in experimental spot asset markets," *Econometrica*, 56, 1119–1151.

SNOWBERG, E. AND L. YARIV (2021): "Testing the waters: Behavior across participant pools," *American Economic Review*, 111, 687–719.

SOLNICK, S. J. (2001): "Gender differences in the ultimatum game," *Economic Inquiry*, 39, 189–200.

STAHL, D. O. AND P. W. WILSON (1995): "On players' models of other players: Theory and experimental evidence," *Games and Economic Behavior*, 10, 218–254.

STAHL II, D. O. AND P. W. WILSON (1994): "Experimental evidence on players' models of other players," *Journal of Economic Behavior & Organization*, 25, 309–327.

STRAUB, P. G. (1995): "Risk dominance and coordination failures in static games," *Quarterly Review of Economics and Finance*, 35, 339–363.

SUTAN, A. AND M. WILLINGER (2009): "Guessing with negative feedback: An experiment," *Journal of Economic Dynamics and Control*, 33, 1123–1133.

SVORENČÍK, A. (2015): "The experimental turn in economics: a history of experimental economics," *University of Utrecht: Utrecht School of Economics Dissertation Series*, 29.

TAJFEL, H. (1974): "Social identity and intergroup behaviour," *Social Science Information*, 13, 65–93.

TAYLOR, J. B. (1993): "Discretion versus policy rules in practice," in *Carnegie-Rochester conference series on public policy*, Elsevier, vol. 39, 195–214.

TIROLE, J. (1982): "On the possibility of speculation under rational expectations," *Econometrica*, 1163–1181.

——— (1985): "Asset bubbles and overlapping generations," *Econometrica*, 1499–1528.

TULLOCK, G. (1980): "Efficient rent seeking," in *Toward a Theory of the Rent-seeking Society*, ed. by J. M. Buchanan, R. D. Tollison, and G. Tullock, College Station: Texas A & M University Press, 97–112.

UMER, H., T. KUROSAKI, AND I. IWASAKI (2022): "Unearned endowment and charity recipient lead to higher donations: A meta-analysis of the dictator game lab experiments," *Journal of Behavioral and Experimental Economics*, 97, 101827.

VESTERLUND, L. (2016): "Using experimental methods to understand why and how we give to charity," in *Handbook of Experimental Economics Volume 2*, ed. by J. H. Kagel and A. E. Roth, Princeton University Press Princeton, NJ, USA, 91–151.

VICKREY, W. (1961): "Counterspeculation, auctions, and competitive sealed tenders," *Journal of Finance*, 16, 8–37.

VOSLINSKY, A. AND O. H. AZAR (2021): "Incentives in experimental economics," *Journal of Behavioral and Experimental Economics*, 93, 101706.

WEBER, M. AND C. F. CAMERER (1998): "The disposition effect in securities trading: An experimental analysis," *Journal of Economic Behavior & Organization*, 33, 167–184.

WEITZEL, U., C. HUBER, J. HUBER, M. KIRCHLER, F. LINDNER, AND J. ROSE (2020): "Bubbles and financial professionals," *Review of Financial Studies*, 33, 2659–2696.

WILSON, R. (1977): "A bidding model of perfect competition," *Review of Economic Studies*, 44, 511–518.

XIAO, E. AND D. HOUSER (2005): "Emotion expression in human punishment behavior," *Proceedings of the National Academy of Sciences*, 102, 7398–7401.

ZHANG, Y. Y., R. M. NAYGA Jr., AND D. P. T. DEPOSITARIO (2019): "Learning and the possibility of losing own money reduce overbidding: Delayed payment in experimental auctions," *PloS One*, 14, e0213568.

ZIZZO, D. J. (2010): "Experimenter demand effects in economic experiments," *Experimental Economics*, 13, 75–98.

Index

A

adaptive learning dynamics, 229
Amazon's Mechanical Turk, 25, 71, 139
animal spirits, 194
artefactual field experiment, 17, 22
asset market experiments, 203
  with multiple assets, 218
asset price bubbles, 206
asset price experiment, 213, 219
  Arrow–Debreu approach, 204
  bubble-crash phenomenon, 208–209
  consumption-based, 213, 215, 217
  expectations-based approach, 213
  greater fool hypothesis, 209
  indefinite horizon, 211
  SSW design, 206–210
  two-assets, 218
asset pricing, 203
auction experiments, 167, 174, 181–182
  all-pay, 112, 178–179

all-pay, overdissipation, 180–181
bidding behavior, 171–172
common-value, 168, 174–175
first-price sealed-bid, 30
house money effect, 173
multi-unit, 182
private value, 167–170
winner's curse, 174, 177
audit studies, 69
auxiliary assumptions, 7–8
average treatment effect, 91

B

backward induction, 107, 110
Banerjee, Abhijit, 20–21
bank run experiments, 233–235
battle of the sexes, 104, 106
  alternation strategy, 107
beauty contest game, 113–114, 116
Becker–DeGroot–Marschak (BDM) mechanism, 47–48, 86
behavioral bet, 5
belief elicitation, 41
Belmont Report, 58
between-subjects design, 29
Big five personality test, 50

binary lottery, 36–39
Binmore, Ken, 6–7
block random assignment, 28
block random termination
    method, 53
bounded rationality, 228
box plots, 77

C

call markets, 190–191, 193, 201
    bid only, 192
causal inference, 1, 16, 11, 28
centipede game, 108
chi-squared test, 83
clustering of standard errors, 93
cognitive measures, 49
cognitive reflection test, 49
collective situations, 142
common knowledge, 98, 115
comparative statics predictions,
    12, 97, 138
competitive market
    equilibrium, 187
computer programs, 70
conditional cooperators, 127–128
confounding factor, 18
consumption/savings decisions,
    224
contests, 111–112
control, 27
control group, 2
control test questions, 67
control treatment, 10
convenience samples, 19–20
coordination games, 104
coordination problem, 106
    macroeconomic, 233
corner solution critique, 123
corner solutions, 88

cumulative distribution functions
    (CDFs), 77, 83–84, 115

D

data analysis, 75
data collection methods, 69–70
deception
    acts of commission, 68
    acts of omission, 68
derivative assets, 220
dictator game, 146–147, 153,
    157, 161
    charitable donations, 148
disposition effect, 219
distinction between lab and field,
    26
dominance, 31–32
dominant strategy, 108
double auction (DA), 186, 188,
    193–194, 207
Duflo, Esther, 20–21
Duhem–Quine thesis, 7–8

E

earned endowments, 148
effect size, 64
efficient markets hypothesis
    (EMH), 204
elements of control, 17
empirical relevance, 8
equilibrium selection, 9
experienced subjects, 71, 176
experimental currency units
    (ECUs), 189
experimental design, 11
experimenter demand effects, 20,
    29, 32
external validity, 15–16, 135–136,
    173, 238

extraneous factors, 17
extrinsic rewards, 32–33

F

field experiments, 16–17, 20–21,
    67, 72, 173–174
Fisher's exact test, 82–83
fractional factorial design, 60
framed field experiment, 17,
    21–22
framing, 148
free-riding behavior, 120
full factorial design, 59

G

game theory experiments, 97
    conceptual issues, 98
generalizability, 16

H

HARKING, 62
hedging opportunities, 35
histograms, 77
how much to pay?, 71

I

image concerns, 157
independence of observations,
    76
induced value theory, 30
inequity aversion, 150–151
inflation, 228–230, 237
informational efficiency of asset
    prices, 204, 206
institutional review
    (IRBs/RECs), 57–59
instructions, 66–67
Inter Ocular Trauma (IOT) test,
    78

interaction effect, 91–92
internal validity, 15–16
intertemporal optimization,
    222–223, 225
intrinsic rewards, 32

K

Kahneman, Daniel, 12
KISS principle, 32
Kolmogorov–Smirnov (KS) test,
    83–84
Kremer, Michael, 20–21
Kruskal–Wallis test, 81–82

L

lab-in-the-field experiment,
    21–23, 108
laboratory experiments, 16–17,
    20
learning-to-forecast experiment,
    211–214
level-k reasoning, 113–116
limited dependent variables,
    92
linear regression analysis, 90
logit regression, 93
Lucas, Robert, 6

M

macroeconomics experiments,
    221, 239
Mann–Whitney U or
    Wilcoxon–Mann–Whitney
    test, 80
markets
    computerized user interface,
    188
    decentralized, 198
    double auction, 199, 201

how to operationalize, 183
numeraire good, 189
posted-offer, 198, 200
search, 199–200
market experiment, 183, 185
market game, 148–149, 151–152
matched pairs design, 28
matching groups, 77
matching, overlapping
    generations, 125
    partners, strangers, 53–54,
    124
matching pennies, 101–102
measurement accuracy, 18
mixed strategy, 179
mixed-strategy equilibrium
    (MSE), 101–104, 106
monetary policy experiments,
    235–236
    Friedman rule, 236
    inflation targeting, 237
    Taylor rule, 236–237
monetary rewards, 31–32
money, 33
multiple equilibria, 6, 9, 195
multiple hypothesis testing
    correction for, 94
multiple price list (MPL), 44–46

N

natural field experiment, 16–17,
    21, 23
negative payoffs, 72–73
non-cognitive (personality)
    measures, 49
non-parametric methods, 78
non-parametric test, 83, 86
non-satiation, 30, 32
Nuremberg Code, 58

O

online workforces, 25–26
order effects, 29
ordinary least squares regression,
    90
other regarding concerns, 143,
    164
oTree, 70, 189
outcome variable, 2, 59
outliers, 77
over-dissipation, 111

P

p-hacking, 61–62
paper and pencil, 69
paradox of voting, 136
parallelism, 32
parametric methods, 78
parametric tests, 88
partner matching, 53–54
payment protocols, 34–36
perfect stranger matching, 54
pit market, 184, 201
pivotal voter model, 136–137
placebo, 2
planned experimental design,
    59–60
Plott, Charles, 4
point predictions, 11, 97
policy questions, 6
posted-offer markets, 199, 201
poverty traps, 231–233
power analysis, 64–66
pre-analysis plan, 61–62
pre-registrations, 61–62
Prisoner's Dilemma, 99, 153
probit regression, 93
Prolific, 25, 71
public economics, 119

public good game, 121–124, 126,
128, 164
confusion or kindness,
126–127
endogenous group
formation, 131
lottery prizes, 132
punishment, 130
public goods, 120, 122, 133, 141

Q

quantal response equilibrium
(QRE), 117

R

random assignment, 2–3, 27–28,
91
random matching, 106
random, no repeat matching, 100
random sampling, 27
random selection, 3
random termination method,
52–53
randomized control trials
(RCTs), 1, 20, 27
rational expectations, 225–227
belief-outcome interaction,
226
Ravens progressive matrices
(RPM) test, 50
real effort, 139
reciprocity, 109, 156–157, 163
intentions-based, 156
recruitment of subjects, 71
regression analysis, 3
replication, 19
revenue equivalence theorem,
170–174, 181

risk dominant equilibrium,
104–105
risk preferences, 36–37, 39,
43–44
robot players, 51–52, 164
robust rank-order test, 81
Roth, Alvin, 4–6

S

salience, 31–32
sample size, 63
scatter plots, 77
scoring rules, 41–42
searching for facts, 5
selection bias, 18
Shapley–Shubik market game,
196–197
show-up payment, 34
sign test, 85
Smith, Vernon, 4, 30, 32
social identity, 160–161
Klee or Kandinsky, 160
social preferences, 143–145,
149, 152–154, 156,
163–165
efficiency concerns, 154
fairness concerns, 149
Fehr–Schmidt specification,
151–153
field experiments, 162
intentions-based models, 156
self-image concerns, 157, 159
social value orientation task, 50,
165
sparsity of effects principle, 60
stag hunt, 104–105
STATA, 65, 81–82, 87
strategic uncertainty, 115, 227
strategy method, 39–41, 165

stratified randomization, 28
subject pool, 1, 15
subjects
    non-students, 24
    professionals vs. households,
        239
    students, 19–20, 24
    students vs. professionals,
        24–25, 211
subjects' beliefs, 97
sunspots, 192, 194
survey software, 70

T

t-test, 88–89
takeover game, 178
tax compliance, 133–136,
    141
text messages, 155
THARKING, 62
theory, 4–9, 11–12
threshold public good game,
    130
time horizons, 52
time preferences, 43, 46–47
Tobit regression, 93
tragedy of the commons, 22
treatment group, 2
trust game, 108–109, 162

U

ultimatum game (UG), 144–147,
    149, 151–153, 155–156
unit of observation, 75

V

variable payment, 72
voluntary contribution
    mechanism (VCM),
    121, 132, 134, 141
voting experiments, 136–140
    team participation game,
        137

W

wealth effects, 35
Wilcoxon signed-rank test,
    86–87, 89
Wilcoxon–Mann–Whitney test,
    79, 81, 89
willingness to accept (WTA),
    47–49
willingness to pay (WTP), 47–49
winner's curse, 176
within-subjects design, 10, 28–29
WTA-WTP gap, 48–49

Z

z-Tree, 70

Printed in the United States
by Baker & Taylor Publisher Services